DATE DUE			

KNOWLEDGE AND MEMORY:
THE REAL STORY

Advances in Social Cognition,
Volume VIII

Edited by

Robert S. Wyer, Jr.
University of Illinois, Urbana–Champaign

Lead Article by

Roger C. Schank and Robert P. Abelson

LAWRENCE ERLBAUM ASSOCIATES, PUBLISHERS
1995   Hillsdale, New Jersey   Hove, UK

Lawrence Erlbaum Associates, Inc., Publishers
365 Broadway
Hillsdale, New Jersey 07642

Cover design by Kate Dusza

Library of Congress Cataloging-in-Publication Data

Knowledge and Memory: The Real Story
Advances in Social Cognition, Volume VIII

ISSN: 0898-2007
ISBN: 0-8058-1445-0 (cloth)
ISBN: 0-8058-1446-9 (paper)

Books published by Lawrence Erlbaum Associates are printed
on acid-free paper, and their bindings are chosen for strength
and durability.

Printed in the United States of America
10 9 8 7 6 5 4 3 2 1

Contents

Preface

This is the eighth volume of the *Advances in Social Cognition* series. From its inception, the purpose of the series has been to present and evaluate new theoretical advances in all areas of social cognition and information processing. An entire volume is devoted to each theory, allowing the theory to be evaluated from a variety of perspectives and permitting its implications for a wide range of issues to be examined.

The series reflects two major characteristics of social cognition: the high level of activity in the field and the interstitial nature of the work. Each volume contains a target chapter that is timely in its application, novel in its approach, and precise in its explication. The target chapter is then followed by a set of companion articles that examine the theoretical and empirical issues that the target has raised. These latter chapters are written by authors with diverse theoretical orientations, representing different disciplines within psychology and, in some cases, entirely different disciplines. Target authors are then given the opportunity to respond to the comments and criticisms of their work and to examine the ideas conveyed in the companion chapters in light of their own. The dialogue created by this format is both unusual and, we believe, extremely beneficial to the field.

Narrative forms of mental representation, and their influence on comprehension, communication and judgment, have rapidly become one of the main foci of research and theory in not only psychology but also other disciplines, including linguistics, sociology, and anthropology. No one has been more responsible for the awakening of interest in this area than Roger Schank and Bob Abelson. Both are eminent scholars whose well-known conceptualization of cognitive scripts has been greatly refined and extended since it was first developed in the mid-1970s. In their target article, they argue that narrative forms of mental representation, or "stories," are the basic ingredients of social knowledge that play a fundamental role in the comprehension of information conveyed in a social context, the storage of this information in memory, and the later communication of it to others. After explicating the cognitive processes that underlie the construction of narratives and their use in comprehension, memory, and communication, the authors consider the influence of stories on a number of more specific phenomena, including political judgment, marital relations, and the sorts of memory distortions that underlie errors in eyewitness testimony.

The provocativeness of the target chapter is matched by that of the companion articles, each of which not only provides an important commentary on Schank and Abelson's conceptualization but makes an important contribution to knowledge in its own right. The diversity of perspectives reflected in these chapters, whose authors include researchers in linguistics, memory and comprehension, social inference, cognitive development, social judgment, close relationships, and social ecology, testifies to the breadth of theoretical and empirical issues to which the target chapter is potentially relevant. We believe that the volume as a whole is a timely and important contribution to research and theory not only in social cognition but in many other areas as well.

In addition to the authors themselves, we want to acknowledge the invaluable assistance of Lawrence Erlbaum Associates. Their continued support and encouragement of the *Advances* series, and their commitment to the publication of a high-quality set of volumes, is deeply gratifying. It is a genuine pleasure to work with them.

—Robert S. Wyer, Jr.

1

Knowledge and Memory: The Real Story

Roger C. Schank
Northwestern University

Robert P. Abelson
Yale University

In this chapter, we argue that stories about one's experiences and the experiences of others are the fundamental constituents of human memory, knowledge, and social communication. This argument includes three propositions:

1. Virtually all human knowledge is based on stories constructed around past experiences,
2. New experiences are interpreted in terms of old stories,
3. The content of story memories depends on whether and how they are told to others, and these reconstituted memories form the basis of the individual's *remembered self.*

Further, shared story memories within social groups define particular social selves, which may bolster or compete with individual remembered selves.

Our style of presentation is discursive and probably prone to overstatement, as we seek to emphasize the differences between our position and competing views in cognitive psychology and cognitive science. Where suggestive empirical research is available, we adduce it. However, we do not believe that a definitive body of empirical evidence is presently available on one side or the other, and we have not attempted to fashion a fully databased theory here.

In the first major section, we lay out the shape of our overall argument. In following sections, we discuss each of our premises in more detail.

STORYTELLING AND UNDERSTANDING: THE BASIS
FOR HUMAN MEMORY

For thousands, maybe millions of years, people have been telling stories to each other. They have told stories around the campfire; they have traveled from town to town telling stories to relate the news of the day; they have told stories transmitted by electronic means to passive audiences incapable of doing anything but listening (and watching). Whatever the means, and whatever the venue, storytelling seems to play a major role in human interaction.

However, the role of storytelling and story understanding is far more significant in human memory than simply representing one kind of human interaction. The reason that humans constantly relate stories to each other is that stories are all they have to relate. Or, put another way, when it comes to interaction in language, all of our knowledge is contained in stories and the mechanisms to construct them and retrieve them.

Philosophers, psychologists, artificial intelligence types, and occasionally even linguists concern themselves with discussions of "knowledge." We talk about what people know, attempt to formalize what they know, make rules about what can follow from what they know, and so on. But, except in one part of the Artificial Intelligence community, the subject of how people use what they know rarely comes up. It is in this discussion of the *use* of knowledge that the *idea* of knowledge as stories becomes significant.

Simply put, humans engage in two broad classes of actions involving language that depend upon knowledge. They try to comprehend what is going on around them and refer to what they already know in order to make sense of new input. Then they attempt to tell things to others, again referring to what they already know in order to do so.

Knowledge is Functional

It is important to recognize that knowledge is functional; it is structured not to satisfy an elegant logic, but to facilitate daily use. However, when we say that all knowledge is encoded as stories (plus mechanisms to process them), we must deal in our analysis with bits of apparent knowledge that don't seem to be stories, such as "Whales are mammals," "I was born in New York," or "Stanford is in California." We discuss this in the next section. In the following sections, we cover the facilitory types of knowledge necessary to process stories.

The idea that knowledge is inherently functional, that it exists to be used for some purpose, imposes a constraint on how we talk about knowledge in this essay. We do not talk about what people know, but about the processes they engage in that utilize what they know. To this end, we can ask what people do that utilizes knowledge. Here are some of these things:

People answer questions.
People make plans and inform others of them.

People comprehend what others are saying.

People inform other people of events that have taken place.

People give advice to other people.

This is not intended to be a complete list of what people do in their mental lives, but it is intended to characterize a great deal of what people do mentally that involves the use of language. In each and every one of the situations listed earlier, the knowledge that people use to help them is encoded in the form of stories.

The Stories Behind "Facts"

When we find ourselves saying, "I was born in New York," we could be doing so for any of the reasons for talking previously listed. We could be answering a question. We could be prefacing some advice that we are about to give, perhaps about what to see in New York, or this could be part of an explanation of some events that have occurred. Whenever such a phrase is used, it is, quite obviously, an abbreviation of a much longer story.

Human memory is a collection of thousands of stories we remember through experience, stories we remember by having heard them, and stories we remember by having composed them. Any story in memory could have gotten there in one of these three ways. The key point is that, once these stories are there in our memory, we rely upon them for all that we can say and understand. Obviously, we can't recall where we were born. We are told the story of our birth, and when required to do so, we can tell others. There are many ways to tell this story, including the very short version: "I was born in New York." That sounds like a mere fact instead of a story.

Such very short versions are not the results of "table-look-up in memory," that is, finding the birthplace slot and reading its value. This may work for computers, but it doesn't make any sense psychologically. Search in human memory is a search for stories. The linguistic expression of those stories can range widely. We can say as much or as little as we like of the story. When we know that a story is funny or weird, we might digress and tell the best part. In fact, when one of us (Roger C. Schank) is asked about his birth by someone who seems willing to listen, he can tell two stories, one about why he was born in Manhattan rather than Brooklyn where his parents lived, and the other about his short-lived middle name (Wilco) that came from having overzealous Air Force officers for parents.

There are several stories of one's birth, and many more stories that comprise one's life. These stories get strengthened in the telling: The memories become more real because we tell them. When we tell them in the abbreviated way, they are simply that, abbreviated stories. Such really small stories should not be confused with factual knowledge. We propose that there is no factual knowledge as such in memory.

What about "Stanford is in California"? Surely this a fact in memory. Actually, it may be more a derived fact than a fact that exists as such in memory. One of us was a professor at Stanford for 5 years. Ask him about Stanford and he can think of hundreds of stories, any one of which could be used to derive the needed information. Just as there is no slot for birthplace in memory, neither is there a slot for Stanford filled in with various characteristics of the place. It is possible to have memorized stuff about the acreage of the campus, for example, but such memorized knowledge is hardly the usual sort of knowledge that we rely upon daily. The issue is not whether we can memorize facts, but whether that process has much to do with normal memory functioning.

Deriving static factual knowledge from stories we have in memory is, of course, quite possible. But, the fact that we can do this should not confuse us. This factual knowledge is yet again a very abbreviated story. In fact, even the phrase "Stanford is in California" is a story for one of us. When he was at Stanford, he took a course in Yiddish. The first sentence the students learned to say in Yiddish was "Stanford is in California" since, as it happens, that sentence sounds exactly the same in Yiddish as it does in English.

Even such banal facts as "Whales are mammals" can be stories. However, we need to guard against thinking that what we are talking about here is the attempt to understand such a sentence. We will deal with understanding later. Here we are discussing where and in what form that knowledge might reside in memory. In any discussion of static knowledge, particularly among those who believe in semantic memory, the whale issue is significant. For instance, knowing that whales are mammals, we can predict things about how they suckle their young. But, as it turns out, we have never needed to use such knowledge. Whale-suckling has simply never come up in any conversation we can remember. What has come up are discussions of how to represent knowledge. In these discussions we have always maintained that, despite what biologists say to the contrary, whales are better treated as fish, because an intelligent system would learn much more about them than this one nonfact. The problem here again is the formalist's view of knowledge that stands in contradistinction to the functionalist's view. Formalists make up names like "mammal" in an attempt to make rules about knowledge that will be predictive. This is handy for them, but it has little to do with what human memory is actually like. In human memory whales are fish if they have to be anything at all, which they probably do not. The real role for whales in memory is to be a part of Jonah stories or Sea-World-visit stories, from which we really derive what we know about whales. Everything else is just rote memorization that we did in school.

Applying Old Stories to New Situations

What we know that seems factual is actually derived from personal stories. Similarly, what we can say about things we believe is usually adapted from personal stories as well. When we ask individuals for their opinion on a subject, and they produce what seems to be a truly creative response, that is, a response that surely they have never uttered before, careful examination tells us that old stories in their memory are the ingredients of the seeming novelty.

To explore this idea, we asked the students in a graduate seminar why Swale had died. Swale was a racehorse that had won many important races and was one day found dead (at the age of three). This was told to the students, and then they were asked to explain what had happened. They came up with some very creative hypotheses, including murder plots, drug overdoses, stress problems, and so on. The more we pushed, the more creative they became, referring, for example, to the "Janis Joplin Memorial Reminding," which basically said that Swale was too rich and too young and couldn't stand the success, so he overdid it by living "life in the fast lane."

The point is that even such new responses, explanations of totally new events, are really just rewrites of existing stories in memory, adapted to fit new circumstances. All of the students' new responses were *already* available in memory, or to put this another way, the responder already knew *an* answer. The problem was selecting from the stories in memory.

People have opinions about a large range of topics derived from the stories that exist in their memories. They know what they think, and more importantly, they have already thought up what they are likely to say long before they say it. The respondent's actual task then is to determine which of the many already known answers is relevant to the question at hand.

Understanding the world means explaining its happenings in a way that seems consonant with what you already believe. Thus, the task of an understander who has a memory filled with stories is to determine which of those stories is most relevant to the situation at hand. The old story is then used as a means for interpreting the new story. Doing things this way makes a seemingly unmanageable task much simpler. Otherwise, understanding the world is phenomenally complex. Finding a story that is like the one you are now seeing is much easier. The fewer stories you have in memory, the easier it is. To a man with a hammer, everything looks like a nail. But if you have many tools, you had better have a good system for knowing when to use them.

Scripts

In the mid-1970s at Yale, in our work on designing programs that understood English or natural language processing (Schank & Abelson, 1977), we applied the concept of a *script*. A script is a set of expectations about what will happen next in a well understood situation. In a sense, many situations in life have the participants seemingly reading their roles in a kind of play. The waitress reads from the waitress parts in the restaurant script, and the customer reads the lines of the customer.

Scripts are useful for a variety of reasons. They make clear what is supposed to happen and what various acts on the part of others are supposed to indicate. They make mental processing easier, by allowing us, in essence, to think less. You don't have to figure out every time you enter a restaurant how to convince someone to feed you. All you really have to know is the restaurant script and your part in that script.

Scripts are helpful in understanding the actions of others as long as we know the script they are following. Scripts also enable computers to understand stories about stereotypical situations (Cullingford, 1979). When a paragraph is about a restaurant, we can realize with very little effort that we need not wonder why the waitress agreed to bring what was asked for, and we can assume that what was ordered was what was eaten. To put this another way, not everything in the world is worthy of equal amounts of thought, and restaurant stories are readily understandable by a computer armed with a good enough restaurant script. In fact, not too much thinking has to be done by a computer or a person if the right script is available. One just has to play one's part, and events usually transpire the way they are supposed to. You don't have to infer the intentions of a waitress if her intentions are already well-known. Why concentrate one's mental time on the obvious?

Taken as a strong hypothesis about the nature of human thought, a script obviates the need to think; no matter what the situation is, people need to do no more in thinking than to apply a script. This hypothesis holds that everything is a script, and very little thought is spontaneous. Given a situation, there are rules to follow for the way things are supposed to be. We can follow those rules and not think at all. This works for all of us some of the time. People have thousands of highly personal scripts they use on a daily basis that others do not share. Every mundane aspect of life that requires little or no thought, such as sitting in your chair or pouring your daily orange juice, can be assumed to be a script. In fact, much of our early education revolves around learning the scripts that others expect us to follow. Yet this can all be carried a bit too far. Situations that one person sees as following a script may seem quite open-ended to another person. However, the more scripts you know, the more situations you will face feeling comfortable and capable of playing your role effectively. On the other hand, the more scripts you know, the more situations you will fail to wonder about, be confused by, and be challenged to figure out on your own. Script-based understanding is, therefore, a double-edged sword.

Scripts are also a kind of memory structure. They tell us how to act without our being aware that we are using them. They store knowledge that we have about certain situations. They serve as a kind of storehouse of old experiences of a certain type in terms of which new experiences of the same type are encoded. When something new happens to us in a restaurant that tells us more about restaurants, we must have some place to put that new information so that we will be wiser the next time. Scripts, therefore, change over time and embody what we have learned. For this reason, my restaurant script won't be exactly the same as yours, but they will both include information such as "one can expect forks to be available without asking, unless the restaurant is Japanese." In most contexts, thinking means finding the right script to use, rather than generating new ideas and questions, so, essentially, we find it easier to apply scripts than to reason out every new situation from scratch. But scripts aren't the complete answer. Obviously, we can understand some novel experiences even if no script seems to apply. We do this by seeing new experiences in terms of old experiences.

Beyond Scripts: Indexed Stories

When a prior experience is indexed cleverly, we can call it to mind to help us understand a current situation. This process can lead to brand new insights. All people reason from experience. The differences among reasoners depend upon how they have coded their prior experiences in the first place. We are not all reminded of the same things at the same time.

If a prior experience is understood only in terms of the generalization or principle behind the case, we don't have as many places to put the new case in our memory. We can tell people abstract rules of thumb that we have derived from prior experiences, but it is very difficult for them to learn from them. It is hard to remember abstractions if they are not anchored in specific experiences, but it is relatively easy to remember a good story. Stories give life to past experience. Stories make events in our memory unforgettable to others and ourselves. This is one of the reasons why people like to tell them.

We are more persuasive when we tell stories. For example, we can simply state our beliefs, or we can tell stories that illustrate them. If John explains to Bill that he is in a quandary about whether he should marry Mary or Jane, and if after listening to John's description, Bill says "Mary," his reply would usually be seen as useless advice. We need justifications for the beliefs of others before we can begin to believe them ourselves. If Bill responds by saying, "Mary because Mary is Irish, and Irish girls make good wives," he is being more helpful, but not necessarily more believable. If Bill, though, responds with a story about a similar situation that he was in, or that he heard about, and how the choice was made in that case, and how it worked out, John is likely to be quite interested and to take the advice offered by the story more to heart. Why? Thinking involves *indexing*. In order to assimilate a case, we must attach it somewhere in our memory. Inaccessible information is not information at all. Memory, in order to be effective, must contain both specific experiences (memories) and labels (indexes) used to trace memories of experiences. The more information we are given about a situation, the more places we can attach it in our memory, and the more ways it can be compared to other cases in our memory. Thus, a story is useful because it comes with many indexes. These indexes may be locations, attitudes, beliefs, quandaries, decisions, conclusions, or whatever. The more indexes we have for a story being told, the more places it can reside in our memory. Consequently, we are more likely to remember the story and relate it to experiences already in our memory. In other words, the more indexes we have, the greater the number of comparisons we can make to prior experiences, and hence the greater our learning.

Telling Old Stories

The "Grandfather Model"

With this in mind, let's consider what we might call the *grandfather model* of memory. The "grandfather" is one who seems to tell the same story over and over again. Everyone has heard his favorite stories many times, but they indulge him in hearing them once again. Every now and then, a new story appears, or at least one that no one is sure he remembers hearing before. When this happens, even the grandfather is surprised, and he enjoys telling the story more than usual. In some sense, the grandfather model is really just a crystallization of something we all do.

The Logician Model

The grandfather model of memory is in opposition to the more common *logician model*. This model is all too common in scholarly attempts to understand the nature of knowledge. For centuries people have been composing lists of what we know and rules for deriving logical inferences, as if such models had something to do with normal memory processes. People are not really logical at all. The idea of logical people is parodied in the popular mind, for example, by the Mr. Spock character in *Star Trek* who projects an image associated with scientists. The idea behind the logician model of intelligence is that every problem can be reduced to first principles and decided on the basis of some logic. Knowledge, in this view, is about rules of inference and principles, not stories. In popular fiction, such logical characters often fail to have some emotional quality that makes them human in the audience's eyes. In fact, any live logician model has two more serious problems in real life. The first is an understanding problem, and the second is a discovery problem.

The understanding problem is simply that humans are not really set up to hear logic. People, however, like to hear stories. The reason that people like to hear stories, however, is not transparent to them. People need a context to help them relate what they have heard to what they already know. We understand events in terms of other events we have already understood. When a decision-making heuristic, or rule of thumb, is presented to us without a context, we cannot decide the validity of the rule we have heard, nor do we know where to store this rule in our memories. Thus, the rule we are given is both difficult to evaluate and difficult to remember, making it virtually useless. People who fail to couch what they have to say in memorable stories will have their rules fall on deaf ears despite their best intentions, and despite the best intentions of their listeners. A good teacher is not one who explains things correctly, but one who couches his explanations in a memorable (i.e., an interesting) format.

Storytelling and Understanding

In the end all we have are stories and methods of finding and using those stories. Knowledge, then, is experiences and stories. Intelligence is the apt use of experience, and the creation and telling of stories. Memory is memory for stories, and the major processes of memory are the creation, storage, and retrieval of stories. To build models of intelligence, or simply to understand the nature of intelligence, we must understand the role that stories play in memory. We must know how events become stories, and how these stories are stored and later retrieved. We must know the indexes we construct that label stories, and we must determine how and why such indexes are created. A good theory of the mind must include ideas about how the stories of others are decoded to provide indexes that enable retrieval and storage; it must also determine how and why our own stories appear in our minds in response. Moreover, the theory must contain a model of how and why we create new stories and of what happens to experiences that do not get encoded as stories. What we know is embodied in what we tell, and as we shall see, what we tell strongly determines what we know. We know what we tell, and we tell what we know.

The process by which this all works is the reminding process. Each story we hear reminds us of one that we know, and in a conversational situation we tell that story if it seems appropriate to the audience, adapting it as we go to make it more relevant.

In this way, it is clear that storytelling and understanding are functionally the same thing. Conversation is no more than responsive storytelling. The process of reminding is what controls understanding and, therefore, conversation. Thus, seen this way, conversations are really a series of remindings of already-processed stories. The mind can be seen as a collection of stories, collections of experiences one has already had. A conversationalist is looking to tell one of his stories. He is looking to tell a good one, a right one, but to do this he must be reminded of one that he knows.

Generating Relevant Stories

We could almost conclude that we never say anything new; we just find what we have already said and say it again. Yet we don't do this freely or randomly. There is a method to this system. We are always looking for closest possible matches. We are looking to say, in effect, "Well, something like that happened to me, too," or, "I had an idea about something like that myself." In order to do this, we must adopt a point of view that allows for us to see a situation or experience as an instance of "something like that." In other words, we must evaluate experiences with an intention of matching them to what we have already experienced.

The story-based conception of *generation* presupposes that everything you might ever want to say has already been thought up. This is not as strange an idea as it seems. We are not suggesting that every sentence we will ever say is sitting in our memory word for word. Rather, adults have views of the world that are expressed by ideas they have already thought up and have probably expressed many times. When asked for your view of Reagan, for example, you don't usually consider the problem for the first time. What you say, however, may not be something you have ever said before. Nevertheless, what you say will have a certain familiarity to it, and will be something that you have thought before and possibly expressed in other words. Your views evolve, so that what you say one time will not be identical to what you say the next time. The relation between the two, however, will be strong and will occur to you as you begin to construct your new thoughts. Thus, new ideas depend upon old ones.

The main issue in generation is really the accessing of whatever you already think about something and the expression of those thoughts. When we tell a story, we are doing the same thing. We are accessing the gist of that story and then re-expressing that gist in English. The words we use are not identical each time, but the ideas behind them are more or less the same. We take the gist of a story as it exists in memory, and then we transform that gist into an English expression, one that perhaps leaves out one point or embellishes another. The words we choose may depend upon the audience. The ideas expressed may depend upon our reinterpretation of past events in the light of events that have occurred since the story we are telling took place.

We get reminded of what has happened to us previously for a very good reason. Reminding is the mind's method of coordinating past events with current events to enable generalization and prediction. Intelligence depends upon the ability to translate descriptions of new events into indexes that help in the retrieval of prior events. We can't be said to know something if we can't find it in our memory when it is needed. Finding a relevant past experience that will help make sense of a new experience is at the core of intelligent behavior.

TYPES OF KNOWLEDGE OTHER THAN
STORY-RELATED KNOWLEDGE

In our introduction, we stated a very strong position on stories as knowledge, claiming that all of what people know is in the form of stories and structures that expedite the storage and telling of stories. There are, of course, other positions. For Tulving (1993), there are five kinds of stored memories, of which the two most prominent are *episodic memory* and *semantic memory*. We maintain that there is no distinct entity called semantic memory. This stance grows out of a point of view in artificial intelligence, where it has proven more fruitful to simulate episodic memory processes (Schank, 1982). Old episodes are applied to such tasks as explanation, planning, learning, and summary description. If there is any semantic content in the propositional knowledge base for these tasks, it comes in the form of generic episodes growing out of clusters of similar events.

A Variety of Theoretical Positions

The "kinds of memory" issue is provocative, and both cognitive psychologists and computer scientists debate it hotly. It would be helpful if the empirical evidence were clear on this issue, but it is not. Even striking case studies of brain-injured amnesiacs can be differently interpreted for their implications about episodic and semantic memory. On the one hand, amnesia can occur in chronological chunks, for example good memory for everything before a given date, but no memory of any experiences after that date (see Sacks, 1985, chapter 2). This phenomenon is consistent with an episodic memory position, although not definitive. Tulving (1993), for example, asserts that amnesiacs suffer from a loss of *semantic* memory.

Our very strong position on the episodic side of this debate will raise some hackles. We here discuss a somewhat milder position that will still maintain the central role of stories. (The one thing we won't do is opt for the theory that all knowledge is propositional, leaving episodes out entirely.)

Facts

It is common in considering two theories, one stronger than the other, to refer to them as "the weak theory" and "the strong theory" (e.g., Searle, 1980). We prefer to follow the scheme used in grading the sizes of olives, thus contrasting "strong theory" and "very strong theory." We will attempt to outline a position that is merely strong. We will do this by considering proposed types of knowledge that, on the face of it, seem unrelated to stories.

One category of knowledge often offered in contrast to the episodic type is knowledge of facts. We discussed this briefly in Story Telling & Understanding: The Basis for Human Memory, where we took the stance that facts either are learned by rote and never used again (except for recitation by rote, perhaps to impress the listener with one's mastery of the subject); or function as indexes to stories (for example, about one's birth in New York or life in California).

This position may seem somewhat cavalier, but we think it holds true for *isolated* facts in social situations where people are genuinely communicating with one another. If we consider *bundles* of facts, such as knowledge of the street map for a particular town, and we ask what such bundles are used for, we run into episodic considerations again. If you stop on the intersection of Main and Lakeside streets and ask a passerby how to get to the Fourteen Carrots health food store, she will probably recite for you a little script for getting there—continue west on Main Street, bear left at the Y-junction, and in three-tenths of a mile you'll see a shopping center on your left, and then . . .

Such a response can, arguably, be interpreted as a narration of experience rather than as a manipulation of propositions about the local geography. The argument here essentially reflects a clash of views about expertise and "expert systems" (see Feigenbaum, Buchanan, & Lederberg, 1971). Should experts be modeled as users of *case-based reasoning* on stores of relevant examples (Kolodner, 1991), or as symbol processors employing *rule-based reasoning*? We are squarely in the first camp.

A more indirect challenge to a strong or very strong position on knowledge as stories arises in the case of beliefs. What, if any, relation could there be between beliefs and stories?

Beliefs

We will not attempt a systematic categorization of types of belief, but we will consider two major varieties: belief in the *existence* of some entity or phenomenon and *ideological* beliefs. Together, these should give us a good feeling for the issues involved. There are some distinctions between belief and knowledge (Abelson, 1979), but these are not especially relevant in the present context.

Existence Beliefs

Popular *existence beliefs* include belief in God, in the reality of UFOs, in the big bang theory of the origin of the universe, and so on. In each case, the core belief is that something that seems fantastic is really there, is really true. Let us take, for example, belief in the existence of extrasensory perception (ESP).

Some years ago, one of us (Robert P. Abelson) undertook an interview study to explore of the nature of belief in ESP, soliciting volunteers with a strong belief in the existence of psychic phenomena. A point of major interest was whether the respondents, when asked, "Why do you believe in ESP?", would respond by reference to some source of data, or to the feats of a purported psychic, or whether they would report a convincing personal experience. External "facts" never turned up. One after another, subjects told stories.

One woman reported that at noon one day, after a fight in the morning with her husband, a construction worker, she suddenly had a feeling of foreboding that her husband had suffered a terrible accident. Sure enough, at 11:59 A.M., a heavy crane had toppled on him and killed him.

An aspiring artist told of an experience that led him to realize that he was clairvoyant. He was on the fifth floor of a well-insulated building when he felt himself suffused in the sound and mood of a particular Mozart quartet. On going downstairs to leave the building, he discovered that someone on the ground floor was playing a record of this very quartet. He attributed this experience to his artistic sensitivity, one aspect of which was the ability to perceive the world in ways going beyond the ordinary five senses.

A third respondent, a man with a 6-month-old son, claimed that a few weeks before, he had noticed when he came into the living room that his son was sitting facing three-fourths the other way. He tried sending a telepathic message to the baby to turn his head and look at him, and it worked! He said that since this incident, he had tried repeating his telepathic commands, and though he wasn't always successful, he felt that his technique was improving.

And so it went, one personal experience followed another. People insisted that ESP was possible because they had witnessed it firsthand. Now a skeptic could readily debunk these reports. For instance, the construction worker was at a site two short blocks from his wife's office, and it is entirely possible that she heard a crash. Furthermore, her ready admission that they had been fighting suggests that she might often have wished him harm, perhaps repeatedly having (gleeful?) forebodings. We might also regard these respondents as naive, neurotic, or what-ever. But such skeptical comments are not to the point. The important observation is that we found ordinary people readily giving autobiographical experiences, not abstractions, as support for their belief in ESP. In fact, we can find very well educated individuals giving comparable testimonials. Irvin Child, a respected scholar who supports empirical study of ESP (Child, 1973), wrote that his view of the possibility of psychic influences was radically altered by an experience reported by his uncle, who accurately predicted a tragedy 30 miles away.

We suspect that several other existence beliefs—those whose truth is known to be subject to intense debate—are also apt to form indexes to stories. A popular sort of competition among UFO buffs consists of trying to tell the most exciting story without violating present lore on the proclivities of space aliens. (You can't say that you were taken to Alpha Centauri, for example.)

On the other hand, belief that commands high cultural consensus, such as belief in God, seems less likely to index striking personal experiences. In our acquaintance, when believers are asked why they believe in God, they tend to say that there *must* be a God, or that everyone in their family believes in one and they never questioned it, or they give other propositional responses. The conclusion for our strong story–based position, therefore, is that, in general, existence beliefs are closely bound to stories, but that there may be exceptions.

Ideological Beliefs

Ideologies, whether political or religious, have morality plays at their core (Roseman, 1994). There are good guys and bad guys, and the bad guys, using illegitimate methods, are trying to bring about an evil state of affairs. This can only be averted if the good guys mobilize their forces, recruit people from the sidelines (who are in danger of being seduced by the bad guys), and press forward to glorious victory. Such a scheme was found in interviews by Roseman to characterize the ideologies of both antinuclear activists and anti-Communist hawks—with different contents, of course. Abelson (1973), in a conceptual and computer simulation of the cold war ideology of Senator Barry Goldwater, outlined a master story, or *master script*, which made possible a large number of coherent (if unsophisticated) hawkish responses to foreign policy questions.

This perspective on ideological systems is consistent with a storytelling model of belief. In effect, when an ideologist is challenged, he will tell you a story with the plot of the morality play or master story. The supportive "facts" given will tend to be stories, too, episodes illustrating the venality of the opponent, or the effectiveness of mobilization of the virtuous.

Which Comes First; the Belief or the Story?

It might be argued that beliefs could stem from other sources, or hidden motivations, and that the personal or political stories are merely justifications for beliefs otherwise formed. A strong case can be made that people have no access to the real reasons for their behavior (Nisbett & Wilson, 1977), and research on *cognitive dissonance theory* indicates the facility with which subjects rationalize foolish or insensitive words or acts (see Aronson, 1969). Politicians are even more facile than others at justifying almost anything, as we will see in the section entitled Story Skeletons. Which, then, comes first, the belief or the story?

With respect to the point of view we urge in this essay, it makes no difference whether the story is the cause or consequence of the belief. They end up packaged together, so that the belief indexes the story, and the story supports the belief. Mention ESP to the wife of the construction worker, and she will tell the story of her husband's death; ask her instead what the foreboding about someone's death might signify, and she will report her belief that it could very well be the omen of an actual tragedy. Ask the model, or the real Barry Goldwater, to defend his foreign policy beliefs, and he will tell you a story of the struggle between good and evil. Tell him a story of communist malfeasance, and he will immediately point out the confirmation of his beliefs. Tell him a story of benign communist behavior, and he won't believe it. We pursue the role

of beliefs in indexing stories further in the section entitled Understanding Means
Mapping Your Stories Onto My Stories.

Lexical Items

Words

How does knowledge of word meanings figure in our position? The lexicon
seems to be preeminently of a semantic rather than an episodic nature, and this
would compromise the very strong position that "all knowledge is stories."

There are a fair number of cases in which individual words, although not
themselves stories, do serve to *index* stories. In Storytelling and Memory, we
discuss "betrayal" as an index favoring a generic story skeleton, to which a number
of particular stories attach. And many names of individuals and places evoke
stories: the Alamo, Paul Revere, and Henry VIII, to name three examples. Yet such
example-giving merely forestalls the inevitable conclusion that the lexicon is really
essentially semantic. To claim that every word is a story would lead to the
unsupportable position that the interpretation of phrases and sentences is achieved
through a process of combining stories. To be sure, a whole sentence might index
a story itself, but it wouldn't be made up of ministories.

Posing such challenges to the very strong version of our position, however, is
like playing the political game of "Gotcha!" It misses what we consider to be the
important issues by switching the level of analysis. Our concern is with meaningful
social communication, and such communication does not ordinarily consist of
single words. To see the significance of this observation, suppose that conversational turns were restricted to a single word at a time. Then these utterances, we
claim, would become a vocabulary of story indexes.

Picture a group of rumpled academics sipping port in the common room. The
college has just passed a regulation that no member may say more than one word
at a time. What sort of conversation can they have? One scenario might go like this.
"Revolution!" says the first speaker, trying to stir up something. A second says,
"French," suggesting a stock example. "Cahiers," chimes in a third, who likes to
put on airs. (He is referring to the bills of complaint sent in by groups of ordinary
citizens during the French Revolution.) "Ineffective," opines a fourth, and so on.
Each word indexes a story, or extends a previous story.

Or imagine a word-at-a-time exchange touching on daily concerns. "Grading,"
says the first professor. "Staircase?", asks the second. The third shakes his head.
"Dean," he warns. Again, each word is a story. Our basic point is that whatever the
size of basic conversational chunks, each chunk will usually be story relevant.
Linguistic units smaller than a chunk shift the focus to a lower level of analysis.

Numbers

Numerical elements, like words, don't seem to be story related. For conve-
nience, let us focus on whole numbers. The situation here is similar to that with
words. We certainly would not deny that people have arithmetic knowledge that
has little to do with stories.

We can't resist, however, pointing out that particular numbers can index stories. As Bill James, the baseball statistician says, "Children . . . love those baseball numbers, even though they might hate math: They love the stories the numbers tell . . . the great rookie year followed by years of unfulfilled potential . . . a trade . . . the slow decline of the aging player. . . ." (James, Albert, & Stern, 1993).

Later in this essay, we refer to the classic story of the prisoners who refer to jokes by number, thus allowing jokes to be efficiently retold simply by calling out numbers. One of us haphazardly chose to illustrate the prisoners' joketelling with the number 42, which reminded the other of a story given in Adams' (1980) zany book, *The Hitchhiker's Guide to the Galaxy*. It seems that a committee of scientists had programmed the most powerful computer in the universe to solve the riddle of the meaning of life, the universe, and everything. The computer whirred and crunched and worked on this conundrum for several million years. Finally, with a breathless crowd waiting for the answer, the computer printed out, "Forty-two."

The astonishing number theorist, Srinivasa Ramanujan, was the protagonist of several number stories. One story tells of the occasion when a colleague visited him and remarked that he had come in a taxi with the dull identification number 1729. Ramanujan instantly replied that on the contrary, 1729 was a very interesting number, being the smallest integer that equals the sum of the cubes of two integers in two different ways (see Humez, Humez, and Maguire, 1993, for this anecdote and many other tales revolving around numbers).

As was the case with words, we concede the reality of a numerical knowledge that, except for a few entertaining exceptions, is basically different from story knowledge. But again, numbers and numerical operations, if engaged in by people at all, do not ordinarily enter into social interaction.

Rule Systems

Another type of knowledge category that does not seem to involve stories might be called *rule systems*. By this we mean a symbolic domain with a set of constraints on permissible transformations of state. The influential work of Newell and Simon (1972) promoted the concept of mind as an information processor analogous to a computer. This analogy focused attention on the particular class of mental activities involving rule systems, such as theorem proving, puzzle solving, and chess playing.

The limitation of all this is that very few people spend time trying to prove theorems (Fermat's Last notwithstanding), and when they do, they don't ordinarily talk about it. The same holds essentially true (with less force) for problem solving and chess playing. When people do talk about these things, they tend to become more storylike.

Grammar

A better candidate for a symbolic domain, universally practiced, in which remembered experiences play little or no role, is grammar. Most people learn grammatical rules without awareness of that learning, and are typically unable to articulate what those rules are. Why does one say, "I can hardly wait," but not "I can wait hardly"? Is it because adverbs go before verbs? No, "I can walk slowly" is all right. There must be a perfectly simple answer, but we confess we don't know what it is, nor, like most people, do we particularly care (except out of idle curiosity). For purposes of dealing with spoken or written language, we can place reliance on subconsciously developed intuitions about what is grammatically correct, and what is not.

Perhaps the best way to characterize our position on memory is that virtually all of its interesting features arise within the context of stories. Stories based on personal episodes have both cognitive and social advantages. Variously experienced by different individuals or groups, they are eagerly shared in conversations and mass communications with other individuals and groups. They span historical time and social space, spreading object lessons and encouraging social solidarity.

Stories are very flexible. They can be copiously indexed to help interpret a variety of new circumstances. They can be jointly constructed by two or more individuals. They are the stuff of conversation. By contrast, we are hard pressed to imagine useful conversations about theorems or grammar or whether a flounder has gills.

Linguists who admire the elegant formal properties of language will disagree (perhaps violently) with our judgment. They might argue, for one thing, that without a knowledge of grammar, communication could not occur, and that grammar is, therefore, the most important knowledge we have. Our counter argument would be that, first of all, communication is certainly possible with a minimum of grammar. For example, make ideas nevertheless scramble him words. Second, grammar is only a vessel for conveying messages, and not to be confused with the messages themselves. When someone gives a great speech, we do not praise the microphone and the amplifier, nor the speaker's grammar. Third, grammar has very little social function other than the unfortunate practice of using grammatical construction to judge the social class background of the speaker.

If you feel that our view overstates the very dominant role of autobiographical experience in the totality of people's knowledge, please wait and see where this position leads us.

UNDERSTANDING MEANS MAPPING YOUR STORIES
ONTO MY STORIES

People are only able to comprehend a small part of what is being said to them. Most of what we attempt to understand contains many aspects, including ideas, people, events, opinions, and so on. It all comes by us at a very rapid rate, and our minds can only do so much with this barrage of information. We get reminded by everything: names, places, words, beliefs, and situations. All these remindings proceed in parallel until we can stand no more, and listen no more.

Once we find an interpretation, we have made our choice. We cannot think about all the possible ramifications of something we are being told, so we pay attention to what interests us. We settle on a story we have been reminded of, and, in effect, we hear no more. On the basis of what interests us, we select the mental paths to take. We express our interests by focusing on certain indexes, those that we can say we have been looking for, ignoring the potential indexes we are not prepared to deal with. Because we can only understand things that relate to our own experiences, it is actually very difficult for us to hear things that people say that are not interpretable through those experiences. In other words, we attend to what we are capable of understanding. When what we are attempting to comprehend relates to what we know, what we care about, or what we were prepared to hear, we can understand quite easily what someone is saying to us. If we have heard the same story or a similar story before, we can also understand more easily what we are being told.

Old Stories

Understanding, for a listener, means mapping the speaker's stories onto the listener's stories. One of the most interesting aspects of the way stories are used in memory is the varied effect they have on understanding. Different people understand the same story differently precisely because the stories they already know are different. When they hear new stories, understanders attempt to construe these stories as old stories they have heard before. They do this because it is actually quite difficult to absorb new information. New ideas ramify through our memories, causing us to revise beliefs, make new generalizations, and perform other effortful cognitive operations. We prefer to avoid all this work. One way to do this is to simply assume that what we are seeing or hearing is just the same old stuff. The real problem in understanding, then, is identifying which of all the stories you already know is the one being told to you yet again.

The Number of Old Stories

In the most shallow form of understanding, a hearer has only one story to tell. No matter what you say to your listener, he tells you this one story, like the grandfather in an earlier discussion. What you say is understood as something that calls to mind the story your listener wanted to tell in the first place. Thus, your listener's understanding algorithm does not need any more in it than a detector for when you have stopped talking, and perhaps your listener doesn't even need that. One typical case of this kind of understanding involves people who we might label as crazy or senile, people who just rattle on without regard to the world around them.

A less shallow form of understanding takes place when a listener with many stories to tell pays enough attention to what you have said to relate the story from a repertoire most closely connected to what you just related. In a sense, this still seemingly shallow understanding may be all we can really expect most of the time.

This view may seem rather radical. After all, we do see and hear new things every day. To say that we never have to understand any brand new story may be overstating the case, we often understand new stories mistakenly. Specifically, we don't understand them as new stories. They may be new enough, but we nevertheless persist in seeing them as old stories.

To understand what we mean here, consider the possibility of this hypothesis in its strongest form. Let us assume an understander who knows three stories. No matter what story you tell one of these three stories will be told back to you. If understanding means matching the story we are hearing to the stories we have already heard, the strong form of our hypothesis states that the understander must decide which of the three stories is most applicable. When the understander has found some way to relate the new story to an old one, we can claim that he or she has understood the new story as well as we could hope.

Seen in this way, the strong hypothesis appears somewhat silly. Why should we label *understanding* as a process that merely differentiates among three stories? In some sense, we should not. But, let us consider the same situation if the understander knows 10,000 stories. When this understander selects a known story as a response to the new one just related, he or she will most likely seem more profound than the understander who has only three stories. If the understander has used sound principles for selecting a story to tell from a database of 10,000, we are not likely to dispute the hearer's having understood the original story. The process of understanding in both cases, however, is identical; only our subjective judgment allows us to decide that one understander seems to have "really" understood. We cannot look inside people's heads to see what the difference in their understanding of a new story is. Therefore, from an objective evaluation of the output alone, we still can only measure understanding by how effectively and reasonably we think the responsive story relates to the input story.

The Selection of Old Stories

Our argument here is that what someone is doing when he or she understands is figuring out what story to tell. Thus, the understanding process involves extracting elements from the input story that are precisely those elements used to label old stories in memory. In other words, understanding is really the process of *index extraction*. This is an idiosyncratic process that depends upon what stories you have stored away and what indexes you have used to label those stories. In some sense, then, no two people can really understand a story in the same way. You cannot understand a story that you have not previously understood because understanding means finding (and telling) a story you have previously understood. Finding some familiar element causes us to activate the story that is labeled by that familiar element. In this way, we find things to say to those who talk to us. These things differ considerably from person to person, thus accounting for the very different ways in which two people can understand the same story.

People have powerful models of the world. Through these models based on the accumulated set of experiences a person has had, new experiences are interpreted. When new perceptions fit nicely into the framework of expectations derived from experience, an understander believes himself to have understood the experience.

Understanding something is, after all, a relative issue. We only understand part of what could have gone on in a situation being described to us, but we can act as if we have understood when we can derive information from the description that we know how to place properly in our memory store. In other words, understanding, rightly or wrongly, usually means being able to add information to memory.

Anomalies in Stories

We dislike failing to understand. When what we have been asked to understand is anomalous in some way, failing to correspond to what we expect, we must reevaluate what is going on. We must attempt to explain why we were wrong in our expectations. A failure to have things turn out as expected indicates a failure in understanding. People desire very much to remedy such failures. We ask ourselves questions about what was going on. The answer to these questions often results in a story.

People are constantly questioning themselves and each other in a quest to find out why someone has done a certain thing and what the consequences of that action are likely to be. Thus, in order to find out how we learn, we must find out how we know that we need to learn. In other words, we need to know how we discover anomalies. How do we know that something does not fit?

The premise here is that whenever an action takes place, we need to discover what might be anomalous about it. Anomalies occur when the answers to one or more questions about an action are unknown. Then we seek to explain what is going on, and then we learn.

To get a handle on this process, we must attempt to sort out different kinds of anomalies. In order for us to see something as anomalous, we must have been unable to answer a question about some circumstance. We must first, then, discover the questions that are routinely asked as a part of the understanding process.

Every time someone tells us something or does something, we, in our attempt to interpret what we are observing, check to see whether the actions involved *make sense*. Actions, however, do not make sense absolutely. That is, we cannot determine whether actions make sense except by comparing them to other actions. In a world where everyone walks around with his or her thumb in his or her mouth, we do not need to explain why a given individual has his or her thumb in his or her mouth. In a world where no one does this, we must explain why a given individual does have his or her thumb in his or her mouth. Clearly, making sense, and thus the idea of an anomaly in general, is a relative thing, relative to the stories one already knows. We are satisfied, as observers of actions, when the stories we hear match our own stories. When the match is very similar, we tell our version of the story. When the match is hardly a match at all, when we have a contradictory story, we tell it. Actually, the middle cases are the most interesting—when we have no story to tell. What do we do then? We look for one. We do this by asking ourselves questions.

People are not processing information with the intent of finding out whether something is anomalous and needs explaining, at least not consciously. In fact, quite the opposite is the case. As understanders we are trying to determine the place for an action we observe. To do this, we must find a place in our memory that was expecting this new action. Of course we may not find one, because not everything in life can be anticipated. Thus, tension exists between the attempt to find a story that allows us to think no more, and the desire to see something as new and worth thinking about. An understander thus asks himself, unconsciously of course, "Do I know a story that relates to the incoming story, and is it one that will allow me to rest from mental processing, or one that will cause me to have to think?"

Examples

Consider the following two stories:

> Once while watching the demolition of a building in Chicago, I was struck by how ineffectively the work was being done. The wrecking ball hit one of the concrete supports near the building's center again and again with little result. It was frustrating to watch the lack of progress.

> This poorly executed demolition reminded me of the time I saw a bullfight in Spain. The matador kept dealing out blows to the bull with his sword with seemingly little effect. The failure to execute a "clean kill" made the whole affair grotesque.

The index that links these two stories has something to do with the way in which the goals of the two observed agents, wrecking–ball operator and matador, were not being achieved. It also has to do with the failure of a prediction task, namely, the prediction that the column (and the bull) will fall. The index is formed from the anomaly of a prediction failure. Anomaly is at the heart of index formation for reminding. Any anomaly is set against the backdrop of expected relationships among the salient details of a story.

Anomalies serve as the trigger for memory access. Because we have found an anomaly, we are forced to think about it. We want stories to be nonanomalous, to match directly to stories we have already understood. In a sense, finding a story to be anomalous forces us to find stories in memory also, but now we are looking for a different type of remembered story, this time one that we have not understood so well. In a sense, there exists a memory base of previous stories that fall into two classes.

The first class includes stories we feel we have understood. An understood story is one for which we have many examples. One could claim that these stories represent our beliefs. A belief under this view is a point of view we can illustrate with a number of good stories. They tend to be of the form, "You know X never works out. Remember that old example of X we both knew? And there was another type of X I saw once, too."

The second type of previous story we use to help us understand consists of stories that we found interesting but somewhat incomprehensible. The "steak and the haircut" story that follows fits into this class. Most obvious remindings, the ones that make us feel that we have been reminded, as discussed in *Dynamic Memory* (Schank, 1982), are of this type. They rely on expectation failure. Expectation failure derives from anomaly. However, the stories of which we are reminded during expectation failure have a different role in understanding. Their role is to begin the process of belief formation.

Thus, in the first case, nonanomalous story reminding, we are reminded of a story by a new story and feel compelled to tell that story as a response. In a sense, our old story is the means for understanding the new story, so overpowering the new story that we remember little of it. In this sense, we cannot understand anything new.

In the second case, anomalous story reminding, we are reminded of an old story, and it feels somewhat peculiar to have that reminding. Rather than feeling compelled to tell our reminded story, we feel curious about the reminding, wondering how we happened to think about it. In the "steak and the haircut" example, one of us was lamenting that his wife never cooked steak as rare as he liked, and the other was reminded of an experience in England years before, when a barber seemed unable to cut his hair as short as he wanted it. This type of story reminding is not reflective of existing beliefs. In fact, we don't yet believe anything because we are at the stage of prebeliefs. We will soon believe something because we are comparing similar anomalous stories in the attempt to form a new generalization that will likely yield a belief. In the steak/haircut example, the emerging belief has to do with the behavior of people who have adapted to a habitual range of variation in activities they perform for others. Requests made outside that range cause disbelief that the request could possibly be so extreme.

The demolition/bullfight reminding is somewhat more elaborate. It may be seen in a variety of ways:

1. The frustrated observer (laborious destruction, botched kill),
2. The inept agent (crane operator, matador),
3. The blocked goal (destroy building, kill bull), and
4. The noble object of destruction that holds up against all odds (pillar, bull).

Although all these interpretations are plausible, only one consistent and coherent rendering is responsible for the formation of an initial indexed probe of memory. From the demolition/bullfight example, aspects of the building demolition situation may give rise to many kinds of causal theories about the origin of the arrangement of collapsed building components, theories of decay to explain the pealing paint of the crane, explanations for the noise of the diesel engine, and so forth. However, for the specific reminding in this example, the anomaly is in the theory of planning that generates the expectations that a worker with a task to do will select an appropriate plan with the right resources (methods and tools) to execute the plan expeditiously. It is also the viewer's inference that the crane operator has selected the same causal model of planning, but has picked an inappropriate method of the plan. Seeing the futility of the crane operator's and matador's actions, in the presence of an aesthetic goal to see the job done cleanly, produces frustration or disappointment, a type of *behavior expectation failure.*

In general, an *anomaly-based index* is a system of interrelated goals, expectations, events, and explanations. The index needs to include causal information about events and expected outcomes as contrasted to real outcomes. It is the contrast between causal theories and causal realities that serves as the means for finding prior stories with the same anomalous character.

Commonalities Between Old and New Stories

We might be tempted to imagine that we create questions for ourselves only when our curiosity is aroused by confusion about something in the world that we have observed, but we are also often forced by social circumstances to create questions for ourselves to answer. When somebody says something to us, we are supposed to say something back. But what are we to say? Is there always something worth saying? Whether or not we have something important to say, given that we have to have something to say, and given that this happens to us all the time, we have developed various methods of coping with this situation. We ask ourselves questions.

Clearly, the questions we ask ourselves about what others have told us cannot be solely dependent upon what we have heard. In a sense, since we are both asking and answering these questions, we need to know that we can answer a question before we ask it. That is, the questions we ask serve as memory calls, requests to get information from memory that will be of use in the formulation of a response to what we have heard.

We are concerned here with input stories that are responded to by stories. In other words, we want to know what questions one might ask oneself in response to a story that would allow a story of one's own to come to mind. We can start simply by considering the paradigmatic case where the response to a story is a story where one says, "The same thing happened to me." However, the call to memory that might retrieve a story where the same thing happened is not likely to be *look for the same thing*.

Obviously, the exact same thing never actually happens to anybody. What actually occurs are episodes in memory that bear some superficial similarity to the input story. Probably more differences exist in an "identical story" than similarities. Certainly places and people, time and context, are usually quite different. What is the same then?

Sameness, at the level we are discussing, exists with respect to plans, the goals that drive those plans, and the themes that drive those goals. Thus, when someone tells you a story, you ask yourself, "Are there any events in my memory where I had a similar goal for a similar reason?" In other words, when we hear a story, we ask whether at the broadest possible level of interpretation, we already know a story like the one we are hearing. Possibly, however, the similarity would not exist at the level of plans. That is, one could easily recognize a similar situation and suggest an alternative plan that might have been followed, based upon one's own experience. We can match new stories to old ones on the basis of identical goals. Therefore, one question we can expect people to ask themselves is, "Do I have a story in memory where the main goal is the same as that being pursued in the story I am hearing?"

One thing we do when we understand a story is to relate that story to something in our own lives. But to what do we relate it? One thing seems clear. Potentially, we can see any story in many ways. What does it mean, then, to see a story in a particular way? It means that one has constructed an index that characterizes a "point" that one derives from the story. This point is usually highly idiosyncratic. Usually the points one derives from stories relate to goals, plans, beliefs, and lessons learned from a story. Here we are back to interestingness again. We don't consider points that fail to relate to beliefs we already have. We look instead for stories that verify beliefs we already have. When a new story can be absorbed into our memories as a "natural fit" with stories we already know, we feel we have understood the story.

Consider for a moment what it might mean for an understander to believe something and not be able to give evidence to justify why he believes what he believes. Certainly inarticulate people have difficulty with that sort of thing. And, in fact, we do treat the ability to justify one's beliefs as a measure of intelligence and reasonableness. In other words, we expect intelligent people to have a story to tell that explains why they believe what they believe. But how can they do this? The mental mechanisms that are available must be ones that connect beliefs to stories. The fact that we can do this is obvious. It follows, therefore, that beliefs are one possible index in memory. Construct a belief, and you should be able to find a story that exemplifies that belief.

We find what we want to say effortlessly and unconsciously, but to do so, we must construct complex labels of events that describe their content, their import, their relation to what we know and what we believe, and much more. Effective indexing is what allows us to have stories to tell, and enables us to learn from the juxtaposition of others' stories and the stories we are reminded of.

How Do We Understand?

A key point is that there is no one way to understand a story. When we hear a story, we look for beliefs that are being commented upon. Any story has many possible beliefs inherent in it. But how does someone listening to a story find those beliefs? We find them by looking through the beliefs we already have. We are not as concerned with what we are hearing as we are with finding what we already know that is relevant.

Picture it this way. As understanders, we have a list of beliefs, indexed by subject area. When a new story appears, we attempt to find a belief of ours that relates to it. When we do, we find a story attached to that belief and compare the story in our memory to the one we are processing. Our understanding of the new story becomes, at that point, a function of the old story. Once we find a belief and connected story, we need no further processing; that is, the search for other beliefs is co-opted. (This is the essence of Kelley's [1971] *discounting principle.*) We rarely look to understand a story in more than one way. The mind cannot easily pursue multiple paths.

Telling Stories Back Implies Understanding

We tell stories for many reasons, one of which is to indicate to our listener that we have understood what he has said to us. Assessing understanding by assessing the relevance of a story that we hear in response may be the only avenue open to us. If we choose to measure understanding by the ultimate impact of a story on our permanent memory structures, we may be very disappointed. To the extent that people do understand anything at all, we can identify three different features of understanding:

1. Matching indexes for story retrieval,
2. Adding aspects of a new story to empty slots in an old one, and
3. Seeking further evidence for stories that were only tentatively regarded as correctly understood.

Thus, the very strong hypothesis is that as understanders we are always looking for stories to tell back. We do this by extracting indexes from what we hear, and by using these indexes to find stories we already know. When we find them, processing stops, and we wait to tell our story. We only incorporate what we have heard into memory when we feel that our own stories are inadequate in some way, for example, if a story is missing a piece. Such pieces can be supplied by other people's stories. We may find a story inadequate when we use it to exemplify a belief that we are not quite sure we hold. We are willing to consider new stories as evidence for or against those beliefs and, therefore, to record and to remember better the stories of others.

Scripts

We all understand differently—this much is obvious. The reason we understand differently is that our memories are different. Our experiences simply are not yours. In order to understand anything, we must find the closest item in memory to which it relates. In Schank and Abelson (1977), we claimed that understanding required one to find the correct knowledge structure, and to use that structure to create expectations for what events were likely to take place, so that new events could be understood in terms of what was normal. Thus, when a story about a cocktail party was being told, an understander brought out his cocktail party script which told him about what ordinarily happens at cocktail parties, and he used that script to guide his understanding of the story he was about to hear.

Idiosyncratic Scripts

In Schank (1982) this concept of scripts was extended to allow a more idiosyncratic view of understanding. The concept of a *dynamic memory* was proposed, one that changed in response to what it had understood as time went on. The conception of understanding developed there was that one's knowledge structures were more idiosyncratic than just standard scripts. Each of us has his or her own conception of a restaurant, formed after numerous restaurant visits. We know what information is shared across a culture about restaurants, but we also know that sometimes what we expect to happen next comes entirely from our own personal experiences. We get reminded of past experiences by current ones, and we use those past experiences as a kind of guide to help us process new experiences.

The reason we get reminded while processing something new is to help us by providing the most relevant knowledge we have in memory. If knowledge of restaurants in general is useful when you enter a restaurant, then it follows that knowledge of *Taillevant* is useful when you enter *Taillevant,* and that knowledge about prior circumstances where you have taken a date to a fancy French restaurant in order to impress him or her is especially useful when you are about to try the same thing again.

Beliefs and Ideas

Reminding is very useful for planning and, therefore, for understanding the plans of others. When someone tells you a story, however, he is talking not only about plans, but often, as we have noticed, about beliefs. When what is to be understood in a story is about beliefs, the kind of guidance we need changes. We do not need to know what will happen next. When we hear these kinds of stories, all we are trying to do is understand them. If we are passively viewing a movie, for example, understanding the movie means being able to follow what is going on by relating what we are seeing to what we know, learning something from the movie in a very weak sense of learning. In a conversation, understanding means being able to respond to a story. In both of these cases, then, understanding means attempting to extract indexes such that old stories can be related to new ones. For movies, the intent is recognition. For conversation, the intent is to be able to respond.

When stories are about ideas rather than plans, the problem for the hearer is to respond to those ideas. But ideas are much harder to grasp than plans. Upon finishing a mystery novel, for example, we may all agree on the plans a murderer was following, but such agreement is more difficult to come by when we attempt to discuss the key ideas in a novel about people and their relationships. A murder mystery has a plot, an involved set of plans, so when the understanding process involves plan extraction from the text, the process is fairly straightforward and not especially idiosyncratic. But when a novel has no plot, when no clear plans are being stated and followed, finding the ideas that are being expressed becomes a problem of *belief extraction.* This extraction of beliefs can be especially difficult because actors and even the writers who create fictional actors often don't know what their beliefs are. Actions can express beliefs, and so as understanders our job is to find the beliefs that are inherent and implicit in a given action.

When the understanding process gets complicated, the primary mechanism we have available to guide our understanding, namely reminding, must work especially hard on rather scanty evidence to find something to get reminded of. The main fodder for reminding in such circumstances comes from beliefs that have been extracted from a text. Such beliefs cause our own personal stories to come to mind when those beliefs happen also to be indexes in our own memories. But then a funny thing happens. We feel compelled to tell those stories. Why we desire so strongly to tell our own stories is something we have already discussed in part, and to which we shall return later. The point here is that once we have found our own story, we basically stop processing.

The reason for stopping is partially based upon our intentions in the first place. Because most of the time we were really just looking for something to say back in response, having found something, we have little reason to process further. But more important, what we have found usually relates to an arguable point, an idea subject to challenge, a belief about which we are uncertain. As understanders, one of our goals is to gather evidence about the world so that we can formulate better beliefs, ones that will equip us better to deal with the real world. Once we have found a match between someone else's experience and our own, we are excited to begin thinking about the connections, so that we can add or subtract beliefs from our own personal database.

The Paradox of Understanding

There is an odd side effect to all this. We are not likely to directly learn from other people's stories. In being reminded of our own stories, ones that of course have more poignancy and more rich detail than the ones we are hearing, we tend to get distracted into thinking more about what happened to us. The incoming story can get recalled in terms of the story of which we were reminded, but in the end, we rarely recall the stories of others easily. More often than not, other people's stories don't have the richness of detail and emotional impact that allows them to be stored in multiple ways in our memories. They do, on the other hand, provide enough details and emotions to allow them to be more easily stored than if the teller had simply told us his or her belief.

Thus we are left with a paradoxical picture of understanding. We do not easily remember what other people have said if they do not tell it to us in the form of a story. We can learn from the stories of others, but only if what we hear relates strongly to something we already knew and causes us to rethink our own stories. We hear, in the stories of others, what we personally can relate to by virtue of having heard or experienced, in some way, that story before. Understanding is an idiosyncratic affair. Our idiosyncrasies come from our stories.

BEHAVIOR IN RESPONSE TO NEW EXPERIENCES

The idea that new experiences get interpreted by adapting old stories is quite closely related to the psychological concept of *stimulus generalization*. The original form of the idea, in Pavlovian conditioning, had to do with the decline in strength of a conditioned response as the conditioned stimulus was shifted along a continuum of stimulus similarity away from its original value.

In this and other simple, well-defined situations, the decline is said by Roger Shepard (1987) to follow a strict mathematical form, which he believed warranted being called the *First Law of Psychology*. As a psychophysical statement based on quantifiable responses to quantifiable stimuli, the First Law is very powerful. Unfortunately, it does not help us much when we ask how interpretations of stories change when they are altered away from prototypical stories. In this context, the idea of similarity is vague, but, nevertheless, compelling. In addressing the nature of similarity of stories, we cite several lines of research, and also tell a story.

Interpreting What You Do Not Understand

Chance Situations With "Skill" Indexes

In her seminal work on the *illusion of control,* Ellen Langer (1975) proposed that people have great difficulty interpreting chance processes such as lottery drawings and roulette wheel spins. The lumpy disorder of chance processes is hard for the ordinary individual to appreciate, much less apply to a single chance event. Accordingly, success and failure at gambling on strictly chance events is typically stored in memory as a set of experiences (e.g., "the time I hit eight in a row at the roulette table at the Taj Mahal"), rather than as summary statistics (e.g., "in roulette, betting on red or black, I won 203 out of 400 bets, but by a chi-square test, this is not significantly different from the expected number, 191 out of 400").

Langer hypothesized that unintelligible abstract chance situations are mentally transformed into skill situations familiar to the individual. There are many features of chance situations that correspond, or can be made to correspond, with features of skill situations. The list of such features would include facing a competitor, having choices, feeling involved, and being familiar with the paraphernalia of the game. These may be thought of as low-level indexes to clusters of past experiences. The more skill-related features a chance situation has, the more it will be understood in terms of skilled activity. A consequence of this misinterpretation is that people come to believe they can, to some extent, be skilled, or at least systematically lucky, in lottery drawings and other totally random events.

In testing this hypothesis, Langer ran a series of experiments following a standard design. A lottery was announced to a pool of subjects. Then, in selling them the tickets, only a random half of the subjects were exposed to one of the skill-related factors. For example, for the "choice" factor, the lottery tickets consisted of bubble gum cards of athletes. The experimental subjects were allowed to choose which athlete they wanted to represent them in the lottery drawing, whereas control subjects were assigned an athlete. Later, under a pretext, all subjects were invited to sell their tickets to one of a group of newcomers who belatedly wanted to enter. For a $1 ticket, the average asking price was above $8 for the choice group, but under $2 for the control group. In other words, chosen tickets were much more highly valued than assigned tickets, despite their objectively equal chances to win the lottery.

In another paradigm, subjects were pitted in a simple card selection game against either a nattily dressed, confident opponent, or a sloppy, indecisive, nerdy competitor. On each trial, the players selected a card blindly from a deck of playing cards, and the player with the higher card won or lost from the experimenter the amount of money he had been willing to bet on that trial, amounts ranging from five to twenty-five cents. Subjects pitted against the confident player risked far less money than those facing the nerd, despite the objective fact that confidence has nothing to do with the proclivity for drawing high cards.

Langer's experiments well illustrate the phenomenon of interpreting poorly understood situations in terms of similar, familiar ones. This research further demonstrates the usefulness of conceptualizing the similarity of new and old experiences by means of "common elements" (Tversky, 1977) or to use shared indexes, in our terms.

A later experiment by Ayeroff and Abelson (1976) applied the same reasoning to an even more unfamiliar experience, a mental telepathy experiment. Subjects were brought into separated rooms and told that they would take turns "sending" a series of impressions of simple objects depicted on a deck of cards as a test of a controversial aspect of extrasensory perception.

These subjects faced an extraordinarily cryptic experience. Not only were they confronted with the trial-by-trial vicissitudes of chance, but almost none of them had ever before participated in a systematic, "scientific" mental telepathy test, and none of them knew exactly how to send or receive telepathic symbols.

Now, what type of familiar experience is similar to this unfamiliar experience? Ayeroff and Abelson asserted that the task is reminiscent of the interpersonal experience of having "good vibes" with someone—feeling that communication is effortless, that two spirits are one. Accordingly, for half of the subject pairs, an experimental manipulation was introduced to produce good vibes between the partners preparing to try telepathy. These pairs were given five warm-up trials in which they could practice their telepathizing while conversing into open microphones. A typical conversation would go something like this:

Sender: I've got it focused now. What are you getting?
Receiver: A top hat?
Sender: That was my second choice. This one is bumblebee.
Receiver: Oh, yeah. Focus it a bit more.
Sender: Okay . . . (Pause) . . . Now I'm beaming it like a laser.
Receiver: . . . (Pause) . . . Oh, wow! I've got a buzzing bee! Great!

Pairs in the control condition also had five warm-up trials, but instead of talking, they practiced with the microphones off, and wrote down what they were thinking. This condition was designed to restrain vibes.

On the 100 real trials following the warm-up, the subjects' belief in their success was measured by having each member of the pair indicate to the experimenter whether he or she thought a hit had been scored on that trial, or not. Because there were five equally numerous symbols in the deck, the chance level of success was 20%. (The actual success rate was 19.6%.) On the average, subjects in the good vibes condition claimed hits on 54% of the trials, compared to the no-vibes subjects' mean estimate of 37%. The authors' interpretation of this result was that the unfamiliar experience of attempted telepathy was interpreted in terms of the very familiar experience of two people attempting to understand one other in a social interaction. When the similarity to successful social episodes was increased by providing warm-up trials with good vibes, the participants' subjective estimates of telepathic success increased significantly.

Thus far, we have reported research on the (mis)interpretation of unfamiliar situations by analogy with familiar situations. We advanced the proposition that the more aspects the new situation has in common with the prototypic familiar one, the greater the reliance on the latter. Let us now consider what specific common aspects (indexes) might be rather compelling, that is, likely to dominate the choice of the particular familiar experience used in interpreting the cryptic one. (Here is where we tell a story.)

The Misunderstood Peace Corps Volunteers

In the early 1960s, an erstwhile Harvard cognitive anthropologist named Volney Stefflre spent some time at Yale working on various eccentric research projects.

His (unpublished) magnum opus was a study of the reactions of Indian natives in remote villages in Chile to the arrival of handfuls of Peace Corps volunteers. These volunteers, fresh from a month of insufficient training, were thrown into strange territory with no clear conception of how to use their limited engineering, public health, or organizational skills to help somebody "down there." (Anybody!) And their Regional Coordinator had long since gone native, and could not be located.

Nevertheless, they were earnest and undaunted, and kept recommending projects to the Indians. These natives, for their part, were puzzled. They had never met any visiting people who behaved quite like this. Why had they come, offering help and advice in such a polite manner? What was the story?

As befits this chapter, Stefflre's hypothesis was that people in unfamiliar situations behave as they would in the familiar situation most similar to the new one. Prior to the arrival of the Peace Corps, the natives had been visited by soldiers, teachers, and government officials, among others. But none of these groups behaved in the eager, earnest, talkative manner of the Peace Corps volunteers. The natives observed for a while, and finally decided that these new people were *ministers.* Thereafter they acted with appropriate reverence but paid no attention whatsoever to advice on medical care, birth control, sewage treatment, and so forth. After all, what would ministers know about medicine, sex, and digging ditches?

In this story we see a tension between different bases for experiential similarity. On the one hand, the personal manner of the unfamiliar volunteers was a very good match to the style of known ministers. On the other hand, the content of the volunteers' apparent interests did not fit with that of the ministers. It is to be expected that, in some ways, the new experience would match the old, and, in other ways, not. If an old experience matched a new one perfectly, then the new experience would not be unfamiliar.

A mix of similar and dissimilar features is found also in metaphor (see Gentner, 1983; Ortony, 1979). Thus one might be tempted to say that remindings are metaphorical. Whether it helps in constructing a theory of reminding to say this, we are not sure. The key question is what aspects of experience (which indexes) are dominant in matching a reminding to a new situation.

The Characteristics of the Story Actor

We have a small hint in the Peace Corps example that matching the personal characteristics of the actors in the new story to actors in the old one may be an especially strong principle of reminding, and thus of understanding. A study by Lamb, Lalljee, and Abelson (1992) makes the same point. Subjects in their study were given thumbnail sketches of four men, each a different prototypical criminal: a purse-snatcher, an embezzler, a terrorist, and a bank robber. Then stories were presented in which each of these men was involved in an ambiguous action sequence that might or might not be interpreted as a particular crime. For example, one character (the embezzler) was previously described as a smooth-talking executive who had been involved in a celebrated stock swindle, and was now in desperate need of money to cover gambling debts. This character then appears in a story as a man sitting in an airplane aisle seat, with an odd-looking package under his seat, and beside an elderly woman with heart problems. He calls the stewardess to give her a note he has just written. She looks troubled, and hurriedly walks front to the pilots' cabin. The task for the subjects is to interpret what is going on. Is it a hijacking, or a medical emergency concerning the elderly woman?

In other combinations presented to different groups of subjects, a prototypical terrorist (interested in political causes, loyal to a group in the Middle East, and so on) appears in the airplane story, and the prototypical embezzler appears in a story about a company vice president who often works late at night at a computer terminal.

There was an almost unanimous tendency for the subjects to infer the presence of a crime when the actor was prototypic for it, but much less a tendency when the actor was nonprototypic (e.g., the terrorist was judged to be hijacking the plane, but the embezzler usually wasn't; he was getting aid for his sick mother).

This notion of story interpretations driven by the perceived personality characteristics of the actor seems of a piece with what Ross (1977) called the *fundamental attribution error.* When we perceive an actor behaving a certain way in a given situation, we tend to perceive the cause of the behavior as something about the individual, rather than something about the situation. An alternative label for this effect might be *personality-driven reminding.* In such a reminding, the personality characteristics of the main actor in the new experience serve as useful indexes for previous experiences with that type of person. This possibility is not always relevant (the lottery example, for instance, has no main actor), but we suggest that when available, personality-driven remindings tend to outcompete remindings driven by other features of the situation.

The Story Model of Juror Decision Making

A vein of relevant research in this regard arises from Pennington and Hastie's (1992) *story model* of juror decision making. They maintain that jurors' natural inclination in making decisions in criminal cases is to organize the evidence into a story structure with initiating events, goals, actions, and consequences. In several mock jury studies, factors facilitating story structures were found to lead to more confident verdicts in the direction of the bulk of the evidence. Interestingly, although subjects in story-inducing conditions organized their stories well, their recall for facts in the case was no better than that of other subjects. This result is consistent with much of the research on *transmission set*. However, the orientation of jurors toward the information about a crime is a mixture of a transmission set (they know they will have to share their judgments with other jurors) and a *receiving set* (they know they should wait for all of the evidence).

Salience

Social psychologists have often relied on the concept of the salience of different features of a situation. In unfamiliar or unstructured settings, there are different interpretations the individual can come up with. What the person is most compellingly reminded of will, we have proposed, guide his or her subsequent behavior. But the reminding process is delicately triggered: An individual placed a second time in the same new situation (with amnesia for the first) might not be reminded of the same prior experience. In part, the salience of one reminding rather than another is due to situational influences: The individual's interpretation of what is going on can be manipulated by hints and symbols. A blatant literary example of this is the influence of Iago over Othello. Iago drops innuendoes of Desdemona's unfaithfulness each time an ambiguous behavior of hers is seen or heard by Othello, until at last the tragic Moor accepts this totally false interpretation.

Experimental Manipulation of Salience

Salience has been systematically manipulated in psychological research on persuasion, impression formation, and other topics. Price (1989), for example, showed that members of a group can be led to the interpretation that their interactions with another group are conflictful by making salient some issue between them. "Humanities and science majors clash over curriculum change," says the bogus headline, and presto— students who happen to be humanities majors start resisting persuasive communications from science majors on other issues. Such demonstrations of the effects of reminding people of their group identities go way back to the 1950s, when Kelley (1953) showed that Boy Scouts sitting at a Boy Scout meeting in full uniform were much more resistant to a speaker who made fun of hiking and camping activities than were Boy Scouts at an undesignated meeting who were exposed to the same speaker.

Availability. Modern research workers in the field of social cognition usually use the terms availability and activation to distinguish two sources of salience. *Availability* (Tversky & Kahneman, 1973) refers to the ease with which a given idea, judgment, or evaluation comes to mind. For the present chapter, we would translate this into "the ease with which a given experience comes to mind." Availability arises from repetition of an experience. Thus scripts in particular have high availability: They tend to be triggered as first-choice interpretations of any situation in which script-related cues are present. Also, strong attitudes have high availability (Powell & Fazio, 1984), which increases with repetitive exercise, especially via the expression of those attitudes (Downing, Judd & Brauer, 1992). This implies, for example, that the bigotry of the bigot increases as his expressions of intolerance increase. In the context of story interpretation, telling someone a story about your experiences might be expected to increase the availability of that story on future occasions.

Activation.   In contrast to availability, which signifies the internal priorities of different experiences, *activation* refers to external factors affecting the choice of interpretation. Iago might be said to have activated Othello's jealousy story. The Boy Scout and humanities majors studies also merit the label of activation. In the former case, the presence of peers in uniform presumably activated Boy Scout camping experiences. If these had been fun, this would undercut the speaker's trash talk about camping.

Currently, a very popular class of experimental methods for producing activation is *priming.* This refers to the incidental or sometimes subliminal introduction of an idea in order to activate extensions or related ideas. As cognitive psychologists and social cognitionists will know, the priming concept was introduced by Meyer and Schvaneveldt (1971) in a study of *semantic priming.* These investigators presented subjects with short strings of letters on a succession of trials, and the subjects' task was to decide as rapidly as possible whether each string was a word or a nonword. The experimenters had the hypothesis that words would prime (activate) the perception of similar words that immediately followed, reducing reaction times to the second word. Sure enough, as illustrated by their now standard example, reaction time to NURSE was faster when preceded by DOCTOR than when preceded by an unrelated word such as LAWYER. Other examples with the same structure also produced the same effect. Activation effects have since been obtained in many areas, the most popular of which appears to be the priming of expectations about the traits of an unfamiliar person (Higgins, Rholes, & Jones, 1977).

Priming also occurs with sentences, and even paragraphs, as stimuli. Sharkey and Mitchell (1985) showed that scripts could be primed with introductory sentences such as "The children all brought their presents to Mary's house." Such introductions speeded the lexical decision response to script-related words presented immediately afterwards. For example, subjects were faster to recognize CANDLES as a word when it followed the introduction of the party script, as opposed to a nonparty introduction. Seifert, McKoon, Abelson, and Ratcliffe (1980) demonstrated a priming effect of proverb-related stories on other stories illustrating the same proverb. Indeed, priming can be conceptualized as the (usually implicit) activation of particular story indexes.

Psychological theorizing and research is amply supportive of the idea that new stories are understood in terms of similar old stories. Search for old experiences from memory requires some kind of indexing scheme for picking relevant stories, and we have suggested three conditions affecting the implicit choice of indexes:

1. When applicable, indexing in terms of the personality characteristics of the main actor in the new story tends to be preferred.
2. When aspects intrinsic to a particular type of old experience are added to the scenario of a new experience, search tends to be influenced by these common aspects.
3. In any experience, situational factors or the actions of other people can affect the interpretation of that experience by selective activation or priming.

STORYTELLING AND MEMORY

Stories, as we have noted, are the basis of our understanding. Understanding means retrieving stories and applying them to new experiences. The consequence of this is profound for models of memory. If active memory is really a beehive of activity involving story retrieval and story application, then what it means to remember needs to be reinterpreted.

Researchers have often viewed memory as a kind of warehouse, a place where events are placed and then retrieved when needed. The problem with this point of view is that it assumes that events are discrete items, made up of discrete parts. Thus we assume that when something happens to you, it is labeled as event 497, with parts 1–27. This view of memory essentially buries two key aspects of memory. First, memories for events are indexed by our understanding of the events themselves. Our trip to Maine is not labeled event 456 or even "trip to Maine, 1975." Rather, the event would be indexed by a characterization of the events it comprises. This means that "the time I almost drowned" or "the best lobster I ever tasted" might be two of the many indexes such an event might have in memory. Second, and most important, we must consider how such indexes might have been constructed in the first place, because in their construction in memory and by memory, they have a serious effect on the stories we subsequently tell.

Constructing the Story of an Experience

When we construct an index, we do so not by saying, "Well, what would be a good name for this event that I wish to store away in memory?" People are not so conscious of their internal processes as to be able to ask such a question. Rather, we proceed through life having experiences and in no way attempting to store them away. We are not trying to remember, at least not consciously. Of course, we are remembering, but how?

Telling Is Remembering

We remember by telling stories. Storytelling is not something we just happen to do. It is something we virtually have to do if we want to remember anything at all. No one who has recalled a lobster dinner as "the best one I ever had" could have possibly have done so without consciously thinking that thought. Furthermore, that person would most likely, have expressed that thought as well to a dinner companion, perhaps, or to someone who asked about his trip to Maine. Although it seems less likely that it would be absolutely necessary to tell someone about a near drowning in order to remember it, people nevertheless do seem to feel compelled to tell about such salient experiences. It is in the storytelling process that the memory gets formed.

This happens in the following way. We form an opinion, a viewpoint, or indeed, a good story about what happened to us. We retrieve other details of the story, such as where we stayed, and who we were with in that context, but, over time, we have difficulty remembering the surrounding details. We tend to just remember the story we have constructed. Everything else has to be reconstructed. To put this another way, the stories we create are the memories we have. Telling is remembering. Everything else, what we fail to tell, gets forgotten, although it can often be reconstructed. The effect of all this is very interesting. Not only do our memories become a function of what we talk about, but if these stories aren't sufficiently rehearsed, that is, told often enough, we begin to forget them as well, and because of this a curious thing happens.

The Dangers of Misremembering

In our desire to tell a story in the first place, we resort to certain standard storytelling devices. Those devices are part of our cultural norms for storytelling and they reflect what is considered to be a coherent story in a culture. Due to the fact that in telling one's story to others one wants to be coherent, one has to structure one's story according to these norms. This means, in effect, that one has to lie. Nothing in life naturally occurs as a culturally coherent story. In order to construct such a story, we must leave out the details that don't fit, and invent some that make things work better. This process was seen in Bartlett's (1932) work on Eskimo folk tales, which were remembered by British subjects many years later as coherent stories, although the original was certainly not coherent in a British context. This same process is at work when we tell our own stories. We tell what fits and leave out what does not. Thus, whereas our lives may not be coherent, our stories are. The danger here is that we may come to believe our own stories. When our stories become memories and substitute for the actual events, this danger is quite real. We remember our stories and begin to believe them. In this way, stories shape memory profoundly.

When something important happens to you, you feel compelled to tell someone else about it. Even people who are reticent to talk about themselves cannot help telling others about significant events that have just happened to them. Let us consider how this process might work.

Imagine, for example, that you have just returned from a vacation, or that you meet someone who knows that you have recently been on a date that you were especially looking forward to. In either of these situations, when you are asked how it went, you can respond with a short pithy sentence or two, or you can begin to tell a story that captures the essential parts of the experience.

Changes in Stories When Retold or Not Retold

Now imagine that another person asks you substantially the same question, about how your recent date went. How different is your second story likely to be from the initial story? Of course, the time you have in which to tell the story, or differences in intimacy with the person you tell it to, may affect the telling, but the likelihood is that on a gross level, the subsequent stories you tell will leave out or emphasize the same things. The stories will be, from an index point of view, substantially the same. In other words, while telling about a trip to a great restaurant, if you don't tell about the lovely park you visited beforehand, the park episode will eventually cease to be part of the story.

The process of story creation, of condensing an experience into a story-size chunk that can be told in a reasonable amount of time, is a process that makes the chunks smaller and smaller. Subsequent iterations of the same story tend to get smaller in the retelling as more details are forgotten. Of course, they occasionally get larger when fictional details are added. The old psychological terms for these two alternatives are *leveling* and *sharpening* (Allport & Postman, 1945). Normally, after much retelling, we are left with exactly the details of the story that we have chosen to remember. In short, story creation is a memory process. As we tell a story, we are formulating the index to the experience that we can use to create a story describing that experience.

Losing Access to Details

If we do not tell the story soon enough or often enough after the experience, or if we do not tell the story at all, the experience cannot be coalesced or indexed because its component pieces begin to mix with the new information that continues to come in. We cannot remember a great restaurant if we keep eating in ones quite like it day after day.

Losing Generalizations

Although parts of the experience may be remembered in terms of the low-level memory structures that were activated—a restaurant may be recalled through cues having to do with food, or with a place, or with the particular company—the story itself does not exist as an entity in memory. Thus, without telling a story, any generalization that might pertain to the whole of the experience would get lost. We could remember the restaurant, but we might forget that the entire trip had been a bad idea. We might be able to reconstruct generalizations about the trip as a whole, but this process would require doing exactly what one would have had to do in the first place. That is, reconstruction with an eye towards generalizations creates indexes as stories. In other words, we tell stories in order to remember them.

Motivated Forgetting

Not only do we tell stories to remember them. The opposite side of the coin is also true. We fail to create stories in order to forget them. When something unpleasant happens to us, we often say, "I'd rather not talk about it," because not talking about it makes it easier to forget. Once you tell what happened to you, you will be less able to forget the parts of the story that you told. In some sense, telling a story makes it happen again. If the story is not created in the first place, however, it will only exist in its original form, for example, in a form distributed among the mental structures used in the initial processing. Thus, in the sense that it can be reconstructed, the experience remains. When the experience was a bad one, that sense of being in memory can have annoying psychological consequences. If we encounter a particular setting or prop, unhappy remindings may well occur when not expected.

Adding Embellishments

When you begin to tell a story again that you have retold many times, what you retrieve from memory is the index to the story itself. That index can be embellished in a variety of ways. Over time, even the embellishments become standardized. An old man's story that he has told hundreds of times shows little variation, and any variation that does exist becomes part of the story itself, regardless of its origin. People add details to their stories that may or may not have occurred. They are recalling indexes and reconstructing details. If, at some point they add a nice detail, not really certain of its validity, telling the story with that same detail a few more times will ensure its permanent place in the story index. In other words, the stories we tell time and again are identical to the memory we have of the events that the story relates. Stories change over time because of the process of telling, because of the embellishments added by the teller. The actual events that gave rise to the story in the first place have long since been forgotten.

Memory for Daily Events

The Man With the Special Day

Let's imagine a day in the life of a man living alone in a city. He works by himself and for himself. He sees and talks to no one about his particular experiences during the course of one day. He gets a haircut. He buys some groceries. He shops for new shoes. He fills out tax forms at home and watches some television. The next day he resumes a more normal life, interacting with people and talking about his experiences, but for some reason he never speaks to anyone about the day we have just described. Now, the question is, what can he remember about that day?

The answer to this is complex because we don't know two things. First, how unusual is this day for him? Second, how much rehearsal has occurred? Let us explain why each of these questions matters.

What makes an event memorable is both its uniqueness and its significance to you personally. For example, we easily remember the first time we do anything of significance. Consequently, if this man has never spent a day alone, or if he was deliberately trying out such a lifestyle, or if he had been designated "King for a Day," he would probably remember the day. Or would he?

At first glance, it seems probable that he would remember such a unique or significant day. Therefore, how easily can we imagine the man never telling anyone about it? If people are incapable of not telling others about significant events, then this man, too, feeling that the day was important, would be likely to mention it to someone.

This brings up the question of *rehearsal*. One phenomenon of memory is that people talk to themselves, not necessarily aloud of course, but they do tell themselves stories, collecting disparate events into coherent wholes. Let's imagine then that while this man talked to no one about his day, he did talk to himself. What might he have said? If rehearsal entails storytelling, he would have needed to compose a story with some pertinent generalizations or observations drawn from the day. Moreover, he would have needed to keep retelling himself that story in order to remember it.

What happens if he fails to tell anyone, including himself, about his day? Does he fail to recognize the grocery store where he shopped when he sees it again next week? Does he fill out his tax forms all over again? Of course not.

Obviously, we can remember events that we have not discussed with anyone, but how? How are events like going to the grocery store remembered? Certainly such events never become stories, so they are not maintained in our memory by repeated telling. How, then, are they maintained?

Many psychologists have claimed that memory for facts must be organized hierarchically in a semantic memory. Others have argued for a memory that is more episodically based, and still others have suggested combining the two. A neatly organized hierarchy of semantic concepts is easy to imagine, but the world is full of oddities and idiosyncratic events that fail to fit neatly into a pre-established hierarchy. For example, we may "know" from semantic memory that female horses have teats, but we may more readily access this fact from an episodic store if we witnessed our pet horse giving birth and then suckling its young. Our first memories of playing ball may very well come to mind when the word "ball" comes up, and the properties we ascribe to "ball" may well be ones that a particular ball we remember actually had. In short, the semantic–episodic distinction does not seem to be sharp and clear.

Story-based Versus Event-based Memory

A more useful, process-based distinction can be drawn between *story-based memory* on the one hand and a generalized *event-based memory* on the other. To understand this distinction, let us go back to the question of where our hero's grocery store, tax form filling, and reading experiences are stored in his memory.

We know that he can recall what he did in each instance, so how is this ability to recall different from his ability to tell a story? Probably, he cannot tell the story of his day, whereas he can recall certain aspects of his day. This difference reflects itself in a kind of abstract idea of "place" in memory. To "recognize" the grocery store visit means he knows he has been there. Had something interesting happened there, especially an event that taught him something new about the operation of grocery stores, for example, we can feel sure that he would remember it. Yet how can we make this assertion when he probably will not be able to recall this day if he never talks about it to anyone? We seem to have paradox here, but, in fact, we do not.

When someone has an experience in a grocery store, they update their knowledge of grocery stores. This is how grocery store scripts grow and change over time, in response to actual changes in grocery stores that occur over time, and as a way of organizing pointers to personal odd experiences that have taken place in grocery stores. When shelf arrangements change in a particular grocery store, the patron's memory must change as well. Sometimes it takes a few trials: A patron might keep looking for milk in its old location for some time after a change in the placement of the dairy section, but eventually changes in memory follow changes in reality. Thus people learn from their experiences, but where does this learning take place in the mind?

People need a file of information about grocery stores that includes specific information about where their favorite grocery store keeps the milk, and what it wants from you in order to cash a check. This file must also include general information about grocery stores apart from your favorite, however. When we enter a new grocery store, we want to be able to utilize expectations about our favorite store that will help us in the new one. For example, we want to predict that the milk will be near the cottage cheese in any grocery store, and that a new one might not take our check. In other words, we are constantly drawing upon our file of knowledge about grocery stores and adding to that knowledge when new experiences teach us something worth retaining.

What we are decidedly not doing, however, is updating our memories on what we might call a daily unit basis. That is, we are not making note that on October 16, we bought a quart of milk and six oranges. We could try to do this, of course, but we would have to try very hard. We might make up a poem about what we bought on that day and then memorize the poem, for example. But if we do not take some extreme measure like that, we will simply fail to remember the experience unless something rather strange or important occurred at the same time. Why can't we remember what we bought in the grocery store on October 16, 1982?

One obvious answer is that it would be absurd to remember such a thing. Human memory must be selective to function well. One aspect of this selectivity in memory is the recognition of the distinction between events that are to be added to one's internal storehouse of generalized events and those that need to be summarized and indexed and told as new stories to be added to one's story-based memory. Memory is looking for knowledge that tells it something about the nature of the world in general. This storehouse of knowledge is, on its face, analogous to the notions of semantic memory, but, of course, because it is based in actual experience, it is really quite episodic. Although the notion that semantic memory should be devoted to such general knowledge seems inherently correct, the notion seems equally wrong that such knowledge would not have at its core a seriously idiosyncratic component. We may all know that a flounder is a fish and that a fish has gills, but we do not all know that our father used to eat flounder every Tuesday, and, therefore, so did we, and we refuse to eat it ever again. Yet, this latter fact is just as much a part of the definition of flounder for us as is the fact that a flounder has gills, maybe more, because one fact is far more real to us than the other.

Building up Event-based Memory

Any general storehouse of knowledge, then, is likely to depend very strongly on the expectations about various objects and situations that have been gathered over a lifetime of experience. Thus, when a new experience occurs that speaks to what we already know about something, perhaps updating it, perhaps overriding it, we add that experience to our memories. This is why we remember filling out the tax form. We add the experience of filling out the tax form to our general storehouse of similar experiences. That experience then becomes part of our general knowledge of tax form filling and updates what we already know.

Similarly, when we read something, the facts we garner from our reading go to particular places in our memory, to the structures that we have that are repositories of information about those subjects. Information about restaurants updates what we know about restaurants. Stories about travel to exotic places causes our memory to add new information to our existing knowledge about those particular places and to general information we may have about exotic places. Of course, the actual updating of knowledge structures is much more complex than this. In *Dynamic Memory* (Schank, 1982) it was proposed that pieces of memory structures, once altered, update those same pieces as instantiated in other structures. Thus, for example, if you learn something about paying with credit cards in a restaurant, that new information needs to update how to pay with credit cards in a department store and at an airport as well. The way this happens is through sharing of standardized smaller knowledge structures of which "paying" would be one, and "credit card paying" would be another even smaller structure.

Through such structures, and through the sharing of smaller structures by larger structures, we build up event memory. Every time we use a particular body of knowledge in our interactions with the world, that knowledge gets altered by the experience. We cannot fill out a tax form without using the prior experiences we had in filling out tax forms as a guide to help us through the experience, but because that knowledge is being used as a guide, it changes. We add new information about tax forms, about the experience of filling them out, that overrides what we previously knew. When we are finished doing anything, therefore, our memories are altered by the experience. We don't know what we knew before.

The process of updating our event-based memory every time we have a relevant new experience has an odd side effect, however. The construction of a memory that organizes information around repetitions of events destroys the coherence of any particular *sequence* of events. The dynamic nature of event memory causes the experiences of walking to be placed with prior ones of walking, those of shopping to be placed together with others of shopping, and so on. Constant updating of a memory for events causes a general storehouse about typical events to be built up by destroying the connectivity of one particular event to another particular event. A particular event of walking, therefore, becomes disconnected from its intended purpose of enabling one to go shopping at one particular time, for example, thus rendering us useless when asked how we got to the grocery store. Our only recourse is to make an educated guess: "I must have walked; it's not far, and I usually walk if it's a nice day, and it was June after all."

The Need for Story-based Memory

Because of our need for memory to effect a constant disconnection of events from those that follow, we feel a need to undo this process when something of significance occurs. We can stop the dynamic disconnection from taking place and remember events in sequence by consciously giving our memories an event to remember that is a unit, specifically, a unit that we have rehearsed, sometimes frequently. In this process, the role of stories in memory comes into play and motivates the concept of story-based memory that is the core of this chapter. Stories are a way of preserving the connectivity of events that would otherwise be disassociated over time.

For stories to be told without a great deal of effort, they must be stored away in a fashion that enables them to be accessed as a unit. If this were not the case, stories would have to be reconstructed each time they were told, a process that would become more and more difficult with time as the connections between events fade from memory. Telling a story would require a great deal of work to collect all the events from memory and to reconstruct their interrelation. Further, stories would be quite different each time they were told. Reconstruction would not be the same each time, and instead, different stories would result, depending upon what parts of memory were looked at during the time of telling. This kind of storytelling does occur, of course, especially when stories are being told for the first time, but most storytelling requires so little work and is so repetitive, with each version so much like the other, that many stories must be stored and retrieved as chunks.

A different type of memory process, then, must be active here. Returning to our example, even if our hero fails to tell one or more stories from his isolated day, he will still understand and remember what has happened to him in the sense that the facts will be available to him. The facts, however, will be available to him only when the various segments of his day are accessed for some reason, when someone asks him about his favorite grocery store, for example. What he will lose is the ability to tell a story about that particular day. The day will disappear as a unit from his memory, as will various aspects of the day. In other words, events of the day will no longer be accessible by asking himself about what happened today. After a while these events will only be found in the other parts of memory which will have subsumed them. What is remembered, then, will be in terms of what he knows about grocery stores, not a story in and of itself arising from the events of that day. To find that kind of story in memory, one must have put it there consciously in the first place, either by telling it to somebody or to oneself.

Story-based memory, then, is a different kind of memory from the memory that contains general event knowledge. Story-based knowledge expresses our points of view and philosophy of life. It depends upon telling and gets built up by telling. The consequences of this process are interesting when one considers what we tell and why, because we are, quite unconsciously, making decisions about what to remember.

THE SOCIAL CONTEXT OF STORYTELLING

Human beings have large collections of stories. They accumulate stories over a lifetime, and when they are given the opportunity, they select an appropriate story and tell it. They determine appropriateness by a variety of factors, such as familiarity, emotion, the potential for shared viewpoint, and the need for approval. As we have seen, the story indexes can be selected for a variety of different purposes. The stories we tell are strongly affected by those to whom we are telling them. In any situation where we find ourselves telling an old story, we might reasonably wonder why we have chosen to tell that particular story.

The Teller and the Listener

The Influence of the Listener

One must decide on the appropriateness of a given story, and one usually seeks the approval of the listener either to elaborate or to tell another story. The listener, then, performs a very important role for a storyteller. He or she reveals, usually implicitly, which stories he or she wants to hear. The listener may like ones that show how important or powerful you are, or he or she may think such stories are exaggerations or simply should not be told. The listener may want to learn some specific thing from your stories, or he or she may simply want you to finish up, so the listener can tell a story in response.

Consequences for the Teller

The trick for any listener is to send out the right signals, those that encourage the telling of the stories that the listener wants to hear. In the selection and evaluation process, eliciting the listener's approval is very important. We want to please our listener, but pleasing is a fairly complicated idea. If we know that we are our listener's hero, we might tell stories about our successful exploits in the world. If we know that our listener admires sensitivity, we might alter our stories to reflect that sensitivity.

A story, however, need not be favorable for the presentation to be favorable. Consider the boy who often tells stories in which he has been a nerdy, sad sack character. He locked himself out of his house at 3:00 A.M. in his pajamas. He called his fiancee by the wrong name. He gave the finger to a motorcyclist who turned out to be a policeman. He painted two sides of his house and then ran out of paint and discovered that the color could no longer be matched, and so on. If these are not the only type of anecdotes he tells, and they are told to share a laugh about human foibles, we do not think ill of the teller. In fact, we may like him the more because he doesn't take himself too seriously. He is prone to "endearing pratfalls" (Aronson, Willerman, & Floyd, 1966).

An interactive storyteller, one who tells a story in parts while being interrupted by his or her listener, alters the story according to the interruptions. Thus, when a listener makes it clear by obvious reactions that certain kinds of stories hold more interest than others, the storyteller is likely to alter the stories being told accordingly. A teller tries to tell the story the listener wants to hear.

The telling of one's old stories is a process with consequences. The outside world determines which of our stories are worthy of telling by the way it listens to them. These stories then become our own definition of self. We are the stories we like to tell. Singer and Salovey (1993), in their book on autobiographical memory, call our biased collection of memories the *remembered self*.

If we surround ourselves with people who agree that certain kinds of stories are wrong to tell, clearly, we will tell those stories less frequently. Stories that make us feel good to tell need willing listeners if we want to feel good. Similarly, those stories that put the teller in a bad light may well find willing listeners, but the effects may be quite harmful in the long run. Being defined by a set of negative stories has its limits. Overdone, it can be deleterious to one's mental health.

Of course, we do not only tell stories we have told before. The events we choose to make part of our stories are important to how we define ourselves: When new stories are constructed for telling, the process of constructing those stories changes memory significantly. The storytelling process relies very heavily on evaluation rules that tend to very strongly reflect one's view of the world, oneself, and the events that have occurred in one's life. Thus, two people might be expected to relate events quite differently, depending upon their individual perspectives of what is worth telling, what is significant, what the listener is interested in, and what the events reveal about themselves. This last dimension alters the story composition process most profoundly. In order to tell a story that reflects well on oneself, one might select quite different episodes to relate than if one wanted to tell the same event in a way that might lead the listener to feel sympathy for oneself.

The story composition process reflects very strongly the view that the teller has combined himself with the view that he wants others to have of him. Any listener who really wants to know the person he is talking to, would, of course, want to hear the person's favorite stories. Similarly, any teller who really wants his listener to know him would want to tell his favorite stories. The more we desire intimacy, the more intimate the nature of the stories we tell (see Taylor, DeSoto, & Lieb, 1979).

Composing Stories

From the memory point of view, the process of telling a story is significant because of the composing subprocess that storytelling entails. In order to compose a story, one has to search memory for relevant episodes to relate, and for episodes to discard that one chooses not to relate. Thus, the composition of a story requires both a search and an evaluative process that selects and discards items found during the search.

Mental Efficiency

Once a story has been composed, it tends to stick around. As we have observed, when you tell the story of your vacation, you concentrate on certain details and leave out others. Relating the same events in a different way becomes more and more difficult. Each subsequent retelling of the story is likely to get shorter, and to enhance the second or third telling of a story so that it is much different from the first becomes much more difficult. Therefore, telling, or more important, composing stories affects memory profoundly. Memory tends to lose the original and keep the copy. The original events recede, and the new story takes its place.

Why does memory work in this way? The story composition process requires a great deal of work; therefore, repeating the process every time for each additional telling of the story is quite costly. Moreover, in a composed story the number of episodes to remember is much smaller than the number of original events themselves. Further, these episodes have a coherence to them that allows reconstruction of missing or loosely connected details. Remembering less is simply easier, especially if what we are trying to remember is all located in the same place in our memory, and we do not have to search for it again. A story, remembered as a story, is a unit that can be easily found, easily told, and made useful for a variety of purposes.

On the other hand, collecting events from the separate places where they were stored is a sloppy process at best. You might find something different each time. You would certainly lose information, or at least fail to find it some of the time. Further, the required attention to detail would be staggering. It would never be safe to forget something because it might be found useful later. Retrieving a story that is stored in only one place in memory is much simpler. It makes retrieval easier; it lets memory work less hard; it allows forgetting; and it provides a constancy of lessons to be learned that does not need to be constantly reexamined.

Telling Negative Stories

Suppose we have a bad experience. Is the best strategy to keep it quiet, to suppress it? What does the storytelling model of memory predict about suppression? We tell stories in order to create records in memory that will coalesce a complex experience into a coherent whole. The story composition process creates a coherent whole that the storytelling process reinforces in memory. When a bad event occurs that we do not want to dwell upon, we should tell someone about it, nevertheless, in order to start the composition process going. You recall that a side effect of the composition process allows memory to forget the details not collected in the composition. After composition, discarded details become harder to remember than if no story had been told at all.

Thus we can try to *edit* the story to make it less painful, and store the edited version that we have told someone. Of course, memory maintains the newly created story, that may still be negative. Here is the key prediction, however. A story must be told fairly often to retain its status as a viable, that is, findable, memory structure. In other words, if you have a bad experience, you should compose the story, tell it once, and never tell it again. The sooner you tell a story, the sooner you can begin to forget it—by never telling it again. If you want to remember the story, on the other hand, keep telling it. Telling stories is fundamentally a memory reinforcing process. The more you tell, the more you remember. The areas you dwell on when you talk are the areas your memory wants to and does reinforce.

Repression

What happens, however, when the negative story you want to tell has no listener available, but you can't stop thinking about it? Or, alternatively, what happens when a negative event occurs, no story is constructed at all, and the negative event doesn't actually disappear? Is this where the phenomenon we commonly refer to as *repression* comes in?

Stories we never tell may illustrate why we are always doing something wrong, or they may be about dark events in our past that we do not really want to admit actually happened. Stories that remain untold have a variety of properties that differentiate them from more normal stories. The major difference is that certain incoherencies are allowed to exist in untold stories. When we tell a story, we make sure it is both coherent and relevant to some point that might interest the listener. When we fail to tell a story, we do not need to examine the story for consistency. We can tell it to ourselves and reinforce it just as we might reinforce a story we actually tell by telling it, but, as we have said, our listener modifies our story by the very act of listening. Ordinarily, this modification does not occur for stories we tell only to ourselves. Here again, we see why it is important to tell one's stories. Therefore, if you cannot easily forget disturbing events and insist on telling the stories to yourself, you would be better off telling them to someone else, a therapist if need be.

Don't Even Think About It

To illustrate the reinforcement principle, imagine a 6-year-old boy coming home from school with a cold, and the next day his mother comes down with a fever and dies. The son assumes he has killed her, especially since he was angry with her the morning of the day he caught the cold. That she was in very poor health at the time, that he often caught a cold, and that he was often angry at her for all the ordinary reasons children might get mad at their parents, does not help him. The causal chain seems so compelling that he concludes he was the killer. As he grows up, he ruminates often about this awful episode and its import, but cannot alter its essential outline. He tries not thinking about it, but as Wegner (1989) has ingeniously shown, the explicit attempt not to think about something only makes things worse in the long run. The best short-run method for avoiding the thought of an object or topic is to substitute a variety of personally meaningful, competing thoughts.

Unfortunately, a side effect of the "don't think about it" strategy is that on later occasions, when the meaningful substitutes come to mind for other reasons, they remind the individual of their previous function. He is thus confronted again with the aversive memory. If he tries new alternative thoughts, they too become contaminated, and in the most extreme version of this scenario, he eventually becomes totally preoccupied with the terrible core memory.

Repeated failures to tell a negative self-defining story can thus establish a spiral of self-abuse, the opposite effect of repeatedly telling and embellishing a self-enhancing story.

An Ambivalent, Neurotic Storyteller

In a rare computer simulation of neurotic thought processes, Colby and Gilbert (1964) developed a knowledge base from a large series of psychoanalytic sessions. The patient, a woman in her 30s, had enormous hostility for her mother, but could not or would not admit it. The computer program imitated several stratagems that the real patient had tried. The most interesting class of these involved transformations of her forbidden story into a related story that was sufficiently different to be acceptable for her to tell. Thus the story, "I hate mother" (embellished with details), raised an anxiety monitor to an unbearable level, and set off a story transformation subroutine that came up with things like, "Actually, my mother hates me," or "I don't hate my mother, but my sister hates dogs." The first of these examples is close to the real story, and, therefore, has good potential for satisfying the need to tell, but this very similarity makes this alternative too dangerous, and it is likely to be rejected. On the other hand, "My sister hates dogs" is safe to tell, but is so disguised that it does not satisfy the goal of expressing the true situation.

Included in the simulation were three affect monitors which went up and down, depending on the nature of what was said. The simulated patient cycled through a number of attempts to tell her story. Whether she succeeded depended on the settings of various initial parameters, but she typically failed. After a number of painful failures, she refused to deal with this topic any more in the analytic hour.

The Fate of the Untold Story

The phenomenon of repression relies upon this idea of the unwanted and untold story. When we have no listener for a story, we tend to bury it. It may well go away; indeed, without rehearsal, it should go away. Certain events, however, are too important to go away simply because we fail to tell their story. Stories about the grocery store will go away if we don't tell them, partly because they are not so interesting or important, and partly because we replace such stories with similar ones. However, stories about significant episodes in our childhood, for example, do not go away so easily, partly because our childhood does not keep recurring, and partly because significant episodes are, by definition, different from the norm, and thus unlikely to repeat. Episodes that define a situation will tend to remain in our memory, looking for a repetition that will allow us to make the appropriate generalizations, but we cannot easily check out our generalizations and explanations if the events that concern us do not replicate. Furthermore, childhood explanations are childish and often inadequate. Because explanations are often the indexes or labels for stories, bad explanations may not easily find another situation for comparing.

Thus, untold stories tend to stick around when they are unique in some way, waiting for a similar story to occur and create generalizations. If such stories are very negative stories and remain untold, they can indeed affect a person's psyche.

This phenomenon of the untellable story is familiar to psychoanalysts. They typically regard the dangerous content as repressed, and not available to consciousness. With this view, one of the goals of analysis is to undo repression and enable the patient to have insight into the hidden motives. We prefer to think that untold, negative autobiographical experiences are partially conscious but surrounded by confusion resulting from many unsuccessful attempts to edit and tell them, leading to the absence of useful indexes.

Stories Based on Shared Experiences

A very interesting property of experiential memories is that two or more people may go through the same set of activities or events at the same time, and each come away with variations in the stories they tell about it.

Rashomon

The famous Japanese movie, *Rashomon,* acts out four different versions of an encounter in the woods between a bandit, a woman, and her husband. Each of these main characters tells a face-saving story of the encounter. The "truth" may be somewhere in-between, but by the time a fourth version from a supernatural presence is heard, the audience begins to doubt whether there is such a thing as the true story.

Japanese metaphysics notwithstanding, biased testimony by participants in conflictful events has a bearing on the outcomes of legal proceedings, and this certainly merits psychological analysis. However, we are going to bypass this application, and concentrate instead on the social consequences of similarities and differences in memories of shared episodes.

Co-biographical Memories

Meaningful (and sometimes meaningless) experiences are told and retold soon and/or long afterwards by couples ("the time we sneaked out and went swimming in the moonlight"), families ("the way Grandma sold a house before she bought it, and made a big profit"), office mates ("the time they put in the first computers"), political activists ("that was a terrific rally"), and so on. Couples, friends, or groups with close, long-lasting relationships accumulate a great many shared experiences. We will refer to memories of these episodes as *co-biographical memories.*

There are also many groups that form around mutual recreational or professional interests. Even though they may encounter one another only intermittently, with participants possibly changing over time, such groups, too, have shared, collective memories. Examples might include casual friends who share an interest in movies ("I thought the mathematician was going to get eaten") or follow sports news ("Buckner couldn't take it any more, so he moved to Idaho"). Such stories have some properties of autobiographical memories, as each person has had the experience. The stories also have some different properties, because the experiences of the participants cannot have been exactly the same, and their interpretations of these experiences almost certainly differ somewhat. If the individual versions are rather close, and each person knows that the other person has approximately the same memory, then the individuals have established what linguists call *common ground* (Clark & Marshall, 1981). For our purposes, this means that they can talk about the topic in a highly condensed way. Here is an example as overheard by one of us: Two New York Knicks basketball fans encountered one another in the departmental mail room early one morning in June 1993. They looked at each other and shook their heads sorrowfully. One said to the other, "How in hell did he miss!"

As a stand-alone linguistic utterance, this is completely unintelligible. How did who miss? Miss what? The listeners in the room who knew nothing about the basketball playoffs found this sentence baffling. How did the listener know what the speaker was talking about?

The listener must have presumed the meaning, knowing that the fifth playoff game between the New York Knicks and the Chicago Bulls had taken place the night before, and that every true fan (which the speaker was known to be) would almost certainly have watched it on TV. With the Bulls ahead by one point in the final few seconds, Charles Smith of the Knicks missed four straight apparently easy shots, dooming the Knicks to lose the playoff. For intense fans, such co-biographical memories, even though they were only seen and not a result of participation, are shaped over time to become the lore of the game. Every sport or recreation has such legends, which are, in effect, subcultural memories.

Although many individuals participate in conversations about a vivid event seen or heard by an interest group, we cannot claim that the event is biased by exactly the same processes as is a strictly autobiographical memory. Yet the distortions may well have the same meanings. The stories become "leveled" (with details dropping out), and "sharpened" (with the core aspect exaggerated), as also happens in rumor transmission (Allport & Postman, 1945).

Frozen Historical Stories

Consider "Merkle's Boner," a famous 1908 baseball incident that occurred in the last half of the ninth inning of a crucial game between the Giants and the Cubs.

The actual details of this event are extremely complicated (Fleming, 1981), with crowds on the field, a couple of baseballs in play, disagreement about what Merkle did, and bitter controversy over the umpires' ruling for weeks (even years) afterwards. Yet what remains of this story in the minds of all but the most erudite fans is that some guy named Merkle didn't touch second base in the ninth inning and the Giants lost. The tag line, "Merkle's Boner," freezes this attribution of blame in what turns out to be an unjust way if one examines the original accounts.

If blatant story shaping of a "minor" public event such as a single play in a baseball game can survive for a century through storytelling and retelling, the fragility of accounts of defining events in the history of kingdoms, religions, and nations is mind-boggling.

Sometimes the stories of history get frozen, as in the (possibly false) attribution of child murders to Richard III. Sometimes competing versions have currency for quite a while, as in the Kennedy assassination. Although falsehoods in group stories may occasionally be due to connivance, distortion can readily occur without political intervention. Autobiographical experiences, certainly, are shaded away from the truth by fairly mundane processes.

One Experience, Two Stories

For social psychologists, analyzing dyadic relationships is preferable to analyzing the quagmire of human history. Let us consider the case of two people in an intimate relationship who have participated in the same event, with each of them wanting to tell the story about it. First of all, there is the question of whether they will agree about the event. Ross and Holmberg (1990) asked husbands and wives to recount various benchmark episodes, such as their first date, that had occurred up to 20 years before. A surprising number of discrepancies of various types occurred in recountings of a couple's first date. Many details emphasized by one spouse could not be recalled by the other.

An incidental finding of note was that wives recalled more details, and said that they had retold and rehearsed first date episodes more than their husbands had. These two findings can be variously interpreted, but they are at least superficially consistent with the notion that, in general, men are more indifferent to matters of sentiment than are women.

Why Couples Fight Over the Story Both Are Telling

Now let us picture the commonly enacted scene of a husband and wife jointly telling a co-biographical memory at a dinner party. Suppose it is the first time that this particular experience has been told. Typically, the two spouses will disagree about what is important to tell, and about the interpretation of the events, as well as about irrelevant details like how many steps they climbed, or whether the tour guide was Greek, or Italian.

There are two issues at stake in such disagreements, one particular to the story being told, the other pertaining to joint storytelling in general. Usually the audience will politely ignore the disagreements and join in the illusion that a single version of the story exists. The partner whose descriptions and interpretations more often command the attention and acceptance of the audience is laying claim to having the authentic co-biographical story. The more passive partner finds that other people take as autobiographical fact the story that the more active partner has imposed upon the audience. We have seen in previous sections that autobiographical stories are self-defining, and influence memory. In this situation, therefore, part of one partner's self is being publicly defined infelicitously by the other partner. The more passive partner is under duress to remember an alien version of the story.

Given this insight, it still is not clear why husbands and wives commonly haggle over the irrelevant details of a story. What difference to either spouse's self-definition does it make if the guide was Greek or Italian? We think such disagreement is a skirmish in a general ongoing battle to exercise the most control over joint storytelling. The loser surrenders the right to individual self-definition, a very threatening eventuality.

We are not certified clinicians (nor even uncertified clinicians), but we suggest that the road to happy "coupledom" in the storytelling scenario is sensitive negotiation of when who says what such that the dignity of both parties is preserved. The major difficulty here appears to stem from failure to perceive the crucial role that storytelling plays in self-definition. Acceptance of a story by one person alone, or by two or more people together, means the acceptance of a new memory, and that is powerful stuff.

STORY SKELETONS

Skeletal Summaries

Consider the following statement made by a woman commenting on the relationship of two friends of hers:

> He used to admire her. She was a rising star in her profession, and he thought that she was terrific. He was willing to make sacrifices for her because he respected what she was doing. He made choices about having children, household chores, and his own career, based upon his attempt to let her be whatever she could be. He believed in the women's movement, and he believed in her. And then, she betrayed him. She stopped caring about her career. She competed with him for the children's attention. She eventually gave up working altogether and spent her time jogging or hanging around in women's support groups. He is tremendously angry at her because he feels betrayed. What were all his sacrifices for—so she could goof off?

How Summary Concepts Determine Story Interpretation

The teller of the preceding story has decided that the marriage of her two friends was an example of a betrayal story. In effect, once she decided to see their situation as one of betrayal, she didn't need to see it any other way. Aspects of the relationship between the two people unrelated to betrayal, or that contradicted the notion of betrayal, were forgotten. Seeing a particular story as an instance of a more general and universally known story causes the teller of the story to forget the differences between the particular and the general. In this instance, the teller of the story can use the word "betrayal" as a very short story for telling on other occasions when time is more dear. In other words, the concept of betrayal becomes what she knows about this situation. It controls her memory of the situation, so that new evidence of betrayal is more likely to get admitted into her memory than contradictory evidence.

It is very convenient that we have words or phrases that are, in essence, stories. We use this convenient feature of language as a means of taking shortcuts when we talk. Instead of telling all the details of a situation, we can index it as "betrayal" or "undermining my confidence" or "ordering me around" or "being inconsiderate." Such prototypic stories need not be negative, of course. We have "heroism" stories and "defense of our nation" stories, and "always there when I need you" stories as well.

The problem with all this is that it allows the possibility of working backwards. That is, instead of considering the facts of the matter and saying to oneself, "Gee, a good way to summarize that would be by using the concept of betrayal," we turn this process around. We decide that betrayal is a good story to tell, based on very little evidence, and then we find facts that support this point of view.

There are a great many words and phrases in English that indicate complex stories, and thus serve to standardize particular situations. These words are stories, or, more accurately, the indexes to stories.

Among the conceptual schemes for classifying complex stories are Schank's (1982) "Thematic Organization Packets" and Lehnert's (1981) "plot units." Most people believe that betrayal is bad. The teller tells the story so that betrayal seems to have happened, using the betrayal skeleton story, and then constructing the story around that skeleton.

In other words, by using a skeleton story for betrayal, the teller could construct only a story of betrayal. Why couldn't the preceding story have been told as if it were a story of "devotion"? Only small changes would be needed to make this such a story. A statement that he still loves her and hopes she will return to her former self would portray devotion, or one that shows he values and will support her in her role as mother. Often, the truth or falsity of such additions is not so easy to determine. We cannot always know every aspect of a situation that we describe. Nevertheless, we could have chosen to tell this story as a story about devotion.

Thinking in terms of standard stories poses a serious danger, although doing otherwise is not so easy. We want to see the situations we encounter in terms that are describable to others. Furthermore, we often have only a short time in which to tell these stories. Thus even if the fit with those stories is not exact, seeing and describing complex situations in terms of standard stories provides an easy shorthand method for communication. However, a problem can arise when we see our own lives that way. That is, if we react to our own situations by understanding them in terms of general standard stories, we can make some serious mistakes.

Different Story Skeletons: The Iranian Plane Case

If we construct our own version of truth by reliance upon skeleton stories, two people can know exactly the same facts, but construct a story that relays those facts in very different ways. Because they are using different story skeletons, their perspectives will vary. For example, a few years ago the United States Navy shot down an Iranian airliner carrying over 200 passengers. Let us look at some different stories constructed to explain this event. All the stories that follow are excerpts from various *New York Times'* reports in the days following this incident:

> Mr. Reagan smiled and waved at tourists as he returned to the White House. But in speaking to reporters he remarked on what he had previously called "a terrible human tragedy. I won't minimize the tragedy," Mr. Reagan said. "We all know it was a tragedy. But we're talking about an incident in which a plane on radar was observed coming in the direction of a ship in combat and the plane began lowering its altitude. And so, I think it was an understandable accident to shoot and think that they were under attack from that plane," he said.

In this quotation from Ronald Reagan, the use of skeletons to create stories can be easily seen. (A *skeleton* is a cluster of motivated events and states, sequential in time.) Mr. Reagan has chosen a common skeleton: *understandable tragedy.* The skeleton looks something like this:

Actor pursues justifiable goal.
Actor selects reasonable plan to achieve goal.
Plan involves selection of correct action.
Action taken has unintended and unanticipatable result.
Result turns out to be undesirable.
Innocent people are hurt by result.
It is not the actor's fault.

Mr. Reagan selected this skeleton and interpreted the events in terms of that skeleton. Had he been asked to tell the story of what happened, he would simply have had to fill in each line of the skeleton with the actual event that matches it. As it is, he merely had to recognize the skeleton that was applicable and to use the phrases "terrible human tragedy" and "understandable accident" that are well-known referents to that skeleton.

Now let's look at some other comments on the event:

> After expressing "profound regret" about the attack, Mrs. Thatcher said: "We understand that in the course of an engagement following an Iranian attack on the U.S. force, warnings were given to an unidentified aircraft. We fully accept the right of forces engaged in such hostilities to defend themselves."

Mrs. Thatcher has used a much more specific skeleton, namely, *the justifiability of self-defense.* This skeleton proceeds as follows:

First actor pursues unjustifiable goal.
First actor selects plan.
Plan has intention of negative effect on second actor.
Second actor is justified in selecting goal.
Second actor selects justifiable plan.
Plan causes action to take place that harms first actor.

Let us look at another version of the story:

Libya's official press agency called the downing "a horrible massacre perpetrated by the United States." It said the attack was "new proof of state terrorism practiced by the American Administration" and it called Washington "insolent" for insisting that the decision to down the plane was an appropriate defensive measure.

Here, two different skeletons are invoked. The first is *state terrorism,* and the second is *insolence.* The insolence skeleton is an amusing one to invoke, but we shall ignore it and concentrate on the terrorism skeleton:

Actor chooses high-level goal.
Country blocks high-level goal.
Actor chooses secondary goal to harm citizens of country.
Actor endangers or actually harms citizens of country.
Actor expects blockage of high level goal by country to go away.

"State terrorism" supposedly means that the actor is a country, not just an isolated naval vessel. However, "state terrorism" is not exactly a well-known story skeleton for an American. In fact, Arab leaders refer to this skeleton quite often, and we can figure out what it must mean and why Arab leaders use it to justify their own actions. Other people's story skeletons, ones that we have not heard before, are usually best understood by analogy to skeletons we already know.

Notice that the events under discussion fit as easily into the state terrorism skeleton as into the other two skeletons. The art of skeleton selection is exactly that—an art. Very little objective reality exists here. One can see and tell about events in any way that one wants to. In each case, certain aspects of the story being transmitted are enhanced, and certain elements are left out altogether. (An exposition of various detailed methods for tailoring a political speech for different audiences is given by Hovey [1987].)

The real problem in using distorted skeletons this way is that the storytellers themselves usually believe what they are saying. Authors construct their own reality by finding the events that fit the skeleton convenient for them to believe. They enter a storytelling situation wanting to tell a certain kind of story, and only then worrying about whether the facts fit onto the bones of the skeleton they have previously chosen. This method has almost comic qualities when various interpretations of an event are so clearly interpretations independent of the event itself. For example, consider the following comment:

A newspaper in Bahrain, Akhbar Al Khalij, said: "No doubt yesterday's painful tragedy was the result of Iran's insistence in continuing the Iran–Iraq war. The United States as a great power does not lack moral courage in admitting the mistake. This will help contain the effects of the accident."

The remarks above refer to two skeletons: *the justifiable bad effects of war on the aggressor* and *moral courage.* Both of these skeletons could have been used to describe nearly any event in the Middle East that Bahrain wanted to comment upon.

Political Storytelling

In the International Arena

The use of new events as fodder for invoking old skeletons is the stuff of which international political rhetoric is made. In the *New York Times* of the same period, we have another reference to how Reagan commented on a similar situation some years back:

President Reagan, in a speech after the Korean plane was shot down after straying over Soviet airspace above Sakhalin Island, said: "Make no mistake about it, this attack was not just against ourselves or the Republic of Korea. This was the Soviet Union against the world and the moral precepts which guide human relations among people everywhere."

"It was an act of barbarism," Mr. Reagan went on, "born of a society which wantonly disregards individual rights and the value of human life and seeks constantly to expand and dominate other nations."

Whereas the Americans used the *barbarism* skeleton, where the Koreans were the victim and the Russians the actor, to describe the shooting down of the Korean airliner, the Russians, in describing the Korean Airlines attack, used the *military aggressor* skeleton, where the Koreans were the actor and the Russians the victim. This same discrepancy occurred in the Russian statement about the Iranian airliner:

The Tass statement said the attack Sunday was the inevitable result of the extensive American military presence in the Persian Gulf.

"The tragedy, responsibility for which is wholly with the American command, has been far from accidental," the agency said. "It has been, in effect, a direct corollary of United States actions over the past year to increase its military presence in the Gulf."

It added: "The Soviet Union has repeatedly warned at different forums that the path of military actions cannot lead to a normalized situation. If the warnings had been heeded, the July 3 tragedy would not have occurred."

Storytelling by Candidates

International politicians are not the only ones who tell stories by selecting their favorite skeleton and fitting the event to the skeleton. United States candidates running for president also had something to say:

Mr. Jackson said there was "no evidence that the U.S. ship was under attack by that plane." But he added, "The issue is not just failed technology, but failed and vague policy for the region." Mr. Jackson argued that the United States should not be in the Gulf unilaterally, but as part of a United Nations peacekeeping effort that would have as its prime goal a negotiated settlement of the Iran-Iraq war.

At a Fourth of July address at the Charlestown Navy Yard in Boston today, Mr. Dukakis described the incident as a "terrible accident," adding: "Clearly we have the right to defend our forces against imminent threats. And apparently, the shooting down of the airliner occurred over what appears to have been an unprovoked attack against our forces."

For Mr. Jackson, the appropriate skeletons were *bad technology causes errors* and *vague policy causes problems.* Mr. Dukakis, on the other hand, looked suspiciously like Mr. Reagan, indicating that he was already acting presidential. Mr. Jackson had already realized that he was not going to be president at this point, but he was still campaigning to be taken seriously. Therefore, he was still raising issues. The Iran incident reminded him of two of his favorite issues, so he chose to see the Iranian airplane event in terms of those issues.

Last, we should look at the Iranian point of view. They, too, had their favorite skeletons in terms of which they could look at this event. First, let us examine the remarks of an exiled Iranian official, a political rival of the government (who was soon assassinated):

"It must be clear that much of the policies in Iran today are dictated by the internal struggle for power," said Abolhassan Bani-Sadr, the first President of Iran. Mr. Bani-Sadr, who spoke in an interview, lives in exile in Paris and opposes the current regime.

"In that sense," Mr. Bani-Sadr said, "this American act of aggression will increase pressure to steer away from conciliatory policies in favor of radicals inside Iran who want to crush all talk of compromise. I am sure the trend now will be toward more mobilization for more war, although it will get nowhere."

Mr. Bani-Sadr was trying to predict the future rather than retell an old story. Nevertheless, he still relied upon a skeleton to create his new story. The skeleton he chose was *fanatics find fuel to add to fire.* Now look at a comment from inside Iran:

Hojatolislam Rafsanjani, who is the commander of Iran's armed forces, warned today against a hasty response to the American action. In a speech reported by the Teheran radio, he told Parliament, "We should let this crime be known to everyone in the world and be discussed and studied."

The Speaker, who has emerged as Iran's most powerful figure after Ayatollah Khomeini, went on to say that the Americans might "want a clumsy move somewhere in the world so that they can take the propaganda pressure off America and transfer it somewhere else."

Hojatolislam Rafsanjani added that Iran retains the right of taking revenge, but that "the timing is up to us, not America." He called the downing of the airliner "an unprecedented disaster in contemporary history" and said it should be used by Iran to "expose the nature of America," statements indicating that for now the Speaker favors a measured response.

Here again, we have a story about the future. Two skeletons are invoked as possible candidates for the basis of this story. One, *force opponents into bad move,* refers to the intentions of the United States as seen by the Iranians and is really a part of a continuing story of conflict between the two countries. The second, *avoid revenge to show up opponent,* is more or less the other side of the same coin. In both cases, we have a kind of conscious admission by Mr. Rafsanjani that the real question is which story skeleton will be followed in the creation of the next set of events. The only problem with this assertion is that Mr. Rafsanjani naively seems to assume that some audience is waiting to see the next act in the play. A more accurate assumption is that no matter what happens next, all the viewers of the play will retell the story according to skeletons they have already selected; for example, they will probably not be moved to reinterpret any new event in terms of some skeleton that they do not already have in mind.

Skeletons and Belief

Political Contexts

Story skeletons can have an important effect on memory. Due to the fact that we see the world according to the stories we tell, when we tell a story in a given way, we will likely remember the facts in terms of the story we have told. This effect on memory has an interesting offshoot. When we select a particular skeleton because we have no real choice from a political point of view, we most likely will begin to believe the story we find ourselves telling. For example, consider the following statement:

Iran Air's senior Airbus instructor, Capt. Ali Mahdaviani, ruled out the possibility of pilot error in the tragedy. He said it was possible that the airliner's captain, Mohsen Rezaian, failed to respond to signals from the American cruiser Vincennes because at that stage in the flight he was busy receiving air controller instructions off two radios and from four control towers, Bandar Abbas, Teheran, Dubai and Qeshon Island in the Gulf.

He insisted that the airliner would not have been outside the flight corridor and certainly would not have been descending, as early Pentagon reports said. He attributed the incident to a panicky reaction from the American cruiser, but did concede that the decision to fire the two surface-to-air missiles was made in difficult circumstances. "I think the decision to shoot down the plane was taken in very nervous conditions," he said.

Now consider an opposing statement:

"We have in this briefing all the facts that were made available to the captain when he made his decision," said Senator John Warner, a Virginia Republican and former Navy Secretary. "We are all of the same view, that he acted properly and professionally."

Senator Sam Nunn, the Georgia Democrat who is the chairman of the Armed Services Committee, agreed. "I find nothing to second-guess him on, based on his information," Mr. Nunn said.

He was quick to add, however, that the information that Capt. Will C. Rogers 3d, the commanding officer of the Vincennes, was working with might be contradicted by information on the computer tapes, which are believed to have recorded every action taken by the ship's operators, every bit of data picked up by its sensors and every communication heard in the region during the encounter.

"It is an entirely different matter to second-guess a decision that had to be made in three or four minutes, to second-guess it over a two-week period," Mr. Nunn said, referring to the deadline for Navy investigators looking into the events.

Each of these statements is what might have been expected from the people who made them. Yet, how were the memories of the spokesmen affected by the stories they told? In some sense, they told stories that they had to tell. Neither of these spokesmen was necessarily 100% sure that the pilot, the captain, or both, were not somewhat wrong in what they did. Situations are rarely that black and white. But, having made a politically necessary statement to support his man, each spokesman probably believed more in his man after defending him.

A Divorce Story

In order to understand an episode in our lives, we must construct a story that makes the episode make sense. We do not like to believe that we act randomly or without reason. When we make a decision or take an action, we like to believe in our choice, especially if that decision or action is a significant one. In a sense, then, we must construct a story before we take an action to ensure that the action we are about to take is coherent. Further, if the action is in any way incoherent, we make it more sensible by putting it into a framework that is acceptable to those who hear the story. In other words, if what we do fits into a well-known, socially acceptable story skeleton, then we can believe that we have acted properly.

The attempt to put things into a framework for the purposes of storytelling has, as we have suggested, a serious impact on memory. In effect, we find ourselves believing our own stories. In reality most people are not nearly as rational as they pretend to be. We make decisions on the basis of what feels right at the time, out of fear or ignorance, on the basis of emotional reactions to events, and so on. Nevertheless, although many of us recognize that this is how we make decisions on a daily basis, we cannot bear to admit it when we are asked about our decisions. We find ourselves constructing a story to serve as the answer to why we changed jobs, got divorced, decided to spend too much money, or mistreated our friends and family. When the answer ought to be, "I don't know why I did it," or "there were a great many factors that went into the decision," we instead construct a good story, one that will be believed and understood as being coherent. To do this, we pick a skeleton that we know will work for our listener. Unfortunately, once we tell a story using such a skeleton, it is difficult not to believe it ourselves.

In order to see this process in action, at least as well as one can really see such a process, we asked people who had been divorced to tell us the story of their divorces. The subjects were all teachers. The stories shown here were edited from longer versions for the purpose of readability. (They were probably edited as well by the tellers as they were telling them, which is, of course, the point here.)

Divorce is a good domain to study with regard to storytelling and story skeletons because the stories are attempts to summarize many complex events. Anyone who has been divorced probably has a story to tell about that divorce. The teller often has a real desire to portray himself as the wronged party and to have the listener express sympathy. However, in the attempt to meld many years' worth of events into one story, the actual events would be too complicated for any standard story skeleton. Coherent stories that rely on a standard story skeleton may well mask, in varying degrees of effectiveness, a less coherent set of events which do not fit neatly into a story skeleton.

Let's look at the first story:

A: I was divorced actually two years ago. I probably would have stayed married for much much longer had Peter stayed working, but he decided to take retirement from his job and start his own business, and I wasn't really thrilled about the idea, but it's not the sort of thing you can talk a man out of. He said "you know you can work with me." I said, "no chance, we'd be divorced in a week." He took it as a joke. He said "we work so well together," and I thought "that's because I do it the way you want to, not the way I like." So, I went out and got a full-time job teaching, and gradually it started to dawn on me how very unhappy I was with having him around.

He was extremely hard-working, very demanding of himself, and extremely demanding of everyone else. Sometimes he'd be critical; sometimes, if I'd take him to task about it and say, you know you're always so critical, he'd say you're the most wonderful, you're the best person I could have married, etc. etc. I realized he was saying to me on the logical plane that I was the best wife he could have had. He certainly wouldn't want to trade me for someone else, but at the same time, I could improve just a few things.

Then I went back to work, and I started saying to myself, wait a minute, I don't have to spend the rest of my life being squashed. I realize I think I was afraid of him in a way, not that he physically abused me or attacked me in any way except verbally. And I think he undermined my ego to a certain extent, and after I started working, and he was home, I really found I didn't like to be home.

Then when I came down here, he started thinking he'd look for a job down here, and I was hoping he wouldn't find one. He didn't, and when he'd come down to visit every couple of weeks, I found I was really not looking forward to seeing him. And he began to realize that he wasn't being particularly welcomed by the people here, and I think the poor man really was quite hurt. When we'd go up to visit him, we'd arrive so tired and find a list of things he wanted us to do. We realized this is not much fun, and we stayed here, and he stayed there and then after about a year, there were a couple of other little incidents with his family and what have you, and he one day said to me, maybe we should get a divorce.

You know, my mother always looked upon divorced women as some sort of fallen woman and fast-living, loose woman. "She's divorced you know." I can't be one of those people, people she would point out and say, "she's a divorcee, you know, what can you expect?" Divorce really has a very bad press, and it took me a couple of months to get into my little head that this was the 80s, and this was the United States, and plenty of people I liked and respected got divorced, and they hadn't turned into scarlet women, so gradually it dawned on me that this is not such a bad idea.

I phoned Peter, and I said you know you're right, we should get divorced, and I think it totally took him by surprise. Peter thought that it would shake me up if he said maybe we should get divorced. I'd say I can't lose this marvelous man, and what have I done wrong. Let me shape up a bit and we'll keep the marriage going.

In fact, once I made the decision, it was a wonderful feeling. I remember going out running one day and thinking, oh, I feel free, I feel as if a sort of load has been lifted. I think what it was was that I no longer had this person standing over me and criticizing whatever it was that I was doing. The longer we were separated with the divorce coming, the more I felt the sense of incredible freedom, and life was almost poetic. Once I made the decision, I never had a moment's doubt. I was thinking one night, well, so it's easy for me to divorce him now. If I was married to him, I'd be with him, and I'd rather be on my own. You know, at least if I were on my own, I could do my job, I could run, I could play tennis. I could go to lectures or whatever, and I basically could enjoy myself on my own. So it was a good feeling to get divorced.

Getting the Reaction You Want

Conflicting Skeletons

What kind of story is this one about divorce? The first problem arises from the story skeleton it uses. A fairly standard story skeleton that some wives use to describe their marriages runs as follows: *man oppresses woman, who in turn demands more independence.* For the woman who is telling this story, this skeleton conflicts with another one from her childhood: *woman leaves man and turns to wanton life.* She clearly had a conflict deciding which of these two skeletons would be her story, and one can guess that she decided to test herself by getting a job in another state away from her husband. The odd thing here is that we can only guess at her motivation, because she says almost nothing about her decision to move out. She just uses the phrase, "then when I came down here," to describe leaving her husband and getting a job elsewhere prior to any talk of divorce. Notice that no standard socially acceptable story skeleton really exists for her sort of separation, and this may be the reason she did not tell that part of the story. What made her decide to split up her family for a job? This behavior is not common and would have to be explained—but she barely mentions it. When no standard story skeleton is available, telling stories is difficult.

Choosing the Right Skeleton

People need to make sense of their own lives. One way of feeling that you have made sense is to tell your story to someone else and hear that person respond in positive, supportive, ways. To make sure that you have expressed your story in terms that others understand, you must use the right skeleton. You wouldn't use the word *rachmones* while talking to someone who, you were sure, did not know the word. Neither would you choose the skeleton *man oppresses woman who in turn demands more independence,* unless you had reason to believe that your hearer knew that skeleton. You could, of course, try to instruct your listener about the meaning of the skeleton, but this would not get you the empathy you were looking for. To avoid this feeling of isolation and lack of understanding when talking to someone from whom one wants support, people naturally use skeletons that they know will get them that support. When people want to make a case for themselves, or when they want to describe a situation to others in order to get a certain kind of reaction, they choose a well-known and culturally agreed upon skeleton, one to which they can predict the reaction of others.

The Annie Hall Sequence

Married couples often comment on a sequence from the Woody Allen movie *Annie Hall.* The sequence involves two scenes, where first the female lead and then the male lead discusses their sex life as a couple with their respective therapists. The woman complains that her boyfriend wants to have sex all the time—two or three times a week. The man complains that they almost never have sex together—only two or three times a week.

This movie scene expresses the essence of story construction. We take the facts and interpret them in such a way as to create a story. In order to facilitate communication and allow easy conversation, we use standard story skeletons that we share as a culture. The choice of which skeleton to use, however, is, in essence, a political choice. We choose to see the world according to a view that we find convenient, and we communicate that view by adopting standard points of view. The stories we tell communicate this view both to others and to ourselves. In the end, we become shaped by the skeletons we use, because we do not remember the facts; we only remember the skeletons we have used. Skeletons are, after all, simply a kind of index. Memory is organized by them, and memories are retrieved with them. Thus the two *Annie Hall* characters, many years later, when asked about their sex lives, can be expected to recall the skeleton they used, not the actual amount of sex they had. Their disagreement was in the story they chose to tell and could not help but remember.

Another way to look at this is to ask which of the *Annie Hall* characters is right. The question is absurd in this context, but it is important to realize that it is also absurd in contexts where we normally think it makes sense. The politicians we quoted earlier are all equally right as well. In a sense, there is no truth apart from interpretation. Memory is not truth; it is merely memory of previous interpretations. Storytelling forces us to adopt a point of view. The skeletons we choose, that we actually select before we have really considered the facts, indicate our prior point of view that alters our interpretations of the facts. Our memories are comprised of the stories we tell, and the stories we tell comprise our memories. In a sense we can see the world only in the way that our stories allow us to see it. Furthermore, storytelling is so altered by the audience that receives them that our audience seriously shapes what we remember.

Thus we and our audience shape our memories by the stories we tell. If we hang around with a "bad crowd," the stories the crowd tells and likes to hear will be the stories we come to believe. Our own experiences are not likely to change the world view of those with whom we surround ourselves. Rather their world view will shape the stories we tell, and thus what we remember and believe. As we come to rely upon certain skeletons to express what has happened to us, we become incapable of seeing the world in any other way. The skeletons we use cause the specific episodes of our lives to conform to one another. The more a given skeleton is used, the more it helps to form our stories so that they begin to cohere in our memory. Consequently, we develop consistent and rather inflexible points of view.

In the process, we distort the facts somewhat. We make our story fit into the skeleton, and tend to leave out the parts that do not quite fit.

Skeletons for Divorce Stories: Emphasizing What Looks Good

To see some of this in action, and to get a feel for some other kinds of skeletons, let us consider another divorce story:

Young Woman Marries Older Man for Guidance

B: I got married when I was 22. I grew up in Colorado in a fairly traditional Western home, had a great college experience, went off to graduate school and stayed in a PhD program. I was in Pennsylvania, an environment that was foreign to me, and I met this man who was older and much more sophisticated, and who had been married.

And in some intuitional ridiculous feminine way I sought him out to help support me and get me through this. I was tired of school by that time, and that was disintegrating. I more and more clutched to this individual. I couldn't possibly imagine life without somebody telling me what to do and how to do it. So, I was Catholic, he was Jewish. I was Western, he was New York City. Many opposites, so we ended up getting married.

And what happened is, I grew up. It sort of was forced on me to become my own person after I became a mother. For the first time, I really had to be conscious of my self and my own motives and how I was doing things because I had this child to take care of, and I also had a full-time job and had to get all this stuff done. I did not need or want to have this oppressive atmosphere created by this person that I married who resented every step of my independence and personal growth.

I found a lot of development of self coming in the classroom relationships with kids, and he would tell me that my relationships were sick. He once said to me, "I've created you, and I want to instill this sort of debt." Interestingly, I ended up in counseling because he said I had a problem. The therapy helped me put some objectivity on this relationship which was really tortuous, very stultifying, very oppressive, as you can imagine. So it began, I think, on a suggestion on his part, I think, to get me to think right. Right thinking, you know, ended up backfiring because I was able to establish some distance from the relationship and finally realize in the long process that I couldn't survive. I was dying in this relationship, and I had to get out. We were married five years. It seemed like one-hundred fifty.

Surely, I would have gotten divorced if I hadn't fallen in love with C. It was going to happen. I had already sort of semi-separated but had gone back. I'd been through therapy, but I think even the moments I spent with C taught me what it was like to be with a real human being male; you didn't have to feel threatened and horrible. It gave me a real glimpse as to what it could be really like, and I was sure that was the impetus. We had seen each other from the start of the affair only once before the lawyers. So it wasn't as though that was the cause. I often think people think well, you've fallen in love, and that's the cause. I have often believed that whatever's wrong is wrong, and you're attracted to other people because things are so wrong.

This story relies upon two standard story skeletons. The first is, *young woman marries older man because she wants guidance; he wants her to remain a child, but she grows up and changes and doesn't need him anymore.* The second is, *partner in bad relationship finds lover to use as means to effect final separation from spouse.* The teller of this story wants the hearer to believe that the first skeleton is operating, and that the second is not. Her story is simple, clear, and obvious, according to her rendition of it. It is quite natural, she is asserting, that a young woman would marry an older man for guidance and then be prevented from growing up by a man who liked being married to a young woman. By relying on this old standard story skeleton, one she can assume that her listener has heard before, she can expect that her divorce will be seen as having been socially acceptable, in other words, reasonable to do. But things are rarely this simple, of course. In this case she mentions a second skeleton that people normally disapprove of, and which, she asserts, was not really operating. The reason she mentions it at all, one can imagine, is because C, her second man, is present and about to tell his story:

Man Tries to Replace Mother with Wife

C: My first marriage took place within hours literally of my graduation from college. I graduated from college at two o'clock in the afternoon and was married at seven o'clock that evening. I promised my father I'd wait until I graduated. I'd not had a lot of relationships with different women. The woman that I'd married I had met in the summer after my sophomore year in college. I was working in a summer camp in upstate New York. We were both on the staff together. It became one of those summer kinds of counselor things that—we got very serious in the course of six weeks. I was going to school and living in Ohio. She was living in Albany, N.Y. For the next two years in the relationship, we saw each other only at vacation times which were, I think, artificial at best. There are all the festivities that surround vacations, and we never had any sense of each other in day-to-day living which proved to be one of the fatal flaws in the marriage.

My mother had died when I was 9 years old—I'm the youngest of 3 children—two older sisters. My sisters were old enough so by the time I was in junior high and high school, it was just my father and I by ourselves, two men. And, I grew up doing lots of the household chores, cooking, cleaning, all the rest of that sort of stuff, sort of envying classmates and friends who had moms, who came home from school, everything was done. So, I really feel that there was some chunk of my psychological development that just was missing, and I think a great force operating pretty subconsciously in my search for a spouse was someone who was going to mother me. Do all of those things, and clearly, that's what Sara, my first wife, was all about. I would say for the first year or so I was having everything that I did not have growing up. I had this woman who really was taking care of me, and it was great, and I think that masqueraded as a deep relationship. There wasn't much what would I say emotional, intellectual exchange between the two of us. I felt I did not have any grand feeling of emotion toward Sara, but I was thinking, well this is just the way marriages are.

Then, we moved to a much larger independent boarding school in Illinois which represented the very best of independent education in that it was a very intellectual community, very diverse, lots of fine minds, and I continued to grow professionally myself there. Found myself very, very comfortable in that community, increasingly comfortable while Sara was finding herself increasingly uncomfortable with that. And, it was at that point that I began to feel that the marriage was not only very empty but was going to continue to be very empty simply because we were two very very different people. The directions that I wanted to move not only professionally but personally and the sorts of people I was attracted to on a social level were not people that Sara was comfortable with.

At the very end of my relationship with Sara, B and I did in fact begin a relationship in which I was discovering what it meant to have the full range of deep feelings for another human being, and that just confirmed my belief that this relationship wasn't going to work, so we separated.

This story relies upon several skeletons at the same time. The first is, *married too young and tried to imitate the idyllic image of a 1950s suburban marriage* (the *Leave It To Beaver* skeleton). The second is, *man tries to replace mother with wife and then decides that's not what he wanted.* Finally, a third is, *one partner grows while other stays the same.* These three are all rather related, and, of course, they are tied together with, *partner in bad relationship finds lover to use as means to effect final separation from spouse,* which was convenient in this case, because he (C) found a woman (B) who had exactly the same story that she wanted to tell. In his story he also denies that this last relationship was the cause of his divorce. We tell the stories that we want to believe, after all.

Man Cannot Commit Himself to Relationship

Now look at the next story:

D: The relationship started. My sister was married to this person's brother. But what I should have known in hindsight is there were certain qualities to this person that I should have known in terms of his attitude towards women and his commitment to one person. We were married in August, and we were divorced August three years later, so it was very short. And, as it turns out, there was someone else, another woman involved before we got married, and there were women involved all the way along. But I didn't know this. I guess I didn't want to know this. So, it was definitely something that I had a hard time getting over. I think that because I was very young, and I had a feeling that divorce meant failure. What I know now is that the failure was not on my part, the failure was on the part of this person toward relationships in general. Matthew came in at a point, and I almost felt guilty that he had come into my life. I knew I wanted out. I knew something was wrong, but I didn't know how to get out of it. I'd just made a move to a new location, and all of a sudden my whole life was changing again. I was seen at that point as being, or I perceived that I was being seen as the one who had found somebody else and so was running off, but, of course, what people didn't realize was that he had somebody in the wings for a long time. So I think that produced a feeling of guilt in me that we had a moral contract. I look back on it as more of a relationship that didn't work as opposed to a marriage that failed, but that's seven years after. I certainly didn't feel that when I first was getting out of it.

Here we have a very standard story skeleton: *man has affairs and cannot commit himself to a relationship, thus he leaves wife to terminate it.* Here again, the teller notices that the skeleton, *partner in bad relationship finds lover to use as means to effect final separation from spouse,* could be inferred from the actual events, so she insists that it was not the dominating skeleton in this story.

Simplifying the World

Humans cannot easily digest the complexity of the world where they live and the actions that they and others take in that world. We look for explanations of our own behavior and of the behavior of others that seem to make sense. Yet what does it mean to make sense of a behavior? When we tell about a series of events that have occurred over a 5- or 10-year period, as in a divorce story, we are looking for overall patterns rather than attempting to relate every event that ever happened. We are looking for generalizations to make. However, what kinds of generalizations can we make? First and foremost, we can look for generalizations that we have seen before and that we believe others have seen before. We can speak in generalizations that our listener can understand.

If we have a set of standard explanations available to us in the form of story skeletons, we can explain the behavior of others by trying to match their behavior to the standard skeletons. In other words, we can try to understand events by referring them to events we have already understood. An available set of skeletons, of old favorites as it were, helps us to impose a uniformity on an otherwise incomprehensible world. We know what patterns to look for, and we insist on finding them.

The Implicit Contrast Between Teller and Listener

This same process works in reverse when we tell a story. If we tell a story that is really brand new, in the sense that none of the behaviors has been seen before, then both the teller and the hearer have a great deal of work to do. The teller must relate almost all the events that took place. No shortcuts can be taken, nor assumptions made that the hearer will infer the details, because the hearer has no basic everyday story to use as a guide. The hearer is trying to match what is heard to what is already known, but if the hearer cannot explain the behaviors in the story being heard, he or she must try to explain things without reference to previous related events in memory. This is very difficult to do.

Consequently, the teller of a story and the listener must have an implicit agreement. The teller will only tell standard stories, stories that are easy to understand. When the teller has to relay some events that are incomprehensible, they may be omitted, or the teller will cast them in a format that makes them look comprehensible. In fact, the teller has no other choice. He or she cannot easily remember events that are incomprehensible, except as a series of isolated occurrences. Thus the teller must also use standard patterns himself to understand the events he is about to relate.

When a person decides to tell about his divorce, he relates the situation the way he understands it, and the way he hopes his hearer will understand it. He is thus forced, in some sense, to make his story acceptable and easily comprehensible, both by his initial attempt to understand the events himself, and by his prior attempts to tell others his story. To achieve this goal, he chooses a standard story to tell, a story skeleton, and forces the facts to fit the skeleton. If parts of the story do not fit the skeleton, he ignores them. If the story also fits a skeleton that is not favorable to the teller, he acknowledges the superficial parallels, and then disputes the accuracy of that skeleton in his case.

Story Fitting

Telling stories of our own lives, especially ones with high emotional impact, means attempting to fit events to a story that has already been told, a well-known story that others will easily understand. *Story fitting,* then, is a kind of deceptive process, one that creates stories that are not always exactly true, that lie by omission. These lies, however, are not necessarily intentional.

A true story could be told, but that would take much more time. Thus time, in many ways, is the villain here. Your listener doesn't have hours to listen to your story, so you create a short version that looks more standard, that fits a well-known story skeleton. The problem with this solution, as we have seen, is that the teller himself begins to believe his edited story. In short, storytelling is a very powerful process. Stories replace the memory of events that actually took place. Therefore, when people tell the kinds of stories we have seen in this section, they usually believe them.

STORY CONSTRUCTION PROCESSES

Although it is convenient to imagine the mind as a collection of thousands of stories all properly stored away and waiting to be told, the situation is considerably more complicated than that. When you tell a story, one reason you feel as though you are thinking of what to say is that this is precisely what you are doing. The *index of the story* is what is held in memory, not the particular words that comprise the story itself. When we tell a story, we are transforming the index into a story about particular actors in a particular setting, told in a particular language with particular words, suitable for telling to the person who is listening.

Adapting a Story for Different Purposes

We can tell the same story in different ways to satisfy different goals. We can, for example, tell a story in different languages, if we speak different languages, so the language itself is not part of the index stored in memory. Also, we can tell a story at different intellectual levels, for example, one version for a child and another for an adult, so, obviously, indexes do not include the way a story is told. Storytelling activates a set of processes that operate on the index of a story in various ways depending upon many factors from the storyteller's environment. The index and the number of possible stories that can express that index are very different entities indeed. Therefore, a set of mental processes that transform indexes into stories must exist.

To get a sense of how such processes might look, examine a story created with different intentions in mind, and thus with different processes operating on the initial index. To explore this, I asked a student with considerable acting experience to tell, in various ways, a story that had happened to him. What follows are the stories he told, each in a very different way, depending upon the intention he was trying to satisfy.

Catharsis

The student first told the basic story from his memory to satisfy a cathartic intention:

> Story 1: I was at a gas station this morning. I have this Volvo. It is a tank. I backed into this planter, this big concrete, made out of mortar, thing and knocked the thing apart. I felt like such a zero. They called the police, and the cop came over, and he didn't give me a ticket because I was on gas station property. But, I can't believe I did that.

Offering an Excuse

The next version of the story was told with the intention of illustrating a point about the student's vision problems:

> I was driving my Volvo once into a gas station, and what must have happened is that I was traveling forward, and I hit this big square concrete thing. It was high enough that I should have seen it, but it was over here in my right visual field. It was just another one of those cases where there is missing field here and I bashed right into it. I mean it was bright daylight, and I drove into it. Sometimes, I just don't see stuff.

Creating an Empathic Reaction

In the next version of the story, the teller tried to make the listener fall in love with him by making himself seem vulnerable:

> I had this old Volvo a few years ago. It was my first car, and people always have a certain special relationship to their first car, and I had one to this. I am not the type of guy that ever thought that I was really fast, the way some people do in a car, but when I was in this car I thought I was invulnerable. One day I drove the car into a gas station and drove right smack into a concrete planter, knocked it to pieces and broke my right headlight. I wasn't injured, but I was so embarrassed. I, I felt like, I felt, I felt just completely devastated. I talked to the guy that was working at the gas station, and he told me that I was an idiot. I was going to have to pay him $10,000 to have the thing installed—it was brand new. I realized that there was a lot more to being safe than being in a car that I wouldn't get killed in; that I was still just as vulnerable and just as potentially damaged as anybody out there. My Volvo wasn't really going to protect me at all in some way or another.

Telling Your Mother

In still another version of the story, the storyteller agreed to recount the events as though he were a teenager telling the story to his mother:

Mother, uhh . . . I hit a cinder block planter with the car today in a gas station. Didn't do any serious damage to the car. Uh, I damaged one headlight. I am fine. Uh, the guy at the gas station on the other hand is very angry. I will take care of it. I will pay for getting the car fixed, and if it turns out there is some damage to the gas station, then, that needs to be taken care of, I will take care of that, too.

Applying for a Job

In the last version of the story, the teller was asked to pretend that he was applying for job as a driver and had to explain a problem on his driving record:

As I recall, I was in a big hurry. I was coming back into town, and at the last minute, I decided to stop for gas. As I was coming in, something happened at the gas station where the cash register and that junk is. I looked over—I must have been coming in about 3 miles an hour—and I nudged this planter about two feet high sitting right out in the middle of the runway where you get gas. I pushed bricks off of it with the front of the car, and the guy comes out screaming bloody murder and says that he has put his life savings into there, and he won't have customers anymore because some of the bricks are missing from the planter and that people will think that the station is rundown and that he is going to sue me for every penny I am worth. So, that is why we called the insurance company at all—otherwise, it was nothing.

Complex Indexes

Actual stories are produced from an index stored in memory. We have thus far presented a rather oversimplified view of indexes. A complex index may include a skeleton at its base with some elements transformed and extra elements added. On the other hand, it may include no standard skeleton at all, being a truly unique story. Each of the preceding stories was produced by transforming either the index or the story. The teller did not have multiple versions of each story stored in memory. Rather, when it was told with a particular intention, the story stored in memory changed form. This transformation of the index used a variety of mental processes to accomplish particular intentions. Consequently, the resulting stories were different because their intentions were different. In other words, stories can differ in intention, but be identical in a content. The index of a story, therefore, is a characterization of the story's events. The communication of those events depends upon the aspects of the index that the teller wishes to highlight. If the same kind of emphasis is placed on a particular interpretation of a story each time it is told, that interpretation will become part of the index. Indexes are mutable entities, changed in the repeated telling. As soon as we begin to tell a story, we also begin to change the original memory index into a story that we think relates to what our listener should hear. The index itself can therefore be changed by telling a story. The behavior of my student who told the preceding stories is not typical after all. Usually tellers adopt one stance for an event and choose one skeleton. Then the combination of the skeleton and the aspects of the event that fit into that skeleton become the index on which any future storytelling must depend. A curiosity here is that it is possible, by choosing a skeleton that is wrong in some sense, to fool ourselves into believing that something did not really take place in that way.

The first version of the preceding story was told upon instruction for a story that was cathartic. Thus, we can assume that the student composed the story by taking its index and transforming it according to the intention of expressing catharsis. However, for the sake of argument, let's assume that the story is identical to the index that is stored in memory. What is wrong with such an assumption? The first problem is that each story had many more events than the ones explicitly related. The Volvo has a color, a year, and a condition. The gas station has a certain look and feel to it. It is modern or old, in a city or on a country road. It sells a particular kind of gas, and so on. The policeman said some things, the station owner said some things, and the teller of the story said some things. All of these have been left out.

In the first telling of a story, a teller decides what to leave out. This decision is based upon a number of factors that include who is listening to the story, why the storyteller is telling it, and how the storyteller now perceives the happenings that occurred. After all, one cannot say everything that has happened. A story about a two-week vacation could take two weeks to tell. A teller must decide what aspects of the index are likely to be of interest to the hearer.

On subsequent tellings of the story, details that have been consistently left out tend to get forgotten, although they can be reconstructed in some instances. The index itself can be changed by the telling of a story over time. Pieces of the index that are never told tend to disappear from the index itself. The location of the gas station is never mentioned in any versions of this story, but if this event took place while the student was at Yale, then the gas station was probably in New Haven, that is, in a city setting and not on a country road. Thus, this aspect of the index is reconstructable. It will never totally be lost because it can be figured out. However, the kind of gas that the station sells, since it is never mentioned and much more difficult to reconstruct, may well be lost forever.

We propose, then, that the index is stored in memory and operated upon in a variety of ways. Now we will discuss the processes that transform various aspects of an index into various aspects of a story.

Distillation

Distillation is a two-part process that reduces the events of a story to a set of simpler propositions, that is, to its index, and then puts those propositions into English. The first part is a memory process. A complex array of memory structures is distilled into a simpler coherent whole when a story is told for the first time. We actively try to figure out what to tell about an experience.

Index Construction

The process of distilling a coherent story from a range of particular experiences causes a memory entity, the index, to be constructed. After an index is constructed, it, in effect, becomes the memory of the original set of events that comprised the story. The events themselves become lost as an easily retrievable entity, while the index is available for use. When someone asks us about an experience, we remember what we have previously told about that experience. Rather than attempting to search all over our memory to find something to say, using what we have already said is simpler. The first part of the distillation process, then, we call *index construction.* This process searches what is known about an event and finds discrete propositions that become the index of the story and can then be told in a given order. Once index construction takes place, the process becomes increasingly difficult to reverse in subsequent retellings because the new story replaces the original memories.

Let's imagine that you have just returned from a week-long vacation touring castles in England. A friend asks you how your trip was. What do you do? First, you must comb through the events of your trip to see how many of them were significant enough to mention. These choices are made in concert with a consideration for the kinds of things your friend might be interested in hearing, and the amount of time your friend is prepared to spend listening to your story. When you are finished finding things that you want to tell about, you have finished the first part of the distillation process. You have constructed a memory representation of the story you are about to tell. You have constructed the index.

Translation

The second part of the distillation process, *translation,* expresses an index in a natural language. There are, as we have seen, many ways to express the same index. The differences depend upon one's intentions and the story skeleton chosen to express those intentions. The translation process takes each of these propositions and translates them from their representation in memory into English. The translation process, then, is not a memory process, but a linguistic process. Events are being translated from a memory format into an English format. This translation proceeds event by event, and thus sentence by sentence. As each sentence appears the memory receives a new call to find the next proposition. These memory calls depend upon what went before. Often, the way an earlier proposition was actually expressed in English can alter what propositions are composed next. Thus, in effect, expressing an index in language can alter the index somewhat by making new demands upon the memory. For example, if you say that a castle you saw was beautiful, and you realize at the moment of expression that your listener might be interested in exactly what was beautiful about it, you can be forced to go back to your memory to find out more. Now, this information may not be in the index, and you might be thus forced to search parts of memory from which it is quite difficult to retrieve information. A possible alternative is to reconstruct the details from what you imagine might have been beautiful about the castle. By this we can see that the translation process depends, in part, upon information about the hearer, as well as upon information in memory that may not be part of the index at all.

An index, therefore, is an evolving kind of entity. If aspects of it are not accessed in future renditions of the story, an index can get smaller. It also can get larger as memory reconstruction adds pieces that may not have been in the original event at all. Further, the process of translation can affect the index. When certain words are chosen, they may express an emotional content that, although not part of the original events, now becomes part of the index. A new point of view in light of subsequent events might cause the translation process actually to change the index. We don't remember how we slanted things during a telling, by and large, but we do remember details that we may have added in translating an index into English, and these additions can become part of a reformulated index.

Index construction is probably a great deal like the memory process that has the responsibility of storing away stories in the first place. We remember only the index of the story, so, in essence, what we are doing when we are initially storing away a new story is consciously trying to remember it. We are rehearsing the telling of the story, distilling it, in other words, for ourselves as part of the memory process. Telling a story for the first time may involve distilling it for the first time for our listener, but, more likely, we probably have already done this in thinking about the experience ourselves.

Nevertheless, more distillation may be done during the actual telling than was done initially. The desire to keep a story short, for example, has the effect of distilling an index so that only the essential details remain. In general, distillation leaves out descriptions of physical items unless those descriptions are critical to the story. Distillation also leaves out the particular words and ideas of the partici- pants in a story, although this distillation tends to occur at the time of storage rather than during generation. In fact, words may be put into the mouths of the participants by another story process, as we shall see in a later discussion. Distillation is a purist's kind of process. It may never really occur in its pure form, however. That is, we like to think that we tell a subset of what we have experienced, and that distillation is the process by which that subset is selected. But, in actual practice, stories add details that may never have occurred at all. We shall see how this process works when we discuss other aspects of story construction.

Combination Processes

Now let's consider again the Volvo story, in which the teller made a point of his vision problems:

> I was driving my Volvo once into a gas station, and what must have happened is that I was traveling forward, and I hit this big square concrete thing. It was high enough that I should have seen it, but it was over here in my right visual field. It was just another one of those cases where there is missing field here, and I bashed right into it. I mean it was bright daylight, and I drove into it. Sometimes, I just don't see stuff.

In this version of the Volvo story, the teller combines the indexes of two stories to make one story. The first or master story is the Volvo story; the second story is about the student's visual problems. Because the vision story has its own point, the effect of the *combination process* is to take everything from the Volvo story that related to the vision story and to tell it while suppressing everything else. Notice how almost nothing unrelated to the teller's visual problems is expressed in the Volvo story. Combining a point with a story means leaving out the parts of the story that don't help make the point, and emphasizing those parts that do.

Suppression

As we have seen, the combination process causes the distillation process to suppress events unrelated to the point of the story to be conjoined. The combination process must integrate two stories by deciding which is the master story and which is "coloration" for this master story. Events are interwoven to make one coherent story. The major subprocesses in combination, then, are *suppression* and *conjunction*. The suppression process examines the index of each story to be combined to see whether it enhances the newly combined story. Aspects of the coloration story that have nothing to do with the point of the master story or with the coherence of the newly created story are thus dropped.

Conjunction

The conjunction process must weave two stories into one by deciding which story is dominant (dominance is often a function of affect), and which story will be used to enhance the dominant story by adding details or evidence. With the vision story dominant, the Volvo story is mined for important details which are then added as evidence for the propositions of the vision story.

When a story is told in order to gain the attention of those around, the teller employs a different kind of story process. Let us consider what processes might have been active in the attention-getting versions of these two stories:

> Let me tell you what happened to me. I was at a gas station, and I was driving this big old Volvo that I have. Let's see, I think I had gotten the gas, and I was—no, I hadn't gotten the gas yet. I was just driving in, and I was trying to get up to the pump, and there was this big planter up there. I don't know, it was this brick thing. It had dirt, and I drove the car into it and mashed the front of the car and really mashed the planter, much worse than the front of the car. So I got out, and I talked to the guy at the gas station. He was really pissed off at me because he couldn't figure out how anybody could be stupid enough to drive into a planter right out there in broad daylight, and so we decided that we had to call the police, and he wanted to know the name of my insurance company. Then, the policeman got there, and I talked to him for a while. He said to me that it wasn't really a problem because I was not out on a road, so he was not going to give me a ticket, but I was still probably responsible for the damage, and the guy could still sue me if he wanted to, or he could go to my insurance company and get the money. So anyway, we exchanged insurance companies.

One difference between this story and the first version is its greater length. Another difference is that this version has more emotional content. Both of these differences are results of the elaboration process.

Elaboration

Stories can be elaborated for a variety of reasons, each relating to the story intentions discussed earlier. For example, a story can be elaborated in order to create an emotional impact on the hearer, or it can be elaborated in order for the teller to hold center stage as long as possible. Each different intention causes the elaboration process to function differently.

Detail Addition. If we want to hold center stage with our story, we might fill in as many details as possible. If we want to make a listener like us, we might elaborate the story with examples of how well we behaved, how poorly we were treated, and so on. Thus elaboration is not the name of one story process at all. Rather, elaboration means finding additional things to say. In the preceding story, the teller elaborated each event by adding details about how he felt to be there.

The elaboration process thus has three major subprocesses associated with it. *Detail addition* is a fairly straightforward process. To make the story take longer or seem more vivid or realistic, details are added to the index. Details can be added by search, by reconstruction, or by adaptation. In other words, we search memory to add details that we actually remember, that we can imagine must have been true, or that we know were true in other similar situations. Although the addition of details may have no point in terms of story content, details matter a great deal in terms of storytelling. The more details the teller adds to the story, the more memorable the story becomes. Thus, details make the story interesting and attention-getting.

Commentary. A second elaboration process is *commentary.* In this process, we embellish by adding our own view of the situation, including comments on how well or how poorly various people behaved, what the right thing to do would have been, what others might say or think about the situation, what we would do the next time, and so on. When we tell the story again, we might add different comments according to our audience and our view of the world at the time. Such comments are rarely part of the story index in memory, but are usually added at telling time.

Role-playing. The third elaboration subprocess is *role-playing,* another part of the telling process and not of memory. Since what people actually say is rarely part of the index, the storyteller imagines what someone might have felt or said in a given situation by accessing other stories where such feelings were experienced and stored. Thus, elaboration via role-playing tends to involve story combination. The combined stories are vestiges of old stories denuded of their actual points and circumstances and added to the current story in order to enhance it.

Consider, for example, the phrase "[the station owner] couldn't figure out how anyone could be stupid enough to. ..." Where does this come from? The teller probably did not recall the station owner's words. He had no real information about the owner's thoughts. Rather, the teller temporarily assumed the role of the owner by remembering his attitude, imagining where that attitude might have come from, and making up the rest. Thus, stories that start out as the telling of factual events tend to become fictional in a sense. Even telling true stories involves making up the events more often than not. The index just doesn't have all you need if you want to tell a story that grabs people's attention.

Other Processes

Captioning

The captioning process is a shorthand way of telling all or parts of a story. *Captioning* is simply the summarization of a larger story used as a means of telling that story. Captioning is a very important storytelling process. It is most commonly used in the telling of those stories that we all share as members of a culture. Because we share them, we need not tell them in detail. We can simply refer to them, so culturally common stories are usually referred to rather than told. A proverb is a captioned culturally common story. For example, the following one-liner from the Woody Allen movie, *Love and Death,* is a reference to stories that we all know about insurance salesmen:

There are worse things in life than death—If you have ever spent an evening with an insurance salesman, you know what I mean.

Our culture's common views of insurance salesmen allows us to communicate in this way about them. The culturally common story here is simply that insurance salesmen are boring and painful to listen to. Some captioned stories get told in their least detailed form, making them understandable only to those who already knew them. Such stories can become so short that they do not in any way appear to be stories, and in some obvious sense, they are not stories. A joke about such "stories" can be seen in the following well-known exaggeration:

The prisoners in a maximum security prison had little to entertain themselves with so they told jokes to each other. But, they had long since run out of new jokes to tell, so they simply numbered the jokes and yelled out the numbers. A new prisoner, hearing "42," "64," "108," being yelled down the hall with raucous laughter following each number asked about what was happening, and it was explained to him. He asked if he could try it, and his cellmate said sure. He hollered "36," and nothing happened. Next he tried "27" and still nothing. The new prisoner finally asked his cellmate what was wrong, and he replied "you didn't tell them so well."

A captioned story that is shortened so much that it ceases to be understood is no longer a story, although what is not understandable to one person may be understandable to another. Thus, the term "story" is clearly relative. In any case, as long as it *is* understood, it remains a story. For this reason, there are some stories that are very short. A really great example of captioning is from the movie *Manhattan:*

A: She's gorgeous.
W: She's seventeen. I'm forty-two, and she's seventeen.

Adaptation

That *adaptation* of a story means taking one story and making another one out of it, for example, taking *Romeo and Juliet* and converting it into *West Side Story*. This involves taking actors, plans, events, and other elements from the source story, and mapping them into analogous entities in the target story.

A CLOSER LOOK AT THE MEMORY EFFECTS OF STORYTELLING

Psychologists might raise several questions for theoretical clarification of our ideas. One theoretical question goes like this: If we grant that telling stories alters our memory of them, how do we know whether this is due to the actual telling, rather than the intention to tell? Presumably, if one has the goal of presenting a laundered version of an episode, some reorganization of memory is required before one tells the story to others. Does the act of telling result in additional alteration, or does it serve to fix this already reorganized memory, or what? This issue might be consequential because it often happens that we prepare to tell a story (or write a letter), and we rehearse it mentally, but for one reason or another, we never actually get to tell it (or send it).

A second, somewhat related question, concerns the distinction between telling stories to others and telling them to oneself, for example, privately reviewing the details of one's experiences. (Psychologists would call this *rehearsal.*) Again, the issue is the contribution of overt conversation, if any, over and above purely cognitive processing of autobiographical stories.

The third question is about the malleability of stories in memory. Suppose the details can't be altered to create a satisfactory version of the remembered self. The person might be too anxious or guilt-ridden about some past episode to dare telling about it. Does this weaken our position about the importance of storytelling for the memory of self? We now consider these questions in turn.

Actual Telling Versus Merely Intending to Tell

What are the effects on memory of preparing to tell a story, as distinct from the effects of actually telling it? Relevant to this point, there has been research on the memory effects of the intention to convey information. This topic goes all the way back to the early 1950s, when Zajonc (1960) considered the purposes of attending to information. There are different reasons why people might want to understand what they are being told, and the reason for attending could influence the way this material is organized in memory. This reminds us of the old joke about a burnt out psychiatrist. A friend asks him how he can stand listening day after day, year after year, to neurotic tales of anguish and distress. He shrugs: "Who listens!"

Cognitive Tuning

Zajonc, in referring to the listener's purpose, used the term *cognitive tuning* to describe how the listener is set mentally to process the incoming information. He drew a major distinction between the *receiving set* and the *transmission set,* each induced by instruction given to experimental subjects who expect to hear some information about a particular person. The receiving set instruction indicated that some material about the person would be given right away, and that more would come later. Subjects were to listen carefully, but to keep in mind that the first batch of information would be incomplete. Subjects in the transmission set condition were told that after hearing material about a person, they would have to describe him to another subject. Subjects were to listen carefully, keeping in mind that they would have to relay the information later.

The information did not come to the experimental subjects as a story of a personal episode. Rather, it was an ambiguous personality description of a hypothetical individual. Characteristic of psychological research on language and memory, Zajonc's study is thus somewhat remote from the realistic scenario we have in mind, which involves the telling of a personal episode. Nevertheless, Zajonc's results make a point about the transmission set: The expectation of telling another subject about the hypothetical person stimulated a better organized memory for the material presented, with fewer inconsistencies. The number of facts remembered did not differ between the two instruction groups, but the selection of facts was more coherent in the transmission condition. We would have expected both better organization and *fewer* facts remembered in the transmission set condition, due to the distillation process.

Recent Research

Research on cognitive tuning has intermittently been followed up. Recently, Lassiter, Pezzo, and Apple (1993) hypothesized that immediately telling a prepared story differentially diminishes memory for it a week later. They established two experimental conditions with subjects hearing a standard story in each. In one condition, they had an opportunity to tell the story; in the other, they did not. The crucial memory test was one week later. Factual memory was better in the group that had *not* had the opportunity to tell the story. The investigator attributed this result to the famous (but fragile) Zeigarnik effect, in which uncompleted tasks command more mental resources than completed tasks.

This experiment was criticized by Boninger, Brannon, and Brock (1993), who doubted the operation of Zeigarnik effects in general. They were also skeptical of the storytelling opportunity provided to the "completed task" group. Subjects had told their story to a computer, a feature employed by the experimenters to rule out variability due to the demeanors of human listeners.

Experimental Difficulties

From these kinds of experimental ambiguities, we can see how difficult it is to combine the usual tight controls of an experiment with the real circumstance of telling a personal experience to a friend. The most straightforward way to distinguish the memory effects of actual telling from those of a mere intention to tell is to have two groups both prepare the same stories for the same prospective listener, with one group telling and the other group not telling. The problem for the experimenter, however, is finding a way to frustrate the intention to tell. Whatever gambit is arranged (running out of time, the listener failing to show up, and so on) introduces an extraneous situational variable. Perhaps it would be best to use a counterbalanced design in which each subject prepares two stories, but actually tells only one. To our knowledge, this has not been tried.

To be truly pertinent to our hypothesis about the memory effects of telling stories, the story material used in experiments should be personally relevant. We have postulated that the shaping of stories is motivated by a more general, long-term desire to shape one's self, particularly for the presentation of that self to others. The transmission of impressions about hypothetical people has little or no consequence for one's "remembered self," unless one's performance reflects on one's own wisdom or empathy.

Is This Issue Critical?

In the end, perhaps it is only a matter of academic interest whether it is the intention to tell or the act of telling that carries the freight of memory alterations. It may be a little of both. A similar issue arises for the counterattitudinal advocacy paradigm in dissonance theory: Is it necessary for the subject actually to give the dissonance-arousing speech, or merely to expect to do so? Ask any two social psychologists this question, and you will get three different answers. What matters for the present discussion is the idea that the individual edits and reorganizes autobiographical experiences for conversational purposes. In the normal course of events, intending to tell is followed by actually telling. The case of the prepared but untold story may only matter if it happens repeatedly. Later, we will discuss the effects of chronic inability to tell one's story.

Rehearsing Versus Telling

Similar to the issue of telling an experience versus merely intending to tell it, is the question of private *rehearsal* versus public presentation. An individual who has had an interesting experience may mentally review it for a number of reasons. One reason may be the intention to tell other people about it, leading the individual to try to organize the interesting parts and drop out the nonessentials, or smooth over the embarrassments. However, planning to tell is not the only reason for rehearsal. There may be a need to ponder the meaning of the experience, which among other things may involve receptivity to remindings from other experiences. The individual may wish to air some feelings internally. The list of reasons for rehearsal could go on.

For the psychological experimenter, it is hard to distinguish the memory effects of rehearsal from those of actually telling about one's experience. The problems are similar to those of trying to separate the influences of intention to tell from actual telling. The major difficulty is in controlling the (privately governed) degree of rehearsal. The apparently straightforward thing for the experimenter to do is to provide time and motivation for some subjects to rehearse their experiences while other subjects have no time to rehearse, but must immediately tell. However, these two manipulations are incommensurate in several arbitrary ways. For example, there is no good way to guarantee that the experience is rehearsed only once, not twice or half a dozen times, so we end up comparing apples and orchards.

Again, however, this distinction between rehearsing and telling may be no more than an academic interest. It seems reasonable to suppose that with most experiences of any importance, rehearsal and telling both occur. There is no doubt that the memory strength of a single item, or list of items, is a monotonically increasing function of the number of rehearsals. Telling, if nothing else, is certainly another rehearsal, so it, too, will strengthen a simple memory. Our interest, however, is not primarily in the strength of experiential memories, but in the system of organizing large numbers of them, and the way this system affects and is affected by storytelling. The social relationship between the storyteller and the listener is consequential for our view of autobiographical memory, but it is not a factor in rehearsal. (Rehearsal with a particular listener in mind is tantamount to the intention to tell, and is not mere rehearsal.)

Children's Memories

Eyewitness Testimony

The memory capabilities of children shed some light on the nature of adult memory. Let us first consider children and adults as eyewitnesses. In many experiments on eyewitness testimony, the basic design is to stage a dramatic episode of possible criminal activity. Then attempts are made to disrupt the accuracy of the observer's memory, for example, by asking misleading questions (Loftus, 1979). Even without disruptive intervention, eyewitness testimony is surprisingly inaccurate. With disruptive interrogation of various types, further error is introduced. At some later time, memory is assessed, and the result of interest is the degree to which inaccuracies are incorporated into the subject's account of the incident.

Such phenomena, of course, hold great legal interest, most poignantly in the area of child abuse (Ceci & Bruck, 1993). Children's testimony on whether an adult has sexually abused them is demonstrably vulnerable to repeated badgering by prosecutors. Induced false memories in preschoolers, after being honed to the satisfaction of the prodding adult, are not infrequently maintained as true, and recounted as such to other adults (Ceci & Bruck, 1993).

In this type of situation, the influence of others on the storyteller is drastic. At first, it seems that the fabrication of facts in the child's testimony under duress has little to do with the voluntary alteration of autobiographical details in the service of self. Still, this example leads us to wonder how a child's memory for experiences develops in the first place. Are there objective autobiographical memories, which may be corrupted by various external and internal influences in the telling and retelling? On the other hand, is there no such thing as unedited memory for experience?

The Invention of Autobiographical Memory

In a very provocative paper on the origins of autobiographical memory, Nelson (1993) defends a highly unusual position, one that is strikingly consistent with our argument in the present paper. It can be paraphrased thus: Autobiographical memory is a social invention.

Nelson first challenges the Freudian construct of repressed memories, which is based on the ubiquitous finding that adults have no memories for experiences prior to age three or four, and very few up to age six or seven. She notes that this finding is rendered moot by studies of the memories of children for prior experiences. Children as young as 24- to 30-months old demonstrate in spontaneous monologues (Nelson, 1989) and in response to questions (Hudson, 1986) that they can occasionally retrieve particular sequences of events from recent novel experiences. Furthermore, 3-year-olds can provide generic event memories (scripts) for routine activities they have repeatedly experienced (Nelson & Gruendel, 1981). Why, then, do these memories disappear by the time the child has reached adulthood?

Nelson's position is that early memories are transient and disorganized, for two reasons: The child lacks the encoding experience to store them systematically, and in any case attaches no particular importance to them. Of what use is the memory of a unique event to a child who doesn't know whether it will ever happen again (and likely does not have the cognitive ability to pose such a question)? The most permanence that Nelson is inclined to accord preschoolers' unique memories is that these memories might remain in a "holding pattern" for up to six months. Reinstatement of the event by the occurrence of a somewhat similar experience within the holding period would increase the potential longevity of such event memories (Fivush & Hammond, 1989). If there were no reinstatement within the holding period, the event memory would be lost. Note the compatibility of this pattern with Tomkins' (1978) notion that a single event in itself is of little cognitive significance to a child, but further events can sometimes evoke the key process of *magnification.*

Several repetitions of very similar events encourage the development of generic memories, such as those of visits to the grocery store or the zoo (Hudson & Nelson, 1986). After five or six repetitions, the individual visits become scrambled in the child's memory, exactly as we have postulated for adults, and a generic memory is formed for a particular kind of activity.

The key part of Nelson's analysis of preschool memory is that parents teach their children how to remember. The transition from the 3-year-old who forgets unique events but retains scripts to the 6-year-old who can intelligently discuss a variety of past experiences is brought about, according to Nelson, by conversational experiences with parents. The parents elaborate ongoing or past episodes with the child, ask questions, share emotions, and so on. Such interactions do not merely serve to reinstate particular experiences; they gradually convey to the child a primary function of event memories: To communicate them to others for the benefits such telling provides. Nelson writes, "The claim here is that the initial functional significance of autobiographical memory is that of sharing memory with other people, a function that language makes possible. Memories become valued in their own right . . . because they . . . serve a social solidarity function. . . . I suggest that this social function of memory underlies all of our storytelling, history-making narrative activities, and ultimately all of our accumulated knowledge systems" (Nelson, 1993, p.12).

Nelson proposed that parents (often implicitly) convey to the child what is important to remember, and, in effect, why and how one has to rehearse an event after its occurrence in order to tell it to others. She offered several corollaries of this proposal, for example, that deaf children of hearing parents and members of cultures that discourage children from speaking with adults should be slower to develop autobiographical memories. There is as yet no evidence on these hypotheses, and hardly any definitive research on her general proposal. Nelson cited an unpublished dissertation by Tessler (1991) showing a strong correlational relationship between mother–child conversation about a museum visit and later memory by the child for objects seen. Another dissertation by Engel (1986) made the distinction between "elaborative" and "pragmatic" styles of parent–child conversations invoking memory.

The pragmatic style concerns itself with serviceable facts such as, "Where did you put your mittens?" The elaborative style provides the basis for storytelling, as it constructs narratives of shared experiences such as museum visits. The obvious prediction is that children of elaborative mothers and fathers who interact often with their children will develop better autobiographical memory facility than children of pragmatic mothers and fathers. The pragmatic group of children, in contrast, might develop memory of a semantic sort. There is sketchy evidence supporting this hypothesis, but it has not been tested longitudinally over long time intervals.

Returning to the topic of the child as an eyewitness, note that the children studied by Ceci and Bruck (1993) were preschoolers, the age range that Nelson proposes as the period during which children learn how to construct and discuss autobiographical memories. Consider the scenario of a sexual abuse accusation in which the child initially denies the evidence for the allegation that is, in fact, false. The repeated badgering by the prosecutor may be seen as a perverse variant of autobiographical memory training: The child learns that one should tell as a memory what a threatening adult tells you to remember. What seems to the adult a capitulation may be to the child a release from confusion, if we accept Nelson's proposal that preschool children don't quite know how to organize and report their fragile memories for events. The prosecutor offers them a compelling method of memory organization, which some of them eventually accept.

SUMMARY

Knowledge

In this chapter, we have claimed that from the point of view of the social functions of knowledge, what people know consists almost exclusively of stories and the cognitive skills necessary to understand, remember, and tell stories.

To be sure, people know various kinds of things that seem to have little to do with stories. These include facts, beliefs, lexicons, rule systems, and grammar. The rhetorical force of these apparent exceptions to our claim, however, is sharply reduced by three considerations discussed in the section Types of Knowledge Other than Story-Related Knowledge. First, there are a great many cases in which items from one or another of these domains serve to *index* stories. This is especially true of beliefs, but applies also to facts, and even to numbers. Second, and more important, people do not ordinarily hold conversations in these domains. The names of state capitals are learned by rote in school, then are unmentioned forever unless the student visits one (when there may be a story in it). And one does not overhear talk of elegant grammatical regularities at family dinners, or golf courses, or on airplanes. Third, such communication as does take place within these domains is largely confined to experts in the subject matter. With increasing expertise comes a tendency toward "storification" on one's subject matter. Mathematicians tell stories about theorem proving; chess players tell stories about legendary chess games, and so on.

What our position comes down to is that it is far more important—certainly for psychologists—to study the cognitive and social nature of storytelling than to pursue abstract, formal domains of information processing. The lack of attention by psychologists to story structure and storytelling seems lately to have been peripherally recognized by the emergence of a specialty called *narrative psychology* (Sarbin, 1986).

Memory

Characteristically, the notable episodes in our lives consist of events and outcomes occurring over a sequence of interrelated scenes. Whether it be a visit to the dentist, a trip to Paris, or the time when you popped the question, the details of an experience can exist in memory in two ways: as a coherent story linking separate scenes, or as a set of disconnected bits of information stored within general scene memories. The main hypothesis of the section on Storytelling and Memory is that if the person experiencing the episode does not tell (or, at least, rehearse) the story soon afterwards, the separate events and outcomes will become disconnected, and memory access to them will operate through independent memories of particular scenes. The episode will lose its coherence—though it may still exert some influence, especially if its outcome was negative. One may regard an encounter with a particular stimulus object as a stressful scene, for example, while being unable to recall the original episode leading up to such an encounter.

On the other hand, if the story is told and retold, it will gradually assume a stable form in memory, and will be indexed in several ways to facilitate access to it. This stable structure will have priority over the bits and pieces originally stored in scattered event memories for the constituent scenes. Thus, a storyteller can suppress memory for raw unpleasant outcomes by embedding them in retold stories, edited to be more benign than the original experience. A variant of this strategy requires that an unpleasant story be edited and told just once in order to co-opt memory for the negative scene(s), and then never told again. This analysis provides an alternative interpretation of the phenomenon of *repression* as a set of mundane storytelling maneuvers to weaken access to bad experiences, rather than as a special, unconscious process sealing off those experiences until you undergo psychoanalysis.

There are other motives and strategies entering into the selective distortion of stories: omitting details or manufacturing excuses for wrongdoing, giving explanations for ambiguities, conforming to the norms of the group, and so on. One of the oldest findings in the social psychological literature, in Allport and Postman's (1945) study of rumor, was that successive communications from one person to another lead to two kinds of distortions away from the original story. These were called *leveling* (the condensation of confusing or awkward details) and *sharpening* (the embellishment of favorable or surprising details). Even prior to that, in Bartlett's (1932) famous study of a weird story retold from an unfamiliar culture, this very point had been anticipated. What has been lacking for 50 or 60 years has been an analysis of the content-sensitive processes that effect the two kinds of distortion. In the sections entitled Story Skeletons and Story Construction Process, we flesh out some of these processes. Much more could be done along these lines. Also, it would be worthwhile to have empirical tests of the hypothesized memory disconnection of untold stories.

Comprehension

If the core of social knowledge and the essence of social communication both consist of a bank of stories and a set of story processing structures, then it should be the case that the understanding of other people's utterances is story-based, too. In the sections Understanding Means Mapping Your Stories Onto My Stories and Behavior in Response to New Experiences, we argue that understanding boils down to finding a story of your own that is similar to the story you are hearing. If there is a very close match, then telling your story in response signals that you have understood, although you will have learned nothing new. If there is not a close match, you will have to work hard to come up with a more remote response, either by locating a partially relevant story, or by constructing one from scene by scene details. If the stimulus story has something anomalous about it, then the retrieval of a partially relevant response story may help you to explain the anomaly. The explanation will then index both stories, and you may, in the process, acquire a new insight, usually in the form of a new belief.

As we show in the section Behavior in Response to New Experiences, similarity is a very powerful construct in psychology, entering into the analysis of many diverse phenomena (Tversky, 1977; Shepard, 1987). Unfortunately, the question of what makes stories similar is a difficult one. No doubt the concept of common elements is pertinent, but we do not yet know what types of elements dominate the matching process, and why they do. We propose that the careful study of *remindings* gives clues to what may be going on. Suppose you are reminded of experience B, apparently unconsciously, when told of experience A. The question, "What does B have to do with A?" can lead to a revealing analysis, both for the individual who got reminded, and to the scholar studying the bases of story similarity.

Other Issues

Other topics of great psychological interest that attach to our story model include the learning of autobiographical storytelling by children, and the phenomenon of socially shared memories. We broached these briefly in sections IX and VI, citing the theoretical paper by Nelson (1993) for the former, and the exploratory research by Ross and Holmberg (1990) for the latter.

We close with the trite but true admonition that our position both requires and deserves much more research. Cognitive and social psychology, in studying knowledge structures, memory processes, and text comprehension, have in our view lost sight of the forest by concentrating on the cellulose in the trees.

REFERENCES

Abelson, R. P. (1973). The structure of belief systems. In R. C. Schank & K. M. Colby (Eds.), *Computer models of thought and language* (pp. 287–339). San Francisco: Freeman.

Abelson, R. P. (1979). Differences between belief and knowledge systems. *Cognitive Science, 2,* 355–366.

Adams, D. (1980). *A hitchhiker's guide to the galaxy.* New York: Harmony Books.

Allport, G. W., & Postman, L. J. (1945). *The basic psychology of rumor.* Transactions of the New York Academy of Sciences, Series II, Vol. 8, 61–81.

Aronson, E. (1969). The theory of cognitive dissonance: A current perspective. In L. Berkowitz (Ed.), Advances in experimental social psychology, Vol. 4 (pp. 1–34). New York: Academic Press.

Aronson, E., Willerman, B., & Floyd, J. (1966). The effect of a pratfall of increasing personal attractiveness. *Psychonomic Science, 4,* 227–228.

Ayeroff, F., & Abelson, R. P. (1976). ESP and ESB: Belief in personal success at mental telepathy. *Journal of Personality and Social Psychology, 34,* 240–247.

Bartlett, F. C. (1932). Remembering: A study in experimental and social psychology. New York: Macmillan.

Boninger, D. S., Brannon, L. A., & Brock, T. C. (1993). Effects of transmission tuning on attitude change persistence: An examination of alternative explanations. *Psychological Science, 3,* 211–213.

Ceci, S. J., & Bruck, M. (1993). Suggestibility of the child witness: A historical review and synthesis. *Psychological Bulletin, 113*, 403–439.

Child, I. L. (1973). *Humanistic psychology and the research tradition.* New Haven: Yale University Press.

Clark, H. H., & Marshall, C. R. (1981). Definite reference and mutual knowledge. In A. K. Joshi, B. L. Webber, & I. A. Sag (Eds.), *Elements of discourse understanding* (pp. 10–63). Cambridge, England: Cambridge University Press.

Colby, K. M., & Gilbert, J. P. (1964). Programming a computer model of neurosis. *Journal of Mathematical Psychology, 1*, 405–412.

Cullingford, R. E. (1979). Integrating knowledge sources for computer "understanding" tasks. *Proceedings of the 1979 Conference of Cybernetics and Society,* Denver, CO, 746–752.

Downing, J. W., Judd, C. M., & Brauer, M. (1992). Effects of repeated expressions on attitude extremity. *Journal of Personality and Social Psychology, 63*, 17–29.

Engel, S. (1986). *Learning to reminisce: A developmental study of how young children talk about the past.* Unpublished doctoral dissertation. City University of New York Graduate Center.

Feigenbaum, E. A., Buchanan, B. G., & Lederberg, J. (1971). On generality and problem solving: a case study involving the dendral program. In B. Meltzer & D. Michie (Eds.), *Machine intelligence* (pp. 165–190). New York: American Elsevier.

Fivush, R., & Hamond, N. R. (1989). Time and again: Effects of repetition and retention interval on two year olds' event recall. *Journal of Experimental Child Psychology, 47*, 259–273.

Fleming, G. H. (1981). *The unforgettable season.* New York: Simon & Schuster.

Gentner, D. (1983). Structure-mapping: A theoretical framework for analogy. *Cognitive Science, 7*, 155–170.

Higgins, E. T., Rholes, W. S., & Jones, C. R. (1977). Category accessibility and impression formation. *Journal of Experimental Social Psychology, 13*, 141–154.

Hovy, E. H. (1987). *Generating natural language under pragmatic constraints.* Unpublished doctoral dissertation, Yale University.

Hudson, J. A. (1986). Memories are made of this: General event knowledge and the development of autobiographical memory. In K. Nelson (Ed.), *Event knowledge: Structure and function in development* (pp. 97–118). Hillsdale, NJ: Lawrence Erlbaum Associates.

Hudson, J. A., & Nelson, K. (1986). Repeated encounters of a similar kind: Effects of familiarity on children's autobiographic memory. *Cognitive Development, 1*, 253–271.

Humez, A., Humez, N., & Maguire, J. (1993). *From zero to lazy eight: The romance of numbers.* New York: Simon and Schuster.

James, B., Albert, J., & Stern, H. S. (1993). Answering questions about baseball using statistics. *Chance, 6*(2), 17–22.

Kelley, H. H. (1953). Group membership and resistance to persuasion. In C. I. Hovland, I. L. Janis, & H. H. Kelley, *Communication and persuasion* (pp. 134–165). New Haven, CT: Yale University Press.

Kelley, H. H. (1971). Attribution in social interaction. In E. E. Jones, D. E. Kanouse, H. H. Kelley, R. E. Nisbett, S. Valins, & B. Weiner. *Attribution: Perceiving the causes of behavior* (pp. 1–26). Morristown, NJ: General Learning Press.

Kolodner, J. (1991). An introduction to case-based reasoning. *Artificial Intelligence Review, 6*(1), 3–34.

Lamb, R., Lalljee, M., & Abelson, R. P. (1992). The role of event prototypes in categorization and explanation. In W. Stroebe & M. Hewstone (Eds.), *European review of social psychology,* Vol. 3 (pp. 153–182). Chichester, England: Wiley.

Langer, E. J. (1975). The illusion of control. *Journal of Personality and Social Psychology, 32*, 311–328.

Lassiter, G. D., Pezzo, M. V., & Apple, K. J. (1993). The transmitter persistence effect: A confounded discovery? *Psychological Science, 4*, 208–210.

Lehnert, W. G. (1981). Plot units and narrative summation. *Cognitive Science, 4*, 293–331.

Loftus, E. F. (1979). *Eyewitness testimony.* Cambridge, MA: Harvard University Press.

Meyer, D. E., & Schvaneveldt, R.W. (1971). Facilitation in recognizing pairs of words: Evidence of a dependence between retrieval operations. *Journal of Experimental Psychology, 90*, 227–234.

Nelson, K., and Greundel, J. (1981). Generalized event representations: Basic building blocks of cognitive development. In M. Lamb & A. Brown (Eds.), *Advances in developmental psychology,* Vol. 1 (pp. 131–158). Hillsdale, NJ: Lawrence Erlbaum Associates.

Nelson, K. (Ed.). (1989). *Narratives from the crib.* Cambridge, MA: Harvard University Press.

Nelson, K. (1993). The psychological and social origins of autobiographical memory. *Psychological Science, 4,* 7–14.

Newell, A., & Simon, H. H. (1972). *Human problem solving.* Englewood Cliffs, NJ: Prentice-Hall.

Nisbett, R. E., & Wilson, T. D. (1977). Telling more than we can know: Verbal reports on mental process. *Psychological Review, 84,* 231–259.

Ortony, A. (1979). Beyond literal conformity. *Psychological Review, 86,* 161–180.

Pennington, N., & Hastie, R. (1992). Explaining the evidence: Testing the Story Model for juror decision making. *Journal of Personality and Social Psychology, 62,* 189–206.

Powell, M. C., & Fazio, R. H. (1984). Attitude accessibility as a function of repeated attitudinal expression. *Personality and Social Psychology Bulletin, 10,* 139–148.

Price, V. (1989). Social identification and public opinion: Effects of communicating group conflict. *Public Opinion Quarterly, 53,* 197–224.

Roseman, I. J. (1994). The psychology of strongly held beliefs: Theories of ideological structure and individual attachment. In R. C. Schank & E. J. Langer (Eds.), *Beliefs, reasoning, and decision making: Psycho-logic in honor of Bob Abelson.* Hillsdale, NJ: Lawrence Erlbaum Associates.

Ross, L. D. (1977). The intuitive psychologist and his shortcomings: Distortions in the attribution process. In L. Berkowitz (Ed.), *Advances in experimental social psychology,* Vol. 10 (pp. 174–220). New York: Academic Press.

Ross, M., & Holmberg, D. (1990). Recounting the past: Gender differences in the recall of events in the history of a close relationship. In J. M. Olson & M. P. Zanna (Eds.), *Self-inference processes: The Ontario Symposium,* Vol. 6 (pp. 135–152). Hillsdale, NJ: Lawrence Erlbaum Associates.

Sacks, O. (1985). *The man who mistook his wife for a hat.* New York: HarperCollins.

Sarbin, T. R. (Ed.). (1986). *Narrative psychology. The storied nature of human existence.* New York: Praeger.

Schank, R. C. (1982). *Dynamic memory.* Hillsdale, NJ: Lawrence Erlbaum Associates.

Schank, R. C., & Abelson, R. P. (1977). *Scripts, plans, goals, and understanding.* Hillsdale, NJ: Lawrence Erlbaum Associates.

Searle, J. R. (1980). Minds, brains, and programs. *Behavioral and Brain Sciences, 3,* 417–457.

Seifert, C. M., McKoon, G., Abelson, R. P., & Ratcliffe, R. (1980). Memory connections between theoretically similar episodes. *Journal of Experimental Psychology: Learning, Memory, and Cognition, 12,* 220–231.

Sharkey, N. E., & Mitchell, D. C. (1985). Word recognition in a functional context: The use of scripts in reading. *Journal of Memory and Language, 24,* 253–270.

Shepard, R. (1987). Toward a universal law of generalization for psychological science. *Science, 237,* 1317–1323.

Singer, J. A., & Salovey, P. (1993). *The remembered self: Emotion and memory in personality.* New York: Free Press.

Taylor, R. B., DeSoto, C. B., & Lieb, R. (1979). Sharing secrets: Disclosure and discretion in dyads and triads. *Journal of Personality and Social Psychology, 37,* 1196–1203.

Tessler, M. (1991). *Making memories together: Influence of mother-child joint encoding on the development of autobiographic memory style.* Unpublished doctoral dissertation. City University of New York Graduate Center.

Tomkins, S. S. (1978). Script theory: Differential magnification of affects. *Nebraska Symposium on Motivation, 26,* 201–236.

Tulving, E. (1993). What is episodic memory? *Current Directions in Psychological Science, 3,* 67–70.

Tversky, A. (1977). Features of similarity. *Psychological Review, 84,* 327–352.

Tversky, A., & Kahneman, D. (1973). Availability: A heuristic for judging frequency and probability. *Cognitive Psychology, 5,* 207–222.

Wegner, D. M. (1989). *White bears and other unwanted thoughts: Supression, obsession, and the psychology of mental control.* New York: Viking.

Zajonc, R. (1960). The process of cognitive tuning in communication. *Journal of Abnormal and Social Psychology, 61,* 159–168.

2

Celebrating the Story in Social Perception, Communication, and Behavior

John H. Harvey
René Martin
University of Iowa

Schank and Abelson have made an important contribution to our understanding of how people understand and make inferences about their social world. In the theoretical tradition of their influential conception of the role of scripts in social behavior (Schank & Abelson, 1977, and Schank's 1991 book *Tell Me a Story*), they have provided a compelling treatment of stories and storytelling that is informative to our understanding of social cognition. Their analysis cogently points to the need for the field of social cognition to give more emphasis to molar aspects of how people construct meaning and communicate in the social context. What we wish to do in this commentary is three-fold:

1. Relate Schank and Abelson's analysis to Heider's (1958) naive psychology.
2. Extend Schank and Abelson's treatment to other parts of the burgeoning literature developing in diverse fields on stories, narratives, and accounts.
3. Address further questions regarding the role of stories and story-making in social cognition (we use the term "story-making" to represent the more comprehensive class of activities including story-comprehending, -remembering, -constructing, and -telling).

NAIVE PSYCHOLOGY AND STORY-MAKING

Heider's (1958) naive or common sense psychology contained a seed for the present emphasis on stories and storytelling in psychology. His rich portrayal of social perception processes involves many implications for how people use stories in their daily lives. Although Heider did not use the story metaphor per se, his naive psychology is a theory about how people impart chunks of meaning to events occurring in their world. These chunks of meaning are often both remembered and communicated to other people in storylike forms. Heider's book, *The Psychology of Interpersonal Relations* (1958), is replete with references to novels and plays as examples of naive psychology. For example, Heider used lines from the character Edmund in Shakespeare's *King Lear* to illustrate egocentric attribution: "This is the excellent foppery of the world, that, when we are sick in fortune, often the surfeit of our own behaviour, we make guilty of our disasters the sun, the moon, and the stars; as if we were villains on necessity. . . ." (Heider, 1958, p. 119).

What Schank and Abelson call a story skeleton contains multiple attributions of causality, responsibility, or both from Heider's perspective. Heider (1976) himself used a story to illustrate how quickly people blend information to form attributions. He told of a loud bang he heard one day at his backdoor and of the immediate interpretative process he engaged in to explain the noise. His interpretation involved the rudiments of a story: His wife had gone to town and had returned home with her hands full of groceries just as a gusty wind made contact with the opened backdoor. There was an immediate attribution for the noise, and the attribution essentially was a partial story.

Heider suggested that this type of interpretive storylike construction was part of our cognition of the world. He argued that we often do not engage in elaborate deduction in our attributional activities (as in Kelley's 1967 version of attribution). Rather, these activities occur almost instantaneously. He said, "Attribution is part of our cognition of the environment. Whenever you cognize your environment you will find attribution occurring" (Heider, 1976, p. 18). Consistent with Schank and Abelson's analysis, we would extend Heider's statement to read, "Whenever you cognize your environment, a story may be born or remembered, and within that story will be attributions about self, other people, and/or the environment."

In Heider's conception, people understand actions by analyzing the underlying dynamics, such as people's intentions, motivations, and skills, as well as the environmental influences on the actions. Schank and Abelson's fascinating story skeletons may be construed as naive attributional analyses that probe the underlying dynamics of actions. Story skeletons often pertain to the justifiability as well as the causality of actions, and they may develop either in social or self-perception. The illustrative skeleton Schank and Abelson present, in which a woman analyzes her husband Matthew's inability to commit himself to a relationship, could have been a story about herself, as well. She also was making attributions about her failure to "read" her husband's true tendencies, given the available evidence when she married him. Heider along with Schank and Abelson suggest that people tell stories to make their lives meaningful and to understand events in their lives. As Frankl (1959) contended, people can more readily live without food than they can live without meaning.

Abelson and colleagues (e.g., Abelson & Lalljee, 1988) previously have articulated a knowledge structure theory of explanation that may provide a more sufficient theory of attributional processes than was provided by early models. This work addresses how knowledge is used, and analyzes the processes of explanation (see also Read,1987, for a similar contribution). The idea of a knowledge structure is not too different from that of a schema as a mediator of attributional activities. *Schemata* are mentally constructed configurations of features associated with people and events that help people quickly engage in cognitive activities such as attributional analyses (Kelley, 1972; Wyer, 1981).

The present analysis by Schank and Abelson, however, is more far-reaching in its implications. Stories, knowledge structures, and schemata may be distinguished. Unlike knowledge structures and schemata, stories, however, are part of folk culture, or *folk psychology,* to use Bruner's (1990) term that invites psychology to be more sympathetic to what "real people" do and say in their daily interactions. Indeed, the idea and value of a story are its aspects of life that most people throughout the world readily understand and embrace in their behavior. The recognition of such relevance is at the heart of Schank and Abelson's treatment. Their statement effectively serves as a clarion call for a broader portrayal of attributional processes than one typically finds in the literature of the 1990s, a type of portrayal much more consistent with Heider's conception.

Stories, Narratives, and Accounts: Converging Work From Several Fields

In its endorsement of such larger units of meaning as stories, Schank and Abelson's analysis is revolutionary (or perhaps evolutionary) for the field of social cognition. Nevertheless, it may not go as far as some scholars do in contending that storylike constructions that we call accounts (Harvey, Weber, & Orbuch, 1990) represent the *principal* grounds for understanding and conveying meaning, generally, in social discourse. There would be no discourse nor meaning in social acts without the drive and ability to construct and report stories.

One of the most comprehensive statements about the potency of story-making was provided by the cognitive psychologist Frank Smith in a book entitled *To Think* (1990). He said:

> Most of the beliefs we have about the world and our place in it come in the form of stories. Most of the beliefs we have about other people, and the way we regard and treat them, are in the form of stories. Stories are the mortar that holds thought together, the grist of all our explanations, rationales, and values.

> Thought is inseparable from a literally fabulous conglomeration of personalized stories—religious, social, economic, philosophical, and psychological. . . . Armies, terrorists, and bigots are motivated by the stories they believe—and so are peacemakers, philanthropists, and martyrs. (p. 144)

In yet another far-reaching argument about the value of stories, Howard (1991) said:

A life becomes meaningful when one sees himself or herself as an actor within the context of a story—be it a cultural tale, a religious narrative, a family saga, the march of science, a political movement. . . Early in life we are free to choose what life story we will inhabit—and later we find we are lived by that story. . . . Thus, a paraphrase of one of Shakespeare's more dire warnings becomes appropriate: "Beware of the stories you tell yourself—for you will surely be lived by them." (p. 196)

The writers of these quotes are, respectively, a cognitive psychologist and a counseling psychologist. They are among the many scholars from the sciences and the humanities who are now arguing that stories, narratives, and accounts, and the processes of developing them are vital elements in the understanding of human activity and interaction. One of the boldest voices advocating a "psychology as story" is Jerome Bruner (1987). Bruner's argument is consistent with Schank and Abelson's position. Bruner believes that the cognitive revolution he was so instrumental in helping develop has been subordinated to the *zeitgeist* of cognitive sciences with its computational metaphor. Bruner claims that the cognitive sciences are wary of the concept of *human agency and purpose*. Accordingly, the view of the human as engaged in a quest for meaning is not a mainstream direction in the cognitive sciences. To Bruner, however, this quest is one of the principal causes of human action. In this vein, Bruner (1987) argues, "I cannot imagine a more important psychological research project than one which addresses itself to the 'development of autobiography'—how our way of telling about ourselves changes, and how these accounts come to take control of our ways of life" (p. 15).

Another emphasis on the story can be found in the study of personality. For example, McAdams (1993) argues that each of us is a natural storyteller and that we create a personal identity via the stories that guide our lives and what we tell to others. There is a plethora of writing about the importance of stories in helping people deal with dilemmas of living. Probably the most able spokesperson for this literature is the psychiatrist Robert Coles (1989), who for many years has stressed the value of the narrative in the lives of people, rich and poor, well educated and little educated, and the way their storytelling helps them overcome adversity. In counseling and psychotherapy, a rich literature also exists that endorses the use of stories and storytelling as intervention for a variety of human problems (see Meichenbaum & Fitzpatrick, 1992). Finally, an edited collection by Harvey, Orbuch, and Weber (1992) brings together writings by scholars in different fields whose work involves foci on attributions, stories, narratives, and accounts in the domain of close relationship phenomena.

Further Questions in the Study of Stories and Storytelling

"The Rest of the Story."   It is likely that many of the skeleton stories used as illustrations by Schank and Abelson would not be perceived as complete stories by most people. Rather, they would be perceived as fragments of the complete story.

In our work on accounts, we have argued that people often report the gists of stories or key story lines to others in the interests of economy or for self-presentational reasons. But there likely are many other details or angles that they could report and do report on occasion when pressed for details, or when motivated to do so. Actually, Schank and Abelson suggest such a position when they argue that people often vary their stories to match the nature of their audience and their goals in addressing that audience.

Harvey, Weber, and Orbuch (1990) proposed that people develop "master accounts," that contain many subaccounts. For example, a person may have a master account of his love life over many years and subaccounts for each of the people with whom love relationships occurred. It also is likely that the master account will contain threads that are perceived to coherently connect the different love stories and make the whole more meaningful.

Gender and Personality Differences. In the study of close relationships, it has been contended that women engage in more relationship storytelling and listening than do men (Kelley et al., 1983). If this is true with regard to close relationships, does a general gender difference exist between women and men in their inclinations to tell and be receptive to stories? We doubt it. Men can become just as interested in and involved with telling relationship stories as are most women. Perhaps it would be more relevant to ask when women and men may differ systematically in their story-making activities.

There may be, however, individual difference variables associated with story-telling inclinations. Baumeister and Wotman (1992) describe findings that the level of self-esteem is related to differences in people's accounts of failure experiences. In this study, individuals low in self-esteem conveyed more distress in their stories and were less likely than high self-esteem people to integrate past failures with current experience. One of us (Martin) has an ongoing study examining whether individuals high on trait hostility tell stories differently than do people low on trait hostility. Are the high hostility people, for example, more defensive and oriented toward blaming others in their presentations than low hostility people are? Martin is also investigating whether self-esteem, depression, and age are associated with people's use of social comparison information in narrative self-evaluations of their abilities in various areas.

Stories, Emotion, and Imagery. "Your glory is your story" (Franklin Greenwald, 1991, Greeting Card). A strong implication of Schank and Abelson's analysis is that stories and story-making are not vapid, sterile enterprises. People often delight in stories, as evidenced by the audience for afternoon soap dramas on television. They also are likely reinforced by the act of telling stories and by perfecting their own style of storytelling. Schank and Abelson make much of the value of stories in knowledge, understanding, and memory. But again, there is "more to the story." As a number of scholars have argued with evidence, storytelling in the form of confiding one's troubles and feelings helps people deal with major stressors and losses in their lives. Pennebaker (1990) has shown this effect of confiding quite impressively, and we have found that people coping with hurts as diverse as divorce and incest report that they felt and coped better when they had the opportunity to confide parts of their oppressive stories to caring others (see Harvey, Orbuch, Chwalisz, & Garwood, 1991).

What about imagery in stories and story-making? We would suggest that this is an area where a lot of useful work could be done. Some of Schank and Abelson's story skeletons invoke vivid images of events. Harvey, Flanary, and Morgan (1986) found that women rated their memories of the events surrounding the ending of close relationships as more vivid than men did (i.e., they had more "vivid memories of vivid loves gone by"). Essentially, the design of this study invited participants first to tell stories of the close relationship that had ended, and then to pick out five main memories and rate their vividness. Consistent with the earlier point about gender differences in close relationship story-making, women reported longer stories and more vivid memories than men did. Further, their memories were more negative in valence than were men's memories. For example, one woman recalled her ex-lover's last act of throwing rocks at her car as she left him! Whether or not this line of inquiry takes us back to the gender question, it does argue for more emphasis than is found in current research on social cognition upon the qualities of imagery in people's stories and memories. As much as any social psychological phenomenon, story-making combines elements of social behavior, cognition, emotion, and motivation.

The Hows of Studying Stories.   The theoretical emphasis given to stories and story-making activities across several disciplines in the last 15 years has been facilitated by the development of interesting methods for studying these phenomena. Some of the work has involved the development of techniques to code naturalistic material such as people's diaries, newspaper articles, or other written material. Seligman (1991) provided interesting evidence about people's optimistic style of thinking by adapting their attribution style questionnaire so that it could be used to analyze the dimensions of locus, stability, and globality of causality in naturalistic material. This line of investigation follows earlier work in the attribution domain to examine when and how people make spontaneous or unsolicited attributions about events in their environments (see Harvey, Yarkin, Lightner, & Town, 1980; Lau & Russell, 1980).

Applications of naturalistic techniques to probe story-making activities are occurring for investigations of diverse populations that cannot be readily studied in the university laboratory. For example, Tennen, Suls, and Martin are presently examining the narratives of inmates in federal prisons to analyze their attributional tendencies. A fascinating study of grief work in the nineteenth century was conducted by the social psychologist Paul Rosenblatt and reported in his book *Bitter, Bitter Tears* (1983). Rosenblatt developed conclusions about the nature of grief work in that century by examining narratives in hundreds of tattered diaries by persons who were grieving the loss of their close relationships (often from the early death of a spouse or because of partners who had gone West in hopes of making their fortunes).

So-called "qualitative" research is a primary venue for the study of naturalistic storylike material. This type of research differs from the previously discussed approaches mainly in that qualitative scholars do not attempt to code and quantify narrative information. A recent example of such a technique is Hopper's (1993) analysis of divorcing persons' stated motives for the ending of their marriages. Hopper used the theoretical lens of Burke's (1950) analysis of people's vocabulary of motives to pinpoint differences between the initiator's vocabulary of motives and the noninitiator's vocabulary. Similar analyses are now abundant in the literature of close relationships, including Weiss' (1975) and Vaughan's (1986) treatments of individuals' explanations for separation and divorce that show how such explanations are related to their coping and getting on with their lives.

Baumeister and Wotman (1992) and Baumeister, Wotman, and Stillwell (1993) presented a useful experimental approach for studying how people develop micronarratives (or short stories) to explain salient events in their lives. This systematic program of work involves making predictions about the qualities and themes of narratives that will be written by people who are recalling experimentally manipulated types of experience in their past. Baumeister, Wotman, and Stillwell (1993), for example, asked college students to recall and write about instances in which they had been the target of unrequited love by another person, or instances in which they had been the unrequited lover. Baumeister et al.'s coding approach to the narratives permitted the researchers to make inferences about the participants' quest to show themselves as morally innocent, to reduce guilt, and essentially to deal with major residual feelings and possible conclusions others might draw about their behavior in the situation. Baumeister and his colleagues have adroitly used this technique to study recall of feelings in interpersonal situations involving intense emotions such as anger.

The future of the study of story-making will likely embrace more ongoing diary–narrative work by respondents. A difficult issue for much of the published work to date is the fact that the narratives often were told or collected at some distant point in time from the occurrence of the events reported in the narrative. Thus, inaccuracy and distortion in the remembered material are apt to be part of the reported memories. As suggested by the previous chapter Schank and Abelson, autobiographical memory researchers have been inventive in trying to surmount this problem. But it is likely that no retrospective technique can establish the link between event and memory better than ongoing diary-type methods. A problem with such ongoing techniques is the feasibility of inducing people to take the time to write about events in their lives at the very earliest time after the occurrence of the events.

In our own research we have argued that whether accounts are true or fictional, they are meaningful and consequential to account-makers. A person may not be able to capture the key details showing why her or his close relationship ended. The person may also not be able to precisely and comprehensively confide parts of the account to a close other. Yet, those very acts—developing a personal account and confiding parts of it to other—have repeatedly been associated with positive outcomes compared to the result when those acts are not taken (Harvey, Orbuch, Chwalisz, & Garwood, 1991).

CONCLUDING REMARKS

By publishing Schank and Abelson's account of stories in *Advances in Social Cognition* (this volume, chap. 1), Wyer deserves appreciation from workers in the field of social cognition for this reason: The vast literature now associated with stories and related phenomena has not greatly affected or been incorporated into the work of most social cognition researchers. Schank and Abelson's monograph may give that literature greater credibility among social cognition researchers. Indeed, it may stimulate a broader focus than is found both in the standard theory and the method of social cognition research. The celebration of the value of the story is not new in human affairs. Nor is it new in psychology, other social and behavioral sciences, or the humanities. Yet, as with the 1958 presentation by Heider of his analysis of commensense psychology, it sometimes takes a unified, well-illustrated argument to begin to make certain cases more cogent for a field such as social cognition. This field already is vibrant, but a serious consideration of Schank and Abelson's analysis could help it shine even more brightly in the future.

REFERENCES

Abelson, R. P., & Lalljee, M. (1988). Knowledge structures and causal explanation. In D. Hilton (Ed.), *Contemporary science and natural explanation: Commonsense conceptions of causality* (pp. 175–203). London: Harvester Press.

Baumeister, R. F., & Wotman, S. R. (1992). *Breaking hearts: The two sides of unrequited love.* New York: Guilford Press.

Baumeister, R. F., Wotman, S. R., & Stillwell, A. M. (1993). Unrequited love. *Journal of Personality and Social Psychology, 64,* 377–394.

Bruner, J. (1987). Life as narrative. *Social Research, 54,* 11–32.

Bruner, J. (1990). *Acts of meaning.* Cambridge, MA.: Harvard University Press.

Burke, K. (1950). *A rhetoric of motives.* Englewood Cliffs, NJ: Prentice-Hall.

Coles, R. (1989). *The call of stories.* Boston: Houghton Mifflin.

Frankl, V. (1959). *Man's search for meaning.* New York: Washington Square Press.

Harvey, J. H., Flanary, R., & Morgan, M. (1986). Vivid memories of vivid loves gone by. *Journal of Social and Personal Relationships, 3,* 359–373.

Harvey, J. H., Orbuch, T. L., Chwalisz, K. D., & Garwood, G. (1991). Coping with sexual assault: The roles of account-making and confiding. *Journal of Traumatic Stress, 4,* 515–531.

Harvey, J. H., Orbuch, T. L., & Weber, A. L. (Eds). (1992). *Attributions, accounts, and close relationships.* New York: Springer-Verlag.

Harvey, J. H., Weber, A. L., & Orbuch, T. L. (1990). *Interpersonal accounts: A social psychological perspective.* Oxford: Blackwell.

Harvey, J. H., Yarkin, K. L., Lightner, J. M., & Town, J. P. (1980). Unsolicited interpretation and recall of interpersonal events. *Journal of Personality and Social Psychology, 38,* 551–568.

Heider, F. (1976). A conversation with Fritz Heider. In J. H. Harvey, W. J. Ickes, & R. F. Kidd (Eds.), *New directions in attribution research* (pp. 1–18). Hillsdale, NJ: Lawrence Erlbaum Associates.

Heider, F. (1958). *The psychology of interpersonal relations.* New York: Wiley (reprinted by Lawrence Erlbaum Associates).

Hopper, J. (1993). The rhetoric of motives. *Journal of Marriage and the Family, 55,* 801–813.

Howard, G. S. (1991). Cultural tales: A narrative approach to thinking, cross-cultural psychology and psychotherapy. *American Psychologist, 46,* 187–197.

Kelley, H. H. (1967). Attribution theory in social psychology. In D. Levine (Ed.), *Nebraska Symposium on Motivation, Vol. 15.* Lincoln: University of Nebraska Press.

Kelley, H. H. (1972). *Causal schemata and the attribution process.* Morristown, NJ: General Learning Press.

Kelley, H. H., Berscheid, E., Christensen, A., Harvey, J., Huston, T., Levinger, G., McClintock, E., Peplau, A., & Peterson, D. (1983). *Close relationships.* San Francisco: Freeman.

Lau, R. R., & Russell, D. (1980). Attribution in the sports pages. *Journal of Personality and Social Psychology, 39,* 29–38.

McAdams, D. P. (1993). *Stories we live by.* New York: Morrow.

Michenbaum, D., & Fitzpatrick, D. (1992). A constructivist narrative perspective on stress and coping. In L. Goldberger and S. Breznitz (Eds.), *Handbook of stress.* New York: Free Press.

Pennebaker, J. W. (1990). *Opening up.* New York: Morrow.

Read, S. J. (1987). Constructing causal scenarios. *Journal of Personality and Social Psychology, 52,* 288–302.

Rosenblatt, P. (1983). *Bitter, bitter tears.* Minneapolis: University of Minnesota Press.

Schank, R. C. (1991). *Tell me a story.* New York: Scribners.

Schank, R. C., & Abelson, R. P. (1977). *Scripts, plans, goals, and understanding.* Hillsdale, NJ: Lawrence Erlbaum Associates.

Seligman, M. E. P. (1991). *Learned optimism.* New York: Knopf.

Smith, F. (1990). *To think.* New York: Teachers College, Columbia University Press.

Vaughan, D. (1986). *Uncoupling.* New York: Oxford University Press.

Weiss, R. S. (1975). *Marital Separation.* New York: Basic Books.

Wyer, R. S. (1981). An information-processing perspective on social attribution. In J. H. Harvey, W. Ickes, & R. F. Kidd (Eds.), *New directions in attribution research,* Vol. 3. Hillsdale, NJ: Lawrence Erlbaum Associates.

3

The Primacy of Stories, the Primacy of Roles, and the Polarizing Effects of Interpretive Motives: Some Propositions About Narratives

Roy F. Baumeister
Case Western Reserve University

Leonard S. Newman
University of Illinois at Chicago

In their treatise on knowledge and memory in this volume, Schank and Abelson have provided a powerful statement about the importance of narrative forms (i.e., stories) in human cognition. Our commentary is intended to build upon and extend some of their lines of thought. We focus on three issues. First, we extend Schank and Abelson's insistence on the primacy of stories to propose that *propositional knowledge,* while not as irrelevant or trivial as they suggest, is commonly derived from stories, although (because such derivation is commonly anticipated) story making may often be influenced by the wish to promote certain propositional conclusions or inferences. Second, we suggest that stories and scripts are often linked to particular situational roles, so they describe a certain *perspective* on an event rather than the event itself. Third, we propose that when people construct stories to make sense of their experiences, their needs for meaning operate to *polarize* the construction of stories, thereby distorting events toward an extreme position that either confirms or radically disconfirms the motivating point.

RELATION BETWEEN NARRATIVE AND PROPOSITIONAL KNOWLEDGE

Schank and Abelson have taken a radical position regarding narratives: In their view, everything important and interesting in human thought and memory occurs in the form of stories. Meanwhile, propositional knowledge is reduced to a rare and trivial exercise ("just rote memorization that we did in school"). Whether Schank and Abelson truly believe that, or whether they are simply providing a needed corrective to the imbalance in previous work that overemphasized propositional knowledge and ignored narratives, is a question that we have no means to answer. Undoubtedly some critics will reproach Schank and Abelson for seemingly overstating the case and downplaying the importance of the propositional forms of thought to which so many researchers have devoted their careers.

Our goal is to discuss the possible relationship between narrative (i.e., story) and propositional knowledge. We assume, therefore, that propositional knowledge is a legitimate and commonly used form of knowledge, contrary to some of the comments made by Schank and Abelson, yet consistent with some of their other suggestions. We think it is clear that people often make attributions, draw conclusions, formulate general principles or broad lessons, and the like. Indeed, evidence that people spontaneously make trait inferences (e.g., Newman, 1991; Newman & Uleman, 1990; Uleman, 1987) suggests two things: First, people normally do some thinking in general, propositional terms, and second, people find it useful and desirable to do so.

There really do appear to be two forms of knowledge. Despite some borderline cases and overlap, the distinction between a story and an abstract generalization or principle is something that most people can make effectively most of the time. Moreover, we think the existence of the two types of knowledge is very likely based on the fact that both serve valuable functions. Schank and Abelson *may* be correct in suggesting that story-making is more common and pervasive than propositional knowledge, but probably each has an important sphere. If one accepts that both forms of knowledge exist, and that stories predominate in people's everyday thinking, then two questions need to be addressed: First, how are the two related (at least in the sense of what separate functional spheres they inhabit), and second, why do people seem to prefer narratives?

Our conclusion, as we have suggested in a recent review of research using autobiographical narratives (Baumeister & Newman, 1994), is that narrative construction may be the common and nearly universal form in which people interpret their experiences, whereas propositional knowledge may be a less common but still very important *derivative* of narratives. In other words, people will nearly always make sense of their experiences by constructing them in story form, and sometimes (but not always) they will proceed from these stories to infer or deduce generalizations.

This view may seem at odds with Schank and Abelson's position, and indeed if everything interesting and important occurs in stories, then there would almost never be any need to resort to propositional knowledge. On the other hand, Schank and Abelson say elsewhere that "Deriving static factual knowledge from stories we have in memory is of course quite possible to do." They say that people sometimes are asked factual or other general (propositional) questions, and people respond by retrieving a relevant story from memory and deriving the required generalization. Thus, some of Schank and Abelson's comments are quite consistent with our present argument that propositional knowledge is typically derived from narratives.

Why would this be the sequence? There are compelling reasons to start off in the narrative mode of thought. In our view, stories are easier and less risky than propositional generalizations, because they conform directly to actual experience. It is usually rather easy to tell what happened; it is much more difficult to say what that means, in terms of articulating the causal or moral principles involved, or making other generalizations from a particular event. The preference for stories, as eloquently argued by Schank and Abelson, and attested by the prevalence of narratives in ordinary thinking and talking, may be due in part to this simplicity.

The ease of making a story is partly because there is an element of story narrative inherent in the events themselves as they happen. Stories are not just constructed after the fact as an aid to memory or explanation. Participants in events are aware of plans, goals, conflicts, links between actions, resolutions, and other narrative elements during (and sometimes even before) the episode. Thus, for example, the participants and spectators in a playoff game have some understanding of the story line before the game; the actions and developments in the game are connected by sequential meanings that are understood and often anticipated by those present; the outcome is understood immediately, and so forth. Propositional implications, such as reflecting on the character of the losing team or the particular advantages of various strategies, may be difficult to conclude with finality (indeed, in professional sports a playoff often consists of multiple games between the same antagonists, often with different outcomes), but the story of the game is relatively easy to narrate.

The ease of making stories is related to the second reason for preferring them, which is that they are often less risky than a propositional generalization. When narrating what happened, one can be relatively sure that one is correct. It is true, of course, that people make mistakes, but they still feel confident that what they are narrating is close to what actually happened. In contrast, it is difficult to evaluate a broad generalization, which would involve imagining all sorts of possible tests and conditions, evaluating counterfactual circumstances, and the like. Thus, one can be reasonably sure that Harry left the window open, but it takes considerably more information and thought to be equally sure that Harry is a careless person. Social scientists are quite familiar with this problem from their own research: It is easy to narrate what happened in one's experiment, but drawing the general (propositional) conclusions is risky and difficult, and there is often an anonymous reviewer who, while not disputing the "story" of what happened in the experiment, will disagree fundamentally with the abstract conclusion.

Social scientists are not the only ones who have discovered the relative safety of storytelling. Many speakers, including politicians and religious figures, rely on stories rather than making definite propositional statements that could be disproven. For example, the evangelist speaker, Billy Graham, is often confronted with difficult propositional questions, such as "Why does God allow innocent young children to suffer and die?" To furnish a propositional answer to such a question would clearly entail multiple risks of disconfirmation, heresy, and presumption; yet to say only that he cannot give an answer might reduce his hearers' confidence in him. In his speeches and in books such as *Facing Death* (Graham, 1987), he handles such questions deftly by telling stories. By describing a particular child's death that led to some spiritually positive outcome, for example, he can seem to answer the question without making a risky commitment to a general principle.

What we are saying is that narratives are typically full of propositional implications, some of which are valid, whereas others may not be. Everyone knows, for example, that Vincent Van Gogh once cut off part of his ear, but the reason for his action is not well known. In a well-known article, Runyan (1981) proposed 17 different possible explanations for Van Gogh's action. Clearly, not all 17 are correct, but each was possible given the action itself. Moreover, people interested in knowing what kind of person Van Gogh was may find it important to decide which interpretation of that story is correct. A central point of the phenomenological analysis of literature and art is that a given story is always capable of supporting multiple possible interpretations (i.e., propositional conclusions) (e.g., Heidegger, 1968).

For this reason, stories may often be constructed in such a way that the propositional implications are manipulated. In other words, the propositions may shape the story, at least in the retelling. We propose that factual or other propositional knowledge is derived from stories. and people seem to know this, at least to the extent that they will construct the story in a way that points toward the desired conclusion. An allegory is not simply a randomly occurring event that happens to lead some people to draw a particular conclusion; rather, allegories are selected, edited, and probably often even entirely invented for the sake of the propositional "moral" that is to be derived from them.

Stories told in courts of law may often reflect the manipulation of stories to anticipate the derivation of propositional conclusions. Courts are often faced with the necessity of making propositional conclusions, particularly as to whether some person is guilty of having violated some legal standard. Everyone present knows this, so the concern with the propositional conclusion is there before all the evidence has been presented. People will narrate what happened in ways that (they hope) will guide the jury toward deriving a particular conclusion. Pennington and Hastie (1988, 1992) have studied this process, and their findings indicate that juries often process information by first constructing a story about what happened, and then deriving the propositional conclusions about guilt or innocence.

Thus, propositional knowledge is typically derived from stories. Stories may be the primary form in which experience is interpreted and preserved. Probably Schank and Abelson are correct in suggesting that people nearly always interpret their experiences by making stories, and that drawing propositional conclusions is less common, probably because it is more difficult and uncertain. On the other hand, it is clear that propositional knowledge is often deeply interwoven into the story, and, indeed, many stories may be constructed with a view toward guiding the hearer to derive the desired (propositional) conclusion.

SCRIPTS, STORIES—AND ROLE PERSPECTIVES

Schank and Abelson have repeatedly pointed out that different people can interpret the same event in different ways. In their view, this follows from the nature of understanding, a process of finding a story in one's own memory that corresponds to the story being told. Because people have different experiences, it would be inevitable that story-based understanding will differ from one person to another. Indeed, if one takes Schank and Abelson's position to an extreme, it becomes difficult to see how two people could ever arrive at the same understanding of an event. The main chance for agreement would involve the use of scripts; if people have similar scripts, their stories then may resemble each other enough for them to interpret similar things similarly.

One of us has been sufficiently fascinated by they way people interpret similar events differently that he has studied it for several years (e.g, Baumeister, Stillwell, & Heatherton, in press; Baumeister, Stillwell, & Wotman, 1990; Baumeister & Wotman, 1992; Baumeister, Wotman, & Stillwell, 1993). This line of work has indicated an important set of reasons for such differences in the stories people tell about similar events, and it has important implications for script theory as well as for narratives.

Essentially, this work has found that stories differ in systematic and predictable ways as a function of the role the person had in an experience. Interpretation is biased by the role the person had. Thus, victims tell stories that differ systematically from the stories told by perpetrators (Baumeister et al., 1990), even when both are describing similar events. Unrequited lovers describe a failed romance in ways that differ systematically from the accounts offered by the individuals who reject them (Baumeister & Wotman, 1992; Baumeister, Wotman, & Stillwell, 1993). People who induce guilt in others tell stories that differ reliably from the accounts people tell about how others make them feel guilty (Baumeister, Stillwell, & Heatherton, in press).[1]

These findings point to the situational role as a vitally important determinant of how people construct interpretations. The reasons for this will be discussed in a moment, but first it is necessary to point out one implication that script theory should emphasize the roles rather than just the events. Many existing social psychology textbooks define a *script* as an *event schema,* that is, a set of information about what constitutes a typical version of that event. Often, however, it is necessary to differentiate scripts by roles. People may not have one standard script for transgressions that lead to anger. Instead, they have at least two versions, one from the transgressor's point of view, and the other from the victim's point of view.

To illustrate the existence of two scripts, one may cite movies, which, after all constitute a major forum in which stories are told and received. Many movies are concerned with violent acts, and audiences seem very sophisticated in knowing more or less what to expect, but usually they need to know whether to regard the violence from the victim's or the perpetrator's point of view so they can anticipate what will happen and respond appropriately. Clover (1992) has pointed out in her

---

[1]In an earlier example, sexual masochists describe episodes of sadomasochistic sex in ways that differ reliably from the accounts of their dominant partners (see Baumeister, 1988a, 1988b).

book, *Men, Women, and Chainsaws,* that audiences of "slasher" or other horror films seem quite able to anticipate what is going to happen, even when seeing the film for the first time, and they often become vocally involved in the action. These audiences often cheer the acts of wanton violence early in the film when innocent victims are slain; late in the film, however, audiences seem to know to shift their allegiance to the final victim, who typically turns into an aggressor and defeats or kills the perpetrator of the earlier violence.

A recent doctoral dissertation by Stillwell (1993) showed the role-based duality of event scripts using experimental methods. All subjects were given identical information about an episode in which one person promised to help another with his or her studies, and then reneged on the promise. Half the subjects were told to identify with the promiser and then to retell the story from that person's perspective; the others were told to identify with the victim and then retell the story from that perspective. Although all subjects had been given exactly the same information, their stories differed systematically on many dimensions. For example, the promisers played up the extenuating circumstances and the inappropriateness of the request, while minimizing the aversive consequences of reneging. The victims emphasized the aversive consequences, left out the extenuating circumstances, and so forth. Thus, even though the subjects began with the same information, their stories differed as a function of their situational (and in this case hypothetical) role. If the subjects had applied only one script for such a transgression, the stories would have all been more or less the same. If each subject had applied a different script (based on unique past experiences), all the stories would have been different, and the data would have reflected nothing but error variance. Nevertheless, Stillwell found that the two roles of promiser and victim yielded systematically different stories, suggesting that people in general have a distinct script for each of the two roles.

The notion that the script goes with the role must also be emphasized in response to a solipsistic conclusion that certain readers might draw from Schank and Abelson's argument, namely the view that differences in interpretation derive simply from the fact that every person has had different past experiences and, therefore, will inevitably interpret a new event in a corresponding unique way. Undoubtedly, individual variation in past experiences will add some variation to the way people interpret each new event, but this should not be overstated. People do agree, by and large, in the way they understand things. Most people will understand a movie or a news report in roughly the same way; the individual variations are often relatively minor.[2]

---

[2]Sometimes there are broad differences in the way people interpret a controversial news story, but these differences often seem to reflect identification with the role rather than a thoroughgoing uniqueness of past experience. In the past few years, public opinion has been divided in response to several such news stories about racial violence, marital violence, and parent–child murder, and we suspect that much difference of opinion seems to be linked to the fact that people find it easier to identify with one or the other role—husbands identifying with the husband in the story, wives with the wife, and so forth. Vallone, Ross, and Lepper's (1985) demonstration of the "hostile media phenomenon," that is, the tendency for people to see news reports as biased against their preferred point of view, presupposes just such a perspectivally based understanding.

There are fewer roles, however, than unique sets of memories, and the common aspects of situational roles may be decisive in enabling people to understand the same story in the same way. In several of our studies, we elicited one story for each role from each subject. Thus, in the Baumeister et al. (1990) study on the interpersonal genesis of anger, every subject was asked for two stories: one victim story and one perpetrator story. The results of that study do not signify that victims and perpetrators are different kinds of people, but rather that the same people interpret similar events differently depending on what role they hold.

One key reason for the differences found in such studies is that motivations are tied to roles. Perpetrators, for example, may be motivated to downplay the consequences of their actions and to emphasize extenuating circumstances to avoid being perceived as wicked or malicious persons (or as people who should be punished). In contrast, victims may be motivated to maximize the harmful consequences, to have a legitimate claim on sympathy and possibly restitution, and they may be motivated to depict the transgressor's actions as especially heinous, so that others will not perceive the victims as being responsible for their own suffering.

Such motivations exemplify what we suggested earlier in this paper: Stories are sometimes constructed to convey a certain propositional message. One possible propositional conclusion from a story about how Cindy offended James is that Cindy is cruel or obnoxious. Although James' story may be set up to favor that conclusion, Cindy's story is likely to discourage the hearer from drawing it. Thus, systematic patterns of story construction often reflect the covert operation of propositional knowledge. James and Cindy know that the listener is likely to derive some propositional inference from the story, so the story construction process is shaped by the motivation to foster (or prevent) one or another inference.

Although our work has emphasized the roles within the story, another set of roles is relevant, namely the roles of storyteller and audience. Gergen and Gergen (1988) proposed that each time a story is told it is a new performance and may be adapted to the immediate situation. Higgins and Rholes (1978) showed that people will modify their narration of an event, depending on whether the listener supposedly likes or dislikes the protagonist in the story, and indeed they found that the storytellers' own memories for the event ended up being altered by the way they had altered the story to accommodate the audience.

More recently, Baumeister and Ilko (1995) had people describe the single biggest success experience they had enjoyed in the previous two years. In the *public condition,* subjects expected to read their stories aloud to the group of other subjects, whereas in the *private condition* people expected to drop their stories off anonymously when they left, with no public reading. The "publicness" manipulation led to several systematic differences in story content, particularly concerning the inclusion of references to help and support received from other people. The public stories gratefully acknowledged how others had helped, but the private stories were largely devoid of such references. Baumeister and Ilko interpreted this "shallow gratitude" effect to mean that people's private recollections of their successes reserve all the credit to themselves and downplay any contributions by others, but when speaking in front of an audience, people alter the story, making it conform to norms of modesty and sharing the credit.

Are there exceptions to our argument that stories and scripts are tied to specific roles? Undoubtedly there are some stories that have this "third person" perspective. We would, in fact, suggest that such stories may contain at least part of the answer to the vexing problem Schank and Abelson raised about how expert knowledge differs from ordinary knowledge. Most researchers consider expertise to be a matter of general, propositional knowledge, so Schank and Abelson's emphasis on stories seems to undercut the very nature of expertise, because in their view an expert understands the same way anybody else does, namely by finding a story in memory that corresponds to the story being told. We suggest that experts' stories may differ from other people's stories in that they are more likely to be told from a detached, third-person perspective. The detachment of the expert (such as a psychotherapist or judge) is often recognized as a powerful aid toward a more correct, "objective" understanding. This detachment may go beyond detachment from the immediate situation to detachment from a large number of the stories that the expert can draw from memory. Experts, in other words, draw upon stories that are not biased by their own direct participation.

MOTIVATED POLARIZATION

Our final concern is to examine the way motivations affect the formation of stories. In this we are assuming that events have a certain objective reality, and that the stories people tell about these events later will depart in various predictable ways from that reality. The study by Stillwell (1993) described in the preceding discussion found more evidence of selective omission than of outright fabrication, but there is little doubt that the final stories departed from the original, objective, factual basis in both informational content and overall implications. The same process is presumed to underlie the many findings in which different roles lead to systematically different stories (e.g., Baumeister et al., 1990, 1993). Two discrepant accounts of essentially the same event cannot both be correct.

One might propose, simply, that motivations will tend to assimilate story content, so that the story tends to satisfy the motivation. In our view, however, the reality is more complex than this. We propose that such motivations will have polarizing effects on story construction.

In a recent paper, we sought to elucidate the motives that guide people's efforts to make sense of their experiences by constructing stories (Baumeister & Newman, 1994). We adapted the scheme of four basic *needs for meaning* (from Baumeister, 1991) to the construction of stories, and showed how much of the literature about accounts and narratives conforms to this pattern of four needs. Many stories are concerned with purposive activity, specifically either the achievement of goals or the enjoyment of fulfillment states. Others are concerned with justifying one's actions (morally) or exemplifying values in other ways. Still other stories revolve around efficacy, as in producing a sense of control, of making a difference in the world, or of exercising power. Finally, other stories are geared toward supporting one's sense of self-worth. (These describe the individual's own needs for meaning; there are also interpersonal motives for making stories, to which we shall return shortly.)

These motives operate on the construction of stories. It will surprise no one if we propose that many stories exaggerate the degree to which the teller's actions were morally justified or that stories seem designed to boost the teller's sense of self-worth. However, it is also clear that not all stories are distorted in that direction. Some stories portray the teller in a bad light that seems likely to detract from self-worth ("I just did an incredibly stupid thing. . . ."). Others, indeed, seem to emphasize a lack of moral justification of one's own—or, especially, of another person's—acts. Still others convey a sense of helplessness (inefficacy), of frustration (nonfulfillment), or, in truth, describe the signal failure to reach one's goals.

The needs for meaning, therefore, should best be understood as central dimensions along which events are interpreted. Moreover, given their motivational force, they do more than simply register what happened: They encourage the person to exaggerate *in either direction* the impact of events.

For example, the average person may (by definition) be a mediocre lover, a so-so parent, and a midrange performer on the job. The stories such a person tells are, however, unlikely to conform to that impression of averageness. Instead, the stories are likely to gravitate toward either extreme. The average person's stories are likely to give impressions of the triumphs or frustrations of one's love life; of the stellar attainments or aggravating, helpless failures of one's offspring; and of the brilliant achievements or humbling misfortunes of one's occupational performance.

A good place to look for evidence of such polarization is in the movies, because these are indeed the stories that are most widely consumed in modern Western society. The polarizing effect of people's needs for meaning on the making of movies is readily apparent. Movies rarely depict indifferent mediocrity or tepid neutrality. Instead, the movies about love depict either ecstatic, happily-ever-after bliss (conforming to the "myth of fulfillment," Baumeister, 1991), or the escalating agony of romantic failure. Movies about work depict either astounding successes or catastrophic failures. The characters and their actions are morally polarized, and many films include both acts of heroic virtue and extremes of depravity and evil.

We noted that there are also interpersonal motives for making stories. That is, people sometimes construct narratives to produce a particular effect on the intended audience. These motives do not seem to operate in a polarizing way. People will rarely tell a story in a way that emphasizes or exaggerates how unfunny it is, or how little there is to be learned from the experience, or how undeserving of sympathy they are. The (intrapsychic) desire for positive self-worth can, paradoxically, induce the person to construct a narrative that emphasizes how a particular experience was humiliating, but the desire to entertain an audience does not seem to induce people to construct stories that are especially dull and boring. Thus, interpersonal motives seem to have unidirectional effects on story construction, whereas intrapsychic or interpretive motives seem to have bidirectional, polarizing effects.

By way of speculation, we can offer some suggestions to explain why the needs for meaning may have such polarizing effects on story construction. The pervasiveness of the four basic needs suggests that they form the core of what makes an experience meaningful to the individual. Thus, a story that had nothing to do with goals or fulfillment, that invoked no values or moral issues, that contributed little to any understanding of efficacy or helplessness, and that was bereft of implications for self-worth would be received by most people as not being very meaningful. Accordingly, these four basic needs are the dimensions people consult when they are interpreting an experience, when they are making sense of a life (Baumeister, 1991), perhaps by constructing a story.

That much explains why these four dimensions constitute the focus of story making. Still, why is there polarization? It may be that stories focusing on the center of the spectrum are perceived as inconclusive. There is a sense in which an action understood as being very good or very evil has been resolved. In contrast, if the action is seen as being in the indeterminate moral gray area, it remains unresolved. A slightly satisfying sexual experience makes a poor story, compared to an intensely fulfilling one or a disastrously frustrating one. Mixed feedback about one's personal worth makes a poor story, as opposed to gloriously self-enhancing feedback or crushingly humiliating feedback, and so forth.

Thus, although professional social scientists have learned to regard most phenomena as distributed along a continuum, the understanding patterns of ordinary people may tend to gravitate toward binary opposites. The preference for binary categories calls attention to the endpoints of the continuum, and stories are made to convey a conclusion that fits one or the other extreme.

CONCLUSION

We have tried to articulate several main points to extend several of the seminal suggestions contained in Schank and Abelson's explication of the centrality of narrative (story) forms in knowledge and memory.

First, we proposed that the relationship between narrative and propositional knowledge is such that people routinely make stories as a way of understanding their experiences, and that they sometimes derive general, propositional conclusions from them. Abstract generalizations, attributions and inferences, moral judgments, and other propositional conclusions are not rare or trivial, but they are typically a derivative form of knowledge. Stories are more commonly used because they are easier to make and more likely to seem correct than are propositional inferences. On the other hand, people know that such inferences or other conclusions are often drawn from stories, and they may often construct their stories to point toward certain, preferred conclusions. In such cases, the propositional statement is hardly secondary or trivial—it is the *point* of the story.

Second, a full understanding of scripts and stories must emphasize situational roles, which determine the perspective (and the attendant motivations) that shapes a story. We cited evidence that the same people tell different stories about similar events as a function of which situational role they adopt. Both similarities and differences in the way different people understand the same event may be traced to these role-based perspectives.

Third, when people use stories to make sense of experiences, their stories seem guided by a small set of four needs for meaning: purpose, efficacy, value or justification, and self-worth. These operate to polarize the content of the story, thereby making it extreme as either a confirmation or a disconfirmation of the meaning the person sought. A sample of stories may, therefore, tend to contain greater extremes (e.g., complete successes and utter failures) than a sample of actual experiences. This too may reflect the influence of anticipated propositional implications: Stories that describe mixed, balanced, or intermediate points may seem inconclusive, while "good" stories make a strong point at one or the other extreme.

REFERENCES

Baumeister, R. F. (1988a). Masochism as escape from self. *Journal of Sex Research, 25,* 28–59.

Baumeister, R. F. (1988b). Gender differences in masochistic scripts. *Journal of Sex Research, 25,* 28–59.

Baumeister, R. F. (1989). *Masochism and the self.* Hillsdale, NJ: Lawrence Erlbaum Associates.

Baumeister, R. F. (1991). *Meanings of life.* New York: Guilford Press.

Baumeister, R. F., & Ilko, S. A. (1995). Shallow gratitude: Public and private acknowledgement of external help in accounts of success. *Basic and Applied Social Psychology, 16,* 191–209.

Baumeister, R. F., & Newman, L. S. (1994). How stories make sense of personal experiences: Motives that shape autobiographical narratives. *Personality and Social Psychology Bulletin, 20,* 676–690.

Baumeister, R. F., Stillwell, A. M., & Heatherton, T. F. (1995). Personal narratives about guilt: Role in action control and interpersonal relationships. *Basic and Applied Social Psychology, 16,* 191–209.

Baumeister, R. F., Stillwell, A., & Wotman, S. R. (1990). Victim and perpetrator accounts of interpersonal conflict: Autobiographical narratives about anger. *Journal of Personality and Social Psychology, 59,* 994–1005.

Baumeister, R. F., & Wotman, S. R. (1992). *Breaking hearts: The two sides of unrequited love.* New York: Guilford Press.

Baumeister, R. F., Wotman, S. R., & Stillwell, A. M. (1993). Unrequited love: On heartbreak, anger, guilt, scriptlessness, and humiliation. *Journal of Personality and Social Psychology, 64,* 377–394.

Clover, C. J. (1992). *Men, women, and chainsaws: Gender in the modern horror film.* Princeton, NJ: Princeton University Press.

Gergen, K. J., & Gergen, M. (1988). Narrative and the self as relationship. In L. Berkowitz (Ed.), *Advances in experimental social psychology,* Vol. 21, (pp. 17–56). San Diego, CA: Academic Press.

Graham, B. (1987). *Facing death and the life after.* Waco, TX: Word Books.

Heidegger, M. (1968). *What is called thinking?* (J. G. Gray, Trans.). New York: Harper & Row. (Original work published 1954)

Higgins, E. T., & Rholes, W. S. (1978). "Saying is believing": Effects of message modification on memory and liking for the person described. *Journal of Experimental Social Psychology, 14,* 363–378.

Newman, L. S. (1991). Why are traits inferred spontaneously? A developmental approach. *Social Cognition, 9,* 221–253.

Newman, L. S., & Uleman, J. S. (1990). Assimilation and contrast effects in spontaneous trait inference. *Personality and Social Psychology Bulletin, 16,* 224–240.

Pennington, N. & Hastie, R. (1988). Explanation-based decision making: Effects of memory structure on judgment. *Journal of Experimental Psychology: Learning, Memory and Cognition. 14,* 521–533.

Pennington, N., & Hastie, R. (1992). Explaining the evidence: Tests of the story model for juror decision making. *Journal of Personality and Social Psychology, 62,* 189–206.

Runyan, W. M. (1981). Why did Van Gogh cut off his ear? The problem of alternative explanations in psychobiography. *Journal of Personality and Social Psychology, 40,* 1070–1077.

Stillwell, A. M. (1993). *Victim and perpetrator accounts in a simulated transgression.* Unpublished doctoral dissertation, Case Western Reserve University, Cleveland, Ohio.

Uleman, J. S. (1987). Consciousness and control: The case of spontaneous trait inferences. *Personality and Social Psychology Bulletin, 13,* 337–354.

Vallone, R. P., Ross, L., & Lepper, M. R. (1985). The Hostile Media Phenomenon: Biased perception and perceptions of media bias in coverage of the Beirut massacre. *Journal of Personality and Social Psychology, 49,* 577–585.

4

To Assert That Essentially All Human Knowledge and Memory Is Represented in Terms of Stories Is Certainly Wrong

William F. Brewer
University of Illinois at Urbana–Champaign

Schank and Abelson argue that stories are "the fundamental constituents of human memory, knowledge, and social communication" (p. 1). They provide many observations about memory and learning that are apparently derived from their theory. My commentary on their framework makes two basic points:

1. Under any theoretically interesting construal of the construct *story,* their claim about the nature of knowledge representation is not correct.
2. Many of the apparently original observations (few references are given to earlier work) have been described and analyzed by other researchers with very different theoretical perspectives. The relationship between theory and data in the paper is so loose that Schank and Abelson's observations provide little specific support for their particular framework.

WHAT IS A STORY?

It is difficult to know how to interpret Schank and Abelson's claim that stories are the building blocks of the mind because no analytic account of the nature of stories is given in the paper. However, in keeping with the authors' beliefs about the role of instances in human knowledge and reasoning, they give many examples of stories, so perhaps it is possible to reconstruct what they had in mind. Therefore, this discussion works through a number of possible interpretations of the core construct—*story*. I start with broader interpretations and work down to more narrow ones. Note that the more narrow the view of stories one adopts, the more extreme become the central claims of their theory.

Knowledge

If we take "stories" to mean "knowledge," then many apparently paradoxical statements in Schank and Abelson's framework are resolved. For example, they say, "Virtually all human knowledge is based on [knowledge] constructed around past experiences" or "New experiences are interpreted in terms of old [knowledge]" (p. 1). However, it seems clear that this is not what is intended, for if "story" means "knowledge," then there is little new content in the proposals in their framework, since the open-ended construct *knowledge* imposes few constraints on theories of the mind. This interpretation of what is intended would simply turn out to be a proposal for a change in vocabulary.

Narrative

If the technical term "stories" as used by Schank and Abelson is not to cover all of human knowledge, then it must be intended to refer to some subset of knowledge. In attempting to give a psychological account of genre types, I once argued (Brewer, 1980) that *descriptive* discourse encodes visual–spatial information; *narrative* discourse encodes event–sequence information (usually human intentional actions); and *expository* discourse encodes abstract–logical information. Given this division of the world of human knowledge, perhaps "story" is intended to mean "narrative." This reading is consistent with the general attempt to argue that most human knowledge is better represented as narrative discourse, and with the implicit argument that only forms of knowledge involved in social conversations are to be taken seriously (e.g., p. 15). This interpretation of the term "story" provides a reading of the proposed framework that makes some strong claims. In fact, the claims are strong enough to be certainly wrong.

Narrative Memory

However, before discussing the fundamental problem with Schank and Abelson's approach, there is an issue about memory for narrative that needs clarification. If one accepts the proposal (Brewer, 1980) that narratives are the text–discourse genre that embodies event sequence information, then one has to distinguish between memory for the underlying events sequence and memory for the particular discourse organization of the underlying events (cf. Ohtsuka & Brewer, 1992). Schank and Abelson are not clear on this issue. In some places they seem to suggest that stories are defined in terms of the characteristics of the underlying events. Thus, they state that story structure includes "initiating events, goals, actions, and consequences" (p. 31). However, in other places they state that there are "certain standard storytelling devices" (p. 34), which sounds as if story structure might be determined by certain cultural linguistic conventions.

However, we do not need to resolve this ambiguity to develop a counterargument since the counterargument applies to both aspects of narrative memory. Asserting that all knowledge is in narrative form runs up against the obvious fact that humans represent and store many kinds of non-narrative information. For example, people represent and store spatial information such as the shapes of the states (Shepard & Chipman, 1970), information about natural reasoning (Johnson-Laird, 1983), and causal–physical information about the physical world (McCloskey, Carmazza, & Green, 1980). None of these forms of information are plausibly represented as narratives.

Story

It appears however, that the construct *story,* as used by Schank and Abelson, is actually intended to be more specific than the construct *narrative.* For example, in the discussion of memory for events (p. 36), Schank and Abelson state that memory for a sequence of events (e.g., going to the grocery store) is not a story, and that if it is to be remembered, it must be reworked into some form of story representation. In addition, a number of early projects out of the Schank and Abelson research group at Yale argued for a distinction between narratives and stories (e.g., Meehan, 1976; Wilensky, 1978). Thus, it appears that the construct *story* is not intended to refer to the general class of narratives, but to a special subset of narratives.

Entertainment Stories

A number of researchers interested in text have made the point that stories constitute a subclass of narratives (de Beaugrande & Colby, 1979; Brewer, 1982; Kintsch, 1980). All of these researchers want to argue, as do Schank and Abelson, that a narrative description of someone going grocery shopping is not a story. Each of these authors (unlike Schank and Ableson) attempts to give a characterization of what constitutes a story, although there is only modest agreement on this issue. Ed Lichtenstein and I have argued that stories are the subclass of narratives that have entertainment as their primary discourse force (e.g., Brewer & Lichtenstein, 1982). We have developed a structural–affect theory of stories, which proposes that stories use affective states such a surprise, curiosity, and suspense to carry out the entertainment function, and we have provided data to support that position (e.g., Brewer & Lichtenstein, 1981). This characterization of stories is consistent with one important line of reasoning in the Schank and Abelson framework. In a number of places (e.g., pp. 15–16), Schank and Abelson attack formal approaches to language and discourse by arguing that these approaches cannot account for why one would tell a story to some other person in the course of a conversation. If by "story" Schank and Abelson mean the same thing that Brewer and Lichtenstein do, then that would explain why people tell a particular subset of narratives (i.e., stories) to others in the course of a conversation (e.g., because they are interesting and entertaining).

Stories with Points

However, examination of the examples of stories given by Schank and Abelson makes it fairly clear that the subset of narratives they refer to as "stories" is not the same as that proposed by Brewer and Lichtenstein. In particular, Schank and Abelson want to account for many nonentertaining, nonaffective aspects of human cognitive processing. The examples of stories given in their discussion suggest that Schank and Abelson may use the term "story" for the subset of stories that have a "point." For example they "index" certain stories with terms such as "betrayal" or "defense of our nation" (p. 50). This construal of their use of stories leads to difficulties, since attempts to analyze the construct *story point* have shown that this is a very hard problem, and that there is little agreement about the nature of story points (cf. Wilensky, 1983). In a recent paper, Dorfman and I (Dorfman & Brewer, 1994) have argued that points are the didactic message embodied in the text that the reader believes the author intends to convey. We proposed a theory of points based on the positive or negative valence of the text's central action, the positive or negative valence of the text's outcome, and the reader's beliefs about the fairness of the outcome. We carried out a number of experiments with fables showing that our theory could account for the points that subjects gave for fables they had never heard before. It seems to me that it is possible to interpret "stories," as used by Schank and Abelson, as being similar to "stories with points," as discussed by Dorfman and Brewer. For example, in one part of their discussion, Schank and Abelson seem to suggest that the appropriateness of story selection in conversations is based on story "points," and they note that "the points one derives from stories relate to goals, plans, beliefs, and lessons learned from a story" (p. 23).

Stereotyped Story Points

Even though Schank and Abelson's use of "story" seems close to Dorfman and Brewer's use of story "points," there are some important differences. Dorfman and Brewer's usage seems to highlight issues of morality to a stronger degree than that of Schank and Abelson. In addition, Dorfman and Brewer intend their approach to be generative (to apply to any new fable), whereas Schank and Abelson emphasize the role of a fixed set of prestored story structures. Therefore, Schank and Abelson's use of the term "story" may come closest to literary analyses of the set of possible plot types. For example, Polti (1977) proposed that all plots can be resolved into 36 basic "dramatic situations." One of Polti's 36 types is "falling prey to misfortune," which could cover Schank and Abelson's story about hitting the planter with the car (p. 66). Another of Polti's plots is "adultery," which might cover aspects of one of Schank and Abelson's divorce stories (pp. 60–62). Thus, after reading Schank and Abelson, and after studying the examples given in the text, the best reading I can give for their technical term "stories" is that it refers to a fixed set of stereotyped story points. I am not sure if I have it right, and I would really have preferred to have Schank and Abelson give an explicit account of the central construct in their chapter.

Implications

If "stories" are to mean a fixed set of stereotyped story points, then what are the implications for the central claims of the Schank and Abelson framework, such as, "Virtually all human knowledge is based on stories" (p. 1) and "New experiences are interpreted in terms of old stories" (p. 1)? The above analysis shows that the claims are false.

The view that "stories" refers to a fixed set of stereotyped story points limits stories to a small subset of the more general class of narratives. Yet, earlier we argued that the assumption that all knowledge and memory is represented in the form of narrative structures was already specific enough to be incompatible with the evidence that people represent and store spatial, logical, and physical explanatory information. Thus, the more specific hypothesis that knowledge is represented in terms of a fixed set of story points provides an even less plausible account of human knowledge representation. In fact, if all knowledge is to be represented by the type of story representations Schank and Abelson discuss, the theory will not even be able to account for the way one represents nonstory narratives such as someone's (uneventful) trip to the grocery store.

MEMORY OVEREXTENDED

Much of the Schank and Abelson chapter is directed at applying their story approach to an analysis of human memory. First, let us examine a few examples of the difficulties that the overextension of the story construct causes for their approach to memory.

All Memory is Story Memory

Schank and Abelson state that "our memories are comprised of the stories we tell and the stories we tell comprise our memories" (p. 60). Story memory is an interesting and important part of human memory, but clearly human memory is a mansion of many rooms, including spatial memory, causal memory, and musical memory. Thus, the expansive claim about story memory is simply false.

Story Memory is Superior to Other Forms of Memory

Schank and Abelson also state that "We do not easily remember what other people have said if they do not tell us in the form of a story" (p. 26). Although the paper provides no empirical evidence for the position that story structure improves recall, it is not hard to find data to support this aspect of their claim. For example Bower and Clark (1969) showed that subjects learning a list of words show enormous improvement if they are instructed to make up a story using the words. However, overextending the role of story structure once again puts Schank and Abelson's larger claim at variance with the facts. Here is one simple example: Probably the other most powerful mnemonic technique known (cf. Bower, 1970) is the "method of loci" invented by the ancient Greeks. This technique involves the placing of mental objects across a mental landscape, and thus gains its enormous power through the use of spatial and event sequence information, not through the use of story structure.

Much of the Schank and Abelson discussion consists of examples of phenomena that they take to provide support for their view. In the next sections of this commentary I will argue that many of the phenomena discussed by Schank and Abelson are well known, and since they have been described and analyzed in frameworks very different from that of Schank and Abelson, it appears that these phenomena do not provide *specific competitive* support for their theory.

MEMORY PHENOMENA

Story Based Errors

Schank and Abelson use their approach to predict that certain autobiographical memories will be distorted by the story structure imposed on them during conversations. They state, "We tell what fits and leave out what does not. So, whereas our lives may be not be coherent, our stories are. The danger here is that we may come to believe our own stories. When our stories become memories, and substitute for the actual events, this danger is quite real. We remember our stories and begin to believe them. In this way, stories shape memory profoundly" (p. 34).

Although this is a hard proposal to test, I think it is quite likely that it is correct. It was also rather nicely stated by William James (1890):

> The most frequent source of false memory is the accounts we give to others of our experiences. Such accounts we almost always make both more simple and more interesting than the truth. We quote what we should have said or done, rather than what we really said or did; and in the first telling we may be fully aware of the distinction. But ere long the fiction expels the reality from memory and reigns in its stead alone. (Vol. 1, pp. 373–374)

Dual Process Theory Repetition

Schank and Abelson assert that we have trouble recalling frequently repeated events such as going to the grocery store and filling out income tax forms. In my study of randomly selected events from the lives of undergraduates (Brewer, 1988), I found that the most powerful predictor of recall of these events was location and event frequency, with rare events and rare locations being well remembered. Thus, the data from autobiographical memory research support Schank and Abelson's claim. They account for this phenomenon as part of a larger memory theory. They ask, "Why can't we remember what we bought in the grocery store on October 16, 1982?" (p. 38). They propose that we add the information "to our general store-house of similar experiences" such that, "that experience then becomes part of our general knowledge . . . and updates what we already know" (p. 39). Finally, they conclude that "the construction of a memory that organizes information around repetitions of events destroys the coherence of any particular *sequence of events*" (p. 40).

The previous reconstruction of their view may not be completely correct, because sometimes they talk as if the repeated events are abstracted into some form of general knowledge, and at other times they assert that the individual repeated instances are retained, but are somehow regrouped into new clusters in memory. Given my account of their views as represented by the quotes just cited from their paper, their proposal is quite similar to that made by a number of different researchers about the general operation of human memory (e.g., Bower, 1974, p. 2; Hintzman, 1978, p. 374). Schank and Abelson apply their view to the specific case of autobiographical memory. Linton (1982, p. 79) was one of the first researchers to adopt this approach in the area of autobiographical memory. In my 1988 paper, I called this position the "dual-process theory of repetition" (Brewer, 1988, p. 76) and had earlier summarized the view by saying that "repetition of events leads to the development of generic personal memories at the expense of the individual personal memories that were repeated." (Brewer, 1986, p. 45) I developed this proposal within a framework quite different from Schank and Abelson's story theory. Thus, it is hard to see how the dual process theory of repetition provides competitive support for Schank and Abelson's theory.

Story Memory Construction

Schank and Abelson hypothesize that there is a complex set of mental operations that is used to convert an event sequence into a story memory. The operations proposed by Schank and Abelson are similar to those that have been developed by previous researchers in the area of text structure and memory. For example, van Dijk and Kintsch (1978) have described a set of "macro-rules" which they state are used to go from the lower-level propositions to the "semantic macro-structures." One of van Dijk and Kintsch's macro-rules is *deletion,* which they describe by stating that, "of a sequence of propositions we may delete all those denoting an accidental property of a discourse referent" (van Dijk & Kintsch, 1978, p. 68). This macro-rule seems fairly close to Schank and Abelson's *distillation,* which they describe as an operation that "leaves out descriptions of physical items unless those descriptions are critical to the story" (p. 70). Examination of these two discussions of this topic suggests that van Dijk and Kintsch give a more complete account of summarization processes, whereas Schank and Abelson give a more complete account of the role the individual's goals in reworking the events for memory.

KNOWLEDGE ACQUISITION

In the course of their discussion, Schank and Abelson make a number of proposals on the issue of how knowledge is acquired.

New Knowledge Is Based on Old

Schank and Abelson are quite clear in proposing that new knowledge must be based on old knowledge. They state that "People need a context to help them relate what they have heard to what they already know" (p. 8) and that "New ideas depend upon old ones" (p. 9). This is a powerful and, I think, fundamentally correct notion. However, the chapter gives the appearance that this is an original idea derived from their theory (no references are given to earlier work). This is, in fact, a very old idea. For example, the German philosopher Herbart (1776–1841) was quite clear on this issue. He referred to an individual's old knowledge as the individual's "apperceptive mass" and drew direct pedagogical implications from his account. His view has been summarized thus: "Since it is on the background of previous experience that a new idea is assimilated in the apperceptive mass, it follows that if information is to be acquired as easily and as rapidly as possible, then in teaching one should introduce new material by building upon the apperceptive mass of already familiar ideas" (Watson, 1971, p. 231). If one prefers a more current cognitive science version, then perhaps a better reference might be Richard Anderson's summary of the conference that was published as *Schooling and the Acquisition of Knowledge.* He uses the term "schema" for old knowledge and states, "Without some schema into which it can be assimilated, an experience is incomprehensible and therefore, little can be learned from it" (Anderson, 1977, p. 429).

New Knowledge Is Based on Old Stories

Actually the previous discussion may not be completely fair. As we have seen, Schank and Abelson are proposing that essentially all knowledge is represented in terms of stories and, therefore, are making a much more narrow, and thus more original, claim (i.e., "New experiences are interpreted in terms of old stories," p. 1). However, for the reasons already discussed above, this claim cannot be supported.

No New Knowledge

Schank and Abelson take a strong position on the impossibility of acquiring fundamentally new knowledge. They state that "everything you might ever want to say has already been thought up" (p. 9) and that "we cannot understand anything new" (p. 21). This position has been attractive to some scholars (e.g., Fodor, 1981). However, it is a very conservative position (it usually requires the proponent to adopt a strong nativist approach). It seems to me that recent thinking on this topic suggests that one can solve the problem of how new knowledge is acquired by assuming that fundamentally new knowledge can emerge from old knowledge (e.g., Carey, 1985; Vosniadou & Brewer, 1987). In fact, work in this area has gone beyond simple speculation. In a recent paper with Stella Vosniadou (Vosniadou & Brewer, 1994) we have shown that old knowledge about the shape of the earth does constrain the acquisition of new knowledge about the day–night cycle. However, with the removal of certain deep-seated presuppositions (e.g., that the earth is flat), new knowledge (new theories) about the day–night cycle can be acquired (e.g., that the sun is fixed and the earth rotates).

CONVERSATIONS

In an attempt to dismiss certain forms of (obviously) nonstory knowledge, Schank and Abelson argue that these forms of knowledge (e.g., numerical information, linguistic information) rarely enter into social conversations (cf. pp. 14–15). The logic here seems to be that if something is not crucial to social conversations, one does not have to consider it in one's theory. Obviously, Schank and Abelson can adopt such a position if they wish, but most of the rest of the world simply is not going to follow. It is clear that it is not just "formalists" who are going to find the restriction of the domain of psychology to the topic of social conversations to be unacceptable.

Storytelling Rounds

Schank and Abelson place an extraordinary emphasis on telling stories in natural conversations. They state that "a conversationalist is looking to tell one of his stories. He is looking to tell a good one" (p. 9). In another place, they state that "as understanders we are always looking for stories to tell back" (p. 24). Finally, they note that "storytelling is not something we just happen to do; it is something we virtually have to do" (p. 33).

The analysis of storytelling given by Schank and Abelson is similar to that developed in the area of conversational analysis (e.g., McLaughlin, Cody, Kane, & Robey, 1981). Researchers in this area have studied sequences of stories in natural conversations and concluded that "any potential succeeding storyteller desiring to create, for whatever reason, a series of stories with a first story, must somehow in the process of constructing his story, orient to and incorporate resources of the prior story" (Ryave, 1978, p. 129). Schank and Abelson discuss "captioning," which they define as "the summarization of a larger story used as a means of telling that story" (p. 73). Ryave (1978) had earlier made a similar point. He noted that one general strategy used in storytelling rounds "is to organize the story in terms of a significance [sic] statement which also serves to formulate a preceding story" (p. 127).

Telling stories is one interesting form of conversation, but so are asking questions, making declarative statements, giving explanations, and so on. It appears to me that Schank and Abelson have taken one particular aspect of human conversations, storytelling rounds, and have reified it as essentially the whole of psychology.

CONCLUSIONS

The assertion that essentially all human knowledge and memory is represented in terms of stories is an extraordinary claim. However, in the philosophy of science there is an rule of thumb that says, "Extraordinary claims must be supported by extraordinary evidence." Schank and Abelson's chapter provides no such evidence.

Schank and Abelson place much emphasis on the functions and goals of the stories people tell. Thus, what could be the goal of the "story" that they tell in their chapter? It seems to me that the extreme overextension of the story construct is an attempt to force this topic to the attention of the cognitive science community. However, if their approach is seen by other researchers as a mere story without logical or empirical support, the conversational ploy they adopt may backfire.

ACKNOWLEDGMENTS

I would like to thank Gregory Murphy and Ellen Brewer for commenting on an earlier (and more vivid) version of this chapter.

REFERENCES

Anderson, R. C. (1977). The notion of schemata and the educational enterprise: General discussion of the conference. In R. C. Anderson, R. J. Spiro, & W. E. Montague (Eds.), *Schooling and the acquisition of knowledge* (pp. 414–431). Hillsdale, NJ: Lawrence Erlbaum Associates.

Bower, G. H. (1970). Analysis of a mnemonic device. *American Scientist, 58,* 496–510.

Bower, G. H. (1974). Selective facilitation and interference in retention of prose. *Journal of Educational Psychology, 66,* 1–8.

Bower, G. H., & Clark, M. C. (1969). Narrative stories as mediators for serial learning. *Psychonomic Science, 14,* 181–182.

Brewer, W. F. (1980). Literary theory, rhetoric, and stylistics: Implications for psychology. In R. J. Spiro, B. C. Bruce, & W. F. Brewer (Eds.), *Theoretical issues in reading comprehension* (pp. 221–239). Hillsdale, NJ: Lawrence Earlbaum Associates.

Brewer, W. F. (1982). Plan understanding, narrative comprehension, and story schemas. In *Proceedings of the American Association for Artificial Intelligence* (pp. 262–264). Pittsburgh, PA: Carnegie-Mellon University, University of Pittsburgh.

Brewer, W. F. (1986). What is autobiographical memory? In D. C. Rubin (Eds.), *Autobiographical memory* (pp. 25–49). Cambridge, England: Cambridge University Press.

Brewer, W. F. (1988). Memory for randomly sampled autobiographical events. In U. Neisser & E. Winograd (Eds.), *Remembering reconsidered: Ecological and traditional approaches to the study of memory* (pp. 21–90). Cambridge, England: Cambridge University Press.

Brewer, W. F., & Lichtenstein, E. H. (1981). Event schemas, story schemas, and story grammars. In J. Long & A. Baddeley (Eds.), *Attention and Performance, IX* (pp. 363–379). Hillsdale, NJ: Lawrence Erlbaum Associates.

Brewer, W. F., & Lichtenstein, E. H. (1982). Stories are to entertain: A structural-affect theory of stories. *Journal of Pragmatics, 6,* 473–486.

Carey, S. (1985). *Conceptual change in childhood.* Cambridge, MA: MIT Press.

de Beaugrande, R., & Colby, B. N. (1979). Narrative models of action and interaction. *Cognitive Science, 3,* 43–66.

Dorfman, M. H., & Brewer, W. F. (1994). Understanding the points of fables. *Discourse Processes, 17,* 105–129.

Fodor, J. A. (1981). The present status of the innateness controversy. In J. A. Fodor (Ed.), *Representations* (pp. 257–316). Cambridge, MA: MIT Press.

Hintzman, D. L. (1978). *The psychology of learning and memory.* San Francisco: Freeman.

James, W. (1890). *The principles of psychology (2 vols.).* New York: Henry Holt.

Johnson-Laird, P. N. (1983). *Mental models.* Cambridge, MA: Harvard University Press.

Kintsch, W. (1980). Learning from text, levels of comprehension, or: why anyone would read a story anyway. *Poetics, 9,* 87–98.

Linton, M. (1982). Transformations of memory in everyday life. In U. Neisser (Ed.), *Memory observed: Remembering in natural contexts* (pp. 77–91). San Francisco: Freeman.

McCloskey, M., Caramazza, A., & Green, B. (1980). Curvilinear motion in the absence of external forces: Naïve beliefs about the motion of objects. *Science, 210,* 1139–1141.

McLaughlin, M. L., Cody, M. J., Kane, M. L., & Robey, C. S. (1981). Sex differences in story receipt and story sequencing behaviors in dyadic conversations. *Human Communication Research, 7,* 99–116.

Meehan, J. R. (1976). *The metanovel: Writing stories by computer* (Research Report No. 74). Department of Computer Science, Yale University.

Ohtsuka, K., & Brewer, W. F. (1992). Discourse organization in the comprehension of temporal order in narrative texts. *Discourse Processes, 15,* 317–336.

Polti, G. (1977). *The thirty-six dramatic situations* (Lucille Ray, Trans.). Boston, MA: The Writer.

Ryave, A. L. (1978). On the achievement of a series of stories. In J. Schenkein (Ed.), *Studies in the organization of conversational interaction* (pp. 113–132). New York: Academic Press.

Shepard, R. N., & Chipman, S. (1970). Second-order isomorphism of internal representations: Shapes of states. *Cognitive Psychology, 1,* 1–17.

van Dijk, T. A., & Kintsch, W. (1978). Cognitive psychology and discourse: Recalling and summarizing stories. In W. U. Dressler (Ed.), *Current trends in textlinguistics* (pp. 61–80). Berlin: Walter de Gruyter.

Vosniadou, S., & Brewer, W. F. (1987). Theories of knowledge restructuring in development. *Review of Educational Research, 57,* 51–67.

Vosniadou, S., & Brewer, W. F. (1994). Mental models of the day/night cycle. *Cognitive Science, 18,* 123–183.

Watson, R. I. (1971). *The great psychologists* (3rd ed.). Philadelphia: J. B. Lippincott.

Wilensky, R. (1978). *Understanding goal-based stories* (Research Report No. 140). Department of Computer Science, Yale University.

Wilensky, R. (1983). Story grammars versus story points & commentary. *Behavioral and Brain Sciences, 6,* 579–623.

5

Why Stories? Some Evidence, Questions, and Challenges

Arthur C. Graesser
Victor Ottati
The University of Memphis

One approach to doing science is to extend and tune the major paradigms of a field. Examples of paradigms in social cognition include the formation of person impressions, the attribution of causes of social behavior, and conversational interaction. Example paradigms in the field of artificial intelligence include knowledge representation, natural language comprehension, pattern recognition, and robotics. There are advantages to working within a paradigm. Researchers accumulate a rich set of data that are collected with established methodologies. There is a sustained collective effort in solving particular problems. But this style of doing science also has its disadvantages, particularly as a paradigm matures. Researchers become locked into conventional tasks, methodologies, and pet theories. At times, also, methodology is given a much higher priority than insight into the phenomenon. Finally, the data generated by standard methodologies often yield very small incremental gains in understanding.

A second approach to doing science is adopting an interdisciplinary stance, which allegedly broadens the theoretical landscape and cracks some barriers of inbred, paradigm-ridden knowledge. This interdisciplinary stance is the hallmark of the cognitive science enterprise. A research team in cognitive science might include expertise in artificial intelligence, linguistics, psychology, and anthropology. The collective interdisciplinary effort encourages multiple perspectives, methodologies, and theories during the study of a particular phenomenon. Insight into the phenomenon is deemed higher in priority than adhering to a particular methodology. There is one unfortunate side effect of this interdisciplinary stance, however. The resulting insights are frequently treated with some skepticism by those who adhere to a particular paradigm, discipline, or methodological gospel.

Those who advocate interdisciplinary efforts can point to the work of Schank and Abelson as an obvious success case. Schank was trained in computational linguistics and artificial intelligence, whereas Abelson was trained in experimental social psychology. Their collaborative interdisciplinary efforts have had a salient, if not revolutionary, impact on cognitive science. Studies of natural language and discourse comprehension, for example, were profoundly changed by their work. Prior to the Schank and Abelson era, linguists and psycholinguists had a skewed emphasis on the lower levels of language processing, such as phonology, syntax, and the lexicon. These levels merited serious attention because they were well-formed and computationally tractable, at least, according to Chomsky and his descendants. Researchers shied away from the deeper levels of language comprehension, such as inference generation, world knowledge, and global discourse coherence. These deeper levels were deemed as inherently problematic because they are open-ended, vague, fragmentary, imprecise, ill-defined, and unconstrained. As one colleague put it, studying world knowledge and inferences is akin to experiencing quicksand. Fortunately, Schank and Abelson's work provided a more solid footing for those who wanted to investigate the deeper levels of language analysis. There they discovered systematicity in the representations and processing mechanisms associated with world knowledge, inference generation, question answering, conversation, and global discourse coherence.

As authors of this commentary, we jointly extend the interdisciplinary foothold. The first author is a cognitive scientist who has investigated text comprehension, conversation, question asking, and question answering. The second author is in the area of social and political cognition. After reading the article by Schank and Abelson, we had a series of lively discussions about the significance of this research in cognitive science and social cognition. We reflected on the value and limitations of some sacred beliefs in our fields. As is the case with most interdisciplinary dialogue, the exchange was enjoyable, sometimes heated, and consistently illuminating. We wondered why more cognitive scientists had not teamed up with social psychologists.

This commentary focuses on two general questions that kept popping up in the course of our discussions. The first question addresses the issue of whether there is empirical evidence for Schank and Abelson's claims about story representations and story indexes. We suspect that this is one of the most frequent questions that social psychologists would ask when reading the article under discussion. Given that Schank is grounded more firmly in computational theories than behavioral science, it is perhaps the most obvious question to ask. The second general question addresses the functional utility of knowledge representations. Schank and Abelson frequently justify the privileged status of story representations on the basis of functional utility, that is, a representation must be useful for solving typical tasks and activities that people face in the real world. In what sense do stories have high functional utility? Do some story configurations have more utility than others? Is there also functional utility in alternative representational schemes, such as traits, beliefs, and facts that are detached from a story context?

EMPIRICAL EVIDENCE FOR STORIES AND STORY
INDEXES

The empirical status of some of Schank and Abelson's claims may not seem very solid from the perspective of many researchers in social psychology. In spite of this, we do believe that the psychological validity of many of their claims is quite on the mark. This section presents evidence that bolsters three of their fundamental claims and shoots down two others.

Stories Do Have a Privileged Status
in the Cognitive System

Long-term memory is frequently viewed as a vast storehouse of *conceptual nodes* (e.g., agents, objects, features, locations, facts, events, goals, rules) that are inter-related by different types of relations (e.g., spatial, temporal, causal, logical, class inclusion, and so on). The nodes are extensively cross-classified and accessible from multiple viewpoints. A relation that connects two nodes either is directly stored in long-term memory or may be indirectly derived when a person uses world knowledge to complete a particular task. This view of long-term memory is widely acknowledged and not particularly controversial. But it has led some researchers to adopt a relativistic, unconstrained view toward long-term memory organization: Because knowledge can be cross-classified in virtually any way one could imagine, and because any two nodes can be connected with most types of relations, it may seem meaningless to argue that the cognitive system is organized in a particular fashion. Simply put, virtually any representational scheme works well enough. Consequently, long-term memory has semantic networks, rule sets, sets of traits that are connected to behavior lists, and so on. All of these are essentially equivalent in status.

Schank and Abelson challenge this unconstrained relativistic view. They argue that the story is the most natural package of organized knowledge in the cognitive system. Stories are indexed with thematic points, goals of main characters, plans that circumvent obstacles, explanations of anomalous information, and other useful features that discriminate one story from alternative stories in memory. Other types of knowledge (such as facts, traits, and semantic networks) are grounded in contextually rich, situation-specific stories. For example, when we are asked whether a person has a particular trait (e.g., "Is Fred lazy?"), we would access stories about Fred and derive an evaluation of Fred on the trait. We would not, as suggested by alternative formulations, access a set of trait-relevant behaviors that are disconnected from any story context. Nor would we access a previously formed trait inference that is detached from situation-specific story content. Schank and Abelson have intentionally taken an extreme nonrelativist position that stories are the basic units of organization in the cognitive system.

It would take less than a minute to convince a scholar in folklore or narratology that stories have a privileged status in the cognitive system. For several millennia, stories were the primary rhetorical structure for passing down the wisdom of a culture from generation to generation. Stories were indeed the primary content of the oral tradition, not semantic networks, person-trait-behavior ensembles, spatial layouts, mental models of causal systems, nor any other structure. An external memory, in the form of written documents or maps, was needed to pass down the wisdom of non-narrative knowledge.

There also is experimental evidence for the privileged status of narrative in memory. Several years ago, Bower and Clark (1969) reported an experiment in which college students memorized and later recalled several sets of 10 unrelated words. In a control condition, the subjects memorized the words within each set in whatever fashion they desired. In a story condition, the subjects constructed a story that incorporated all of the words within each set; there was one story per set. In a delayed recall task, the subjects in the story condition recalled approximately five times as many words as did the subjects in the control condition. Thus, story organization was robustly superior to the college students' subjective organization of the words.

There are two additional implications of these empirical findings. First, when subjects are confronted with unrelated words, they do not spontaneously organize them in terms of a coherent story. Second, cognitive and social psychologists may be missing a fundamental phenomenon by presenting subjects with seemingly unrelated lists of words or behaviors. More naturalistic stimulus materials consist of temporally and causally related event sequences. When presented with such materials, subjects may indeed spontaneously organize the information in terms of a story.

The first author of this commentary has examined reading time and memory for different classes of naturalistic text. The primary contrast was between narrative texts (such as a story about Noah's ark) and expository texts (such as an encyclopedia article about armadillos). The sample of 12 naturalistic texts was scaled on narrativity, topic familiarity, and interestingness (according to college students). The narrative texts were read approximately twice as fast as expository texts (Graesser, Hoffman, & Clark, 1980; Haberlandt & Graesser, 1985). Yet the narrative texts were recalled approximately twice as well as expository texts (Graesser, Hauft-Smith, Cohen, & Pyles, 1980). There was a robust .92 correlation between narrativity and the amount of information recalled from a text. In contrast, topic familiarity and interestingness had very small effects on reading time and recall for these texts.

Studies such as these support the claim that story representations have a privileged status in the cognitive system. Stories are well-remembered and the effect is quite robust. Any theory that fails to recognize this fact is glossing over one of the fundamental constraints of the cognitive system (see also Britton & Pelligrini, 1990; Bruner, 1986; Mandler, 1984).

Important Story Indexes Explain Actions, Events, and States

Schank and Abelson identify some of the important story indexes that are stored in long-term memory. One index is a story skeleton that causally connects events that would otherwise be disconnected in time. The skeleton explains event sequences, character goals, goal conflicts, character plans, emotions, and overall story coherence. An anomaly-based index is formed when input fails to confirm the comprehender's expectations (based on the skeleton that prevails on-line), and the comprehender tries to formulate an explanation for the anomaly. In both of these cases, the comprehender is trying to explain *why* actions, events, and states are mentioned. The content of these explanations consists of motives of characters (i.e., main goals) and causes of events. Explanations also address the pragmatic context of the exchange: Why is the storyteller mentioning something? Explicit information must have some relevance to the global message the storyteller intends to convey.

Do comprehenders normally construct story representations that explain why actions, events, and states occur? There indeed is a substantial body of literature in social cognition that would support such a claim (Hilton, 1990; Pennington & Hastie, 1986; Read, 1987). In the field of discourse processing, Trabasso and his associates (Suh & Trabasso, 1993; Trabasso & Suh, 1993; Trabasso & van den Broek, 1985) have investigated the impact of causal coherence and causal explanations on the recall and importance ratings of story content. In one study, college students were instructed to "think aloud" while they comprehended stories, sentence by sentence. The content in these think-aloud protocols was segregated into explanations (i.e., causes, motives, answers to why-questions) versus nonexplanatory elaborations. Later on, the subjects recalled the stories. Recall of the explicit statements robustly increased as a function of the number of explanations the statements elicited; recall slightly decreased as a function of the number of nonexplanatory elaborations. These results are compatible with the claim that important story indexes address causal explanations.

The inferences that readers construct during story comprehension are also in the service of causal explanations and global coherence. Graesser, Singer, and Trabasso (1994) reviewed an extensive body of literature concerning on-line inference generation during story comprehension. Researchers in discourse processing and experimental psychology have attempted to identify those inferences that are normally generated on-line (i.e., during comprehension) versus those inferences that are generated off-line (i.e., during a later retrieval task but not during comprehension). According to Graesser et al. (1994), on-line inferences tend to be those that explain *why* explicit actions, events, and states are mentioned. These inferences include superordinate goals of story characters that motivate their actions (e.g., the student went to the dance because he wanted to get a girlfriend), causal antecedents of explicit events and actions (e.g., the student left the dance because he felt awkward), and information that fleshes out the main point of the story. In contrast, on-line inferences do not tend to include elaborations about the spatial layout of the story, the manner in which actions and events occur, the properties of inanimate objects, character traits that are not causally relevant, and episodes that are expected to occur much later in the story. It should be noted that the studies included in Graesser et al.'s review had rigorous experimental control over the content of the texts, the selection of test inferences, and the timing of on-line measures.

The preceding studies support Schank and Abelson's empirical claim that important indexes include the story skeletons that causally relate story content and the explanations of anomalous information. Comprehenders want to know why actions and events occur, why the storyteller bothers mentioning something, and what the global point is. Other information is essentially frivolous embroidery that ends up being distilled from the memory representation.

Anomalous Information Is Initially Well-Encoded

According to Schank and Abelson, anomaly-based indexes are formed when input fails to match expectations. These anomalies include obstacles to a character's goals, events that clash with expectations furnished by the story skeleton, and irrelevant information. The comprehender attempts to handle the input by constructing novel explanations; these indexed novelties make the current story discriminable from alternative stories with similar skeletons. Thus, the novel deviations from expectations should be more discriminable in memory than typical skeletal information, which often is filled in by default.

There is ample evidence that memory for obstacles and inconsistencies is initially better than memory for information that is typical of a central organizing schema (e.g., script, stereotype) (Bower, Black, & Turner, 1979; Hastie & Kumar, 1979; Srull, 1981). This result is compatible with the predictions of Schank and Abelson's theory. It is incompatible with filtering models which predict that information is filtered out of the memory representation if it is inconsistent with a central organizing schema. There are some conditions in which the inconsistency bias in memory disappears, or is even reversed, however. First, when the input is extremely ambiguous, and the central organizing schema is fragile at best, then typical information prevails over inconsistent information in memory. Second, the inconsistency bias disappears when the central organizing schema is so loose and indecisive that it could accommodate virtually any input (which is not the case for most story skeletons, but can be the case for personality impressions). Third, as discussed by Schank and Abelson, story skeletons may become distilled over time with repeated retellings; time and retellings may eventually remove the inconsistency bias.

The fate of irrelevant information, which is more controversial, has attracted the attention of the first author of this commentary. On the one hand, irrelevant information would seem to be a good candidate for being distilled because it is difficult to relate it to the causal structure of the story skeleton. On the other hand, it may end up being indexed and somehow explained, under the assumption that it should eventually be relevant to the storyteller's message. The comprehender would essentially adopt the Gricean maxim that whatever the author explicitly mentions is relevant (Grice, 1975). Graesser and his associates (Graesser, Gordon, & Sawyer, 1979; Graesser & Nakamura, 1982) have examined memory for actions that are typical (e.g., customer pays bill) versus irrelevant (e.g., customer reads letter) with respect to a central organizing script (e.g., RESTAURANT). Memory discrimination, as measured in a recognition test that controls for guessing, is better for irrelevant information than for typical script information at all retention intervals (a few minutes to three weeks). A recall measure that controls for guessing shows a somewhat different pattern. Recall memory is initially better for irrelevant information than for script typical information, but the trend reverses with greater retention intervals. Thus, a distillation process trims out irrelevant information as more times goes by.

This initial advantage of irrelevant information in memory has surprised many of our colleagues, particularly those who would have expected an advantage for typical script information. Nevertheless, the effect is quite robust (Graesser & Nakamura, 1982). It is not sensitive to fluctuations in the comprehender's processing objectives (e.g., comprehending for memory versus impression formation). It is not sensitive to the speed in which the actions in the scripted activities are presented to subjects; the effect remains robust even when the speed is so fast that comprehenders would have absolutely no opportunity to engage in elaborative rehearsal. Either the irrelevant information is indexed very quickly, or the typical information is quickly filled in by default. In either case, memory discrimination is substantially superior for irrelevant actions compared to typical script actions. This outcome is compatible with Schank and Abelson's theory, but not compatible with several alternative schema-based models of memory.

Increased recall for script-irrelevant information occurs in situations where application of the Gricean communication maxim is appropriate. That is, when a storyteller explicitly mentions script-irrelevant information, the listener may assume the storyteller has some particular reason for doing so. Recall for irrelevant information in directly observed action sequences may exhibit a different pattern. Furthermore, other research indicates that memory for irrelevant information is lower than memory for typical information when the central organizing structure is a person concept (Hastie & Kumar, 1979; Srull, 1981). There are three plausible reasons for this discrepancy with the previously described script research. First, when confronted with a list of unconnected behaviors about a person, the comprehender may simply abandon the Gricean maxim. Second, unlike a script, a personality impression may be less coherent and more ambiguous with respect to what is relevant. As such, irrelevant behaviors may be less salient. Third, the comprehender may be less prone to fill in information by default when the central organizing structure is a person concept than when it is a script (Wyer & Gordon, 1984).

Most People Do Not Ask Many Questions That Reflect Knowledge Deficits

According to Schank and Abelson's theory, comprehenders ask themselves questions (or ask others questions) when they encounter anomalies, knowledge gaps, and obstacles to goals. They seek answers that explain the glitches they encounter while comprehending stories. Schank has proposed a "question-driven understanding" model that generates good questions and drives the course of comprehension (Schank, 1986).

Alas, the empirical news is not always flattering for Schank and Abelson's theory. Simply put, the vast majority of comprehenders are not very good at asking knowledge-deficit questions. A typical student asks approximately .2 questions per hour in a classroom setting and 6 knowledge-deficit questions per hour in a tutoring session (Dillon, 1988; Graesser & Person, 1994). When students are explicitly told to generate questions while comprehending stories or algebra problems, they entirely miss most occasions where critical information is deleted, inconsistent information is inserted, and irrelevant information is inserted (Graesser & McMahen, 1993). The question asking skills of most individuals is quite unimpressive. Students need to be trained in skills of asking good questions. When trained, students show a substantial improvement in comprehension (Brown & Palincsar, 1989; King, 1989). However, question asking is not a natural skill that pervades comprehension.

Story Remindings Are Not That Frequent During Naturalistic Conversations

According to Schank and Abelson, story remindings sustain many conversations. Person A first tells a story. Then person B tells a similar story that shares many skeletal features of A's story and thereby demonstrates an understanding of A's story. There can be a "one-upsmanship" game between A and B, with each successive story adding interesting features to story skeletons. So a cluster of similar stories evolves during conversation. Understanding is manifested by the judicious selection of stories.

Unfortunately, story remindings are not all that frequent during most conversations. We have analyzed conversation samples in a variety of populations and contexts: business transactions, televised interviews, tutoring, children in free play, children collaboratively solving puzzles, and therapist-client interactions. Story remindings were not very frequent in these contexts, perhaps because most of the conversations were constrained by a conversation script that was appropriate for the situational context. However, this observation does suggest that Schank and Abelson's story reminding mechanism is a particular, rather than a pervasive, conversational frame. Lunchroom conversations and party conversations are contexts where story remindings perhaps prevail. But these contexts also are replete with arguments and griping, rather than remindings per se. Although stories are frequent in many conversations, remindings are not the main generator of conversational coherence.

THE FUNCTIONAL UTILITY OF MEMORY REPRESENTATIONS

Schank and Abelson argue that stories are functional representations in the cognitive system in the sense that they are used for different purposes. Stories are useful packages of knowledge for answering questions, making plans, informing others of events that have taken place, giving advice, justifying beliefs, and so on. We have no reason to doubt that story representations are useful packages of knowledge. However, Schank and Abelson's claim does raise a number of questions and challenges which will be addressed in this section. Responses to these questions and challenges may open up fertile grounds for developing their theory.

Schank and Abelson merely declared that stories are functionally useful memory representations. As readers of their article, we are expected to accept the claim by intuitive appeal or by fiat. It certainly does have intuitive appeal. But the research program could go further by providing a computational defense of the claim. Since Schank is a premier researcher in cognitive science and artificial intelligence, he presumably is no stranger to computational arguments. For example, a good representation is supposed to highlight elements, features, and relations used by computational procedures that operate on the representations (Winston, 1984); it should hide or gloss over unimportant details. All things being equal, a good representation is also concise and economical; a few stored structures should be capable of supporting many structures that are derived via cognitive procedures. So the obvious question arises: How functional are story representations when we apply standard computational methods of evaluating representations? Even an approximate solution would be helpful.

Evaluating the functional utility of a representational system is challenging, but not impossible. We would begin with a laundry list of tasks we would like the cognitive system to perform (e.g., question asking, question answering, summarizing, planning, learning, decision-making, recalling, and so on). We would then postulate a set of theories of representation. The theories would vary in content (spatial, taxonomic, causal, goal structures, and so forth), formats (propositions, conceptual graphs), and packaging. We would then evaluate which representational theory fared best in covering the benchmark cognitive tasks. Presumably, story representations would fare very well. We could then ask what incremental gains exist when we add semantic networks, for example, or what loss exists when we delete spatial composition. This is not merely an exercise in knowledge engineering. It provides an explanatory platform for the theoretical claim that stories have functional utility.

Another approach to evaluating functional utility has a metaphor with genetics (Dawkins, 1976). Biologists evaluate the fitness and survival of genes as they undergo mutation and reproduction in a physical environment. Similarly, we could evaluate the fitness and survival of concepts in a culture as the concepts get transformed by social interactions. Dawkins has, in fact, proposed this approach to evaluating the utility of concepts in a dynamic world; he calls the concepts *memes*, an analogue to the genes in biological systems. Which representational theories would produce memes that have high fitness and survival? Which classes of memes, produced by a single representational theory, would have high fitness and survival values? Once again, this genetic epistemological analysis might provide an explanatory foundation for the claim that stories have high functional utility.

It could be argued that there is functional utility in storing personality traits and behaviors that are detached from a story context. Indeed, numerous models of person representation posit such a representation (Hamilton, Driscoll, & Worth, 1989; Hastie & Kumar, 1979; Srull, 1981; Wyer & Srull, 1986). For example, under the concept "Fred", we might store the trait "lazy" along with any behaviors that are relevant to this trait. In this representational scheme, discrete behaviors are interconnected when they are relevant to the same trait. Person representation models often make the implicit assumption, however, that these behaviors possess no connection in terms of a coherent and organized story. This form of representation may be functional when the perceiver has the objective of forming an impression, as opposed to comprehending an ongoing sequence of behavioral events (Iyengar & Ottati, 1993; Ottati & Wyer, 1991; Wyer & Gordon, 1984; Wyer & Ottati, 1993). Empirical evidence also suggests that trait inferences can become disassociated from the episodic material that originally served to elicit them (Lingle & Ostrom, 1979). This may be especially true when the perceiver is motivated to make semantic or evaluative judgments of a person on-line during encoding. In a job interview, the interviewer may constantly infer from and update an on-line assessment of the applicant's level of competence. This on-line inference may then later be retrieved and used as a basis for a competence judgment, independent of the particular applicant's behaviors and remarks that originally elicited the inference (Hastie & Park, 1986).

On-line trait evaluations, such as those described above, are quite pervasive in the real world. They occur when people date, try to decide which political candidate to support in a debate, choose someone to talk to at a party, and so on. Thus, it could be argued that decontextualized trait attributions have functional utility. Once again, there needs to be an independent explanatory foundation for determining the functional utility of representational systems. Otherwise, a researcher could argue that virtually any representational scheme has functional utility.

There would be another benefit in establishing a defensible explanatory foundation for evaluating the functional utility of concepts and representational systems. Researchers would then be able to evaluate the utility of particular story skeletons and story indexes. Throughout our discussions, the authors of this commentary frequently wondered what makes a good story. What stories are interesting? What stories are humorous? What stories have high aesthetic quality from a literary perspective? Schank and Abelson have, in fact, periodically addressed these questions and have offered some informative insights. But the success of their claims has never been systematically evaluated. For example, how would their analysis of humor compare with alternative psychological theories of humor (Graesser, Long, & Mio, 1989; Wyer & Collins, 1992)?

Aside from the matter of functional utility, it is a good time for psychologists to abandon some of the weary paradigm-ridden research projects, and investigate the properties of good stories.

REFERENCES

Bower, G. H., Black, J. B., & Turner, T. J. (1979). Scripts in memory for text. *Cognitive Psychology, 11,* 177–220.

Bower, G. H., & Clark,, M. C. (1969). Narrative stories as mediators for serial learning. *Psychonomic Science, 14,* 181–182.

Britton, B. K., & Pelligrini, A. D. (1990). *Narrative thought and narrative language.* Hillsdale, NJ: Lawrence Erlbaum Associates.

Brown, A. L., & Palincsar, A. S. (1989). Guided, cooperative learning and individual knowledge acquisition. In L. B. Resnick (Ed.), *Knowing, learning, and instruction: Essays in honor of Robert Glaser* (pp. 393–451), Hillsdale, N.J.: Lawrence Erlbaum Associates.

Bruner, J. (1986). *Actual minds, possible worlds.* Cambridge, MA: Harvard University Press.

Dawkins, R. (1976). *The selfish gene.* Oxford: Oxford University Press.

Dillon, T. J. (1988). *Questioning and teaching: A manual of practive.* Hillsdale, NJ: Lawrence Erlbaum Associates.

Graesser, A. C., Gordon, S. E., & Sawyer, J. D. (1979). Memory for typical and atypical actions in scripted activities: A test of the script pointer + tag hypothesis. *Journal of Verbal Learning and Behavior, 18,* 319–332.

Graesser, A. C., Hauft-Smith, K., Cohen, A. D., & Pyles, L. D. (1980). Advanced outlines, familiarity, text genre, and retention of prose. *Journal of Experimental Education, 48,* 209–220.

Graesser, A. C., Hoffman, N. L., & Clark, L. F. (1980). Structural components of reading time. *Journal of Verbal Learning and Verbal Behavior, 19,* 131–151.

Graesser, A. C., Long, D., & Mio, J. S. (1989). What are the cognitive and conceptual components of humorous texts? *Poetics, 18,* 143–164.

Graesser, A. C., & McMahen, C. L. (1993). Anomalous information triggers questions when adults solve problems and comprehend stories. *Journal of Educational Psychology, 85,* 136–151.

Graesser, A. C., & Nakamura, G. V. (1982). The impact of schemas on comprehension and memory. In G. H. Bower (Ed.),*The psychology of learning and motivation, Vol. 16.* New York: Academic Press.

Graesser, A. C., & Person, N. K. (1994). Question asking during tutoring. *American Educational Research Journal.*

Graesser, A. C., Singer, M., & Trabasso, T. (1994). Constructing inferences during narrative text comprehension. *Psychological Review.*

Grice, H. P. (1975). Logic and conversation. In P. Cole & J. L. Morgan (Eds.), *Syntax and semantics (Vol. 3): Speech acts* (pp. 68–134). New York: Seminar Press.

Haberlandt, K., & Graesser, A. C. (1985). Component processes in text comprehension and some of their interactions. *Journal of Experimental Psychology: General, 114,* 357–374.

Hamilton, D. L., Driscoll, D., & Worth, L. T. (1989). Cognitve organization of impressions: Effects of incongruency in complex representations. *Journal of Personality and Social Psychology, 57,* 925–939.

Hastie, R., & Kumar, P. A. (1979). Person memory: Personality traits as organizing principles in memory for behaviors. *Journal of Personality and Social Psychology, 37,* 25–38.

Hastie, R., & Park, B. (1986). The relationship between memory and judgment depends on whether the judgment task is memory-based or on-line. *Psychological Review, 93,* 258–268.

Hilton, D. J. (1990). Conversational processes and causal explanation. *Psychological Bulletin, 107,* 110–119.

Iyengar, S., & Ottati, V. (1994). The cognitive perspective in political psychology. In R. S. Wyer & T. K. Srull (Eds.), *Handbook of Social Cognition, Vol. 4,* Hillsdale, NJ: Lawrence Erlbaum Associates.

King, A. (1989). Effects of self-questioning training on college students' comprehension of lectures. *Contemporary Educational Psychology, 14,* 366–381.

Lingle, J. H., & Ostrom, T. M. (1979). Retrieval selectivity in memory-based impression judgments. *Journal of Personality and Social Psychology, 37,* 180–194.

Mandler, J. M. (1984). *Stories, scripts, and scenes: Aspects of schema theory.* Hillsdale, NJ: Lawrence Erlbaum Associates.

Ottati, V., & Wyer, R. S. (1991). The cognitive mediators of political choice: Toward a comprehensive model of political information processing. In J.A. Ferejohn & J.H. Kuklinski (Eds.), *Information and Democratic Process* (pp. 186–216). Urbana, IL: University of Illinois Press.

Pennington, N., & Hastie, R. (1986). Evidence evaluation in complex decision making. *Journal of Personality and Social Psychology, 52,* 288–302.

Read, S. J. (1987). Constructing causal scenarios: A knowledge structure approach to causal reasoning. *Journal of Personality and Social Psychology, 52,* 288–302.

Schank, R. C. (1986). *Explanation patterns: Understanding mechanically and creatively.* Hillsdale, NJ: Lawrence Erlbaum Associates.

Srull, T. K. (1981). Person memory: Some tests of associative storage and retrieval models. *Journal of Experimental Psychology: Human Learning and Memory, 7,* 440–462.

Suh, S. Y., & Trabasso, T. (1993). Global inferences in on-line processing of texts: Converging evidence from discourse analysis, talk-aloud protocols, and recognition priming. *Journal of Memory and Language, 32,* 279–300.

Trabasso, T., & Suh, S. Y. (1993). Using talk-aloud protocols to reveal inferences during comprehension of text. *Discourse Processes, 16,* 3–34.

Trabasso, T., & van den Broek, P. (1985). Causal thinking and the representation of narrative events. *Journal of Memory and Language, 24,* 612–630.

Winston P. H. W. (1984). *Artificial Intelligence (2nd ed.).* Reading, MA: Addison-Wesley.

Wyer, R. S., & Collins, J. E. (1992). A theory of humor elicitation. *Psychological Review, 99,* 663–688.

Wyer, R. S., & Gordon, S. E. (1984). The cognitive representation of social information. In R. S. Wyer & T. K. Srull (Eds.), *Handbook of Social Cognition, Vol. 2* (pp. 73–150). Hillsdale, NJ: Lawrence Erlbaum Associates.

Wyer, R. S., & Ottati, V. (1993). Political information processing. In S. Iyengar & W. J. McGuire (Eds.), *Explorations in Political Psychology* (pp. 264–295). Durham, NC: Duke University Press.

Wyer, R. S., & Srull, T. K. (1986). Human cognition in its social context. *Psychological Review, 93,* 322–359.

6

The Big Picture: Is It a Story?

Reid Hastie
Nancy Pennington
University of Colorado

We just read this chapter by Schank and Abelson, who said that stories are the fundamental constituents of human memory, knowledge, and social communication. They are mostly right, and they are completely right that people who study cognitive and social psychology under emphasize the major role that social communication and higher-level mental structures play in everyday memory and thinking.

The authors do an excellent job of arguing that stories are the major form of everyday memory, thinking, and talking. They provide many compelling illustrations of this point, and they show how some obvious counterexamples (e.g., "scientific" facts, numerical cognition, memories of word meanings, and logical reasoning—their heartwarming discussion of whale suckling facts will be with us a long time) are saturated with narrative memory and reasoning processes and are probably not very important in everyday life, outside of the classroom, anyway.

They also provide striking examples of differential interpretation effects in domains where these effects are really dramatic: political "spin" interpretations of events like the Vincennes catastrophe and competing versions of personal conflicts in divorce. For some reason, social psychologists have not been very effective at producing dramatic perspective or role effects under laboratory conditions (there are a few notable exceptions), perhaps because the subjects' motivations for differential interpretation have been weak in the laboratory, or because the experimenters' emphasis on measuring bias has led to a focus on micro-level, quantifiable, dependent variables. This research reminds us of the story about the drunkard looking for his keys under the street lamp. However, Schank and Abelson show us where to look, and encourage future researchers to put the hobgoblins of methodological precision in the peanut gallery where they belong at this stage of the research endeavor.

Schank and Abelson also present useful ideas about how stories are constructed and applied to experience. They hypothesize that experiences "remind" a person of old story "skeletons" stored in long-term memory via "indexes," and that experience (when it is "understood") is fitted into a story form like that of the activated skeleton. They do not attempt to spell out detailed procedures for reminding, skeleton application, or skeleton (and index) creation; this specification is doubtless available in the form of computer programs written by the authors to perform these tasks (e.g., Riesbeck & Schank, 1989) and detailed expositions of the principles underlying the programs (Schank, 1982, 1986). Sometimes the two writers reminded us of the Hindu in the story about the two monks crossing the river. You see, the Hindu just glided across the surface of the torrential river; the Zen Buddhist started to walk across too, but then turned back and scrambled across, emerging drenched and battered, muttering angrily, "That's how you cross a river." The discussions of mechanisms for reminding (salience, availability, activation, and similarity—they warn us that this is an uncertain compass in this domain) and story skeleton modification to achieve different goals (distillation, combination, elaboration, captioning, adaptation—who could ever forget the delightful gas station planter story) are also insightful and instructive.

This chapter is an example of what cognitive science does best: a freewheeling, but rigorous, exploration of genuinely interesting ideas, unfettered by the "methods police" of conventional experimental psychology, or the "logic police" of traditional philosophical and linguistic analysis. In spite of (perhaps because of) the authors' proclivity to illustrate rather than prove, the chapter is worth a dozen or so closely argued essays on the definition of a story, or empirical demonstrations that actors and observers rate causal efficacy as 1.3 points differently on 22-point rating scales. (Of course, Abelson was doing this kind of thinking decades before he helped invent the field of cognitive science [see his many contributions on the subject of "cognitive consistency" and "belief systems," e.g., Abelson, Aronson, McGuire, Newcomb, Rosenberg, & Tannenbaum, 1968], and Schank was kicked out of "The Proper Linguists' Club" many years ago for the same kind of unruly behavior. Does this guy remind us of Groucho Marx, or what?)

However, as fine as this chapter is, it is not perfect. There were some sections that were just not clear to us, where the authors quit writing before we were finished reading. One example is in the second section on "Types of Knowledge Other Than Story-Related Knowledge." We never did understand the sentence that says, "The one thing we won't do is to opt for the theory that all knowledge is propositional, leaving episodes out entirely." What was the "propostional" versus "episodes" distinction? Are episodes complex entities composed of propositions, or what? Similarly, in the fifth section on "Storytelling and Memory," what did they mean by their distinction between story-based versus event-based memories? Were they alluding to a distinction between case-based versus abstraction-based story "skeletons," or what? Sometimes we felt like the characters in the story about the prisoners who told jokes to each other by the numbers.

We are erstwhile fellow-travelers with the authors (Abelson taught one of us most of what he knows about cognitive science), and within our home field of judgment and decision making, we are known as "the story guys." It is not surprising, then, that there were several places in the chapter where we wanted to pitch in and "help" the authors. You see, sometimes Schank and Abelson reminded us of the matador in their story about the bull who would not die. Other times they reminded us of the chef who always over-cooked the steak.

For example, a key precept at the beginning of their chapter is that ". . . knowledge is functional; it is structured not to satisfy an elegant logic, but to facilitate daily use." We couldn't agree more. This is the fundamental premise of our "explanation-based" approach to judgment and decision-making, and it is a good reason to expect that stories will pervade everyones' memories, thoughts, and conversations.

We made this discovery in our own research when we were initially surprised to discover that people making legal, diplomatic (Abelson had his fingers in this pie), business (Schank also had his fingers in this pie), and many other types of decisions talked and reasoned about stories (Pennington & Hastie, 1993a). Why did these people construct *stories* when they were asked to make *decisions?* As Schank and Abelson tell us, what could be more functional than to organize a large, complex, conflict-filled collection of evidence as a temporal narrative summary of "the truth," especially in social situations where communication, argumentation, and revision of both the evidence and the decisions based upon it are sure to follow the original, individual decision process.

However, we have also reviewed research in other decision-making tasks (e.g., medical diagnosis, electronic troubleshooting, software program debugging), and we found that stories were not the common mode for structuring evidence in these situations. We concluded there are many important everyday situations in which spatial (memories for rooms, buildings, geographic layouts), functional (memories for computer commands, physiological, botanical, physical systems), hierarchical (memories for laws and regulations, for rules of proper conduct, for television program and sports event schedules), argumentative (reasons for and against buying a product, supporting a political program, or hiring a job candidate), and other nonstory structures are the fundamental structures in memory (not to mention the many examples of academic knowledge that have been studied by cognitive scientists, but were not completely dismissed by Schank & Abelson).

To put it another way, the authors say that, "The real role for whales in memory is as a part of Jonah stories. . . . Everything else is just rote memorization that we did in school. . . ." Well, this may be true of whales if you live in Boulder or Chicago, but not if you are a whale hunter, and not if we are talking about mountain lions or collies or some other animal you do encounter in everyday life. Useful knowledge often takes forms other than stories. We are saying that sometimes Schank and Abelson reminded us of the kid who gets a new hammer and finds that everything around him looks like a nail.

We believe that a more general version of the "knowledge is functional" principle is the correct assumption. Knowledge in long-term memory will be structured to facilitate its use, but the particular uses will lead to different structures depending on functional considerations. Thus, when the primary uses are social decision making (e.g., jurors' decision making), attribution of responsibility (e.g., political discourse), gossiping and other forms of social storytelling (e.g., talking about a traffic accident or a divorce), we expect to find a lot of story structures. But, when the uses are navigational (e.g., around our office, around our city), mechanical (e.g., computer programming, playing sports), biological (e.g., getting a garden to grow, curing an ailment), and many others, we expect to find other explanatory structures. We believe that structure does follow function, but the most functional structure is not always a story.

Even more generally, we believe that the absolutely fundamental principle of cognitivism is that people attempt to create useful cognitive models of the external world. These situation models, images, mental models, or explanations (as they have been called by various scholars) tend to reflect essential and functionally relevant properties of the world. Because the world is experienced in time, these cognitive models will often have temporal order as a primary organizing feature, and people will often go a step further and structure temporal order as a story. However, spatial relations, causal relations (that are not stories), certain conceptual relations (e.g., in reasoning about mathematical relations, whether academic or everyday reasoning about quantities and other abstractions, and social conventions), even nonstory temporal relations can also compose the structures underlying these cognitive models of the world. What Schank and Abelson tell us, though, that is important, is that story structures are amazingly ubiquitous (but not, we think, universal).

This brings us to the claim that, "Virtually all human knowledge is based on stories." Is this a fruitful assertion, and are the counter arguments against the alternative, that other knowledge structures are common, worth making? This reminds us of the story in the chapter from *Annie Hall* where Woody Allen and Diane Keaton both say the man wants to have sex two or three times a week, but the woman says the man wants to have sex all the time, and the man says they almost never have sex. What are the facts, and what do they mean? What would a census of knowledge structures look like, and what is the definition of "story," so we would know how to count them? Surely, the "methods police" will be after Schank and Abelson for not defining elementary concepts such as "story," nor providing operationalizations so we could count them—this lapse will probably remind some critics of "Merkle's Boner." Even if we could count them and (heaven forfend) if some poor masters student actually did it, could we agree on whether there are too many or too few?

Finally, we suggest a distinction that we find useful in thinking about story construction processes in decision-making tasks. Sometimes a decision-maker is reminded of *one old story* that can be directly applied to comprehend new information. For example, occasionally a juror (much more frequently a judge or attorney) will say, "This case reminds me of another case I know about," or, "This case is just like Macbeth," or, "This is your basic kidnapping." Here comprehension seems to work much like Schank and Abelson have shown that it works when we are reading about airplane trips and visits to restaurants and dentists' offices. First, there is reminding; then there is fitting of the particular new information into the old story framework; then there is modification, often in the service of a social goal (to entertain, to explain, to justify, to persuade, etc.).

A second condition occurs when a person is reminded of *several old stories,* again the authors' theory about comprehension seems appropriate. It gets more complicated, because pieces of different old stories are selected and combined to produce a final framework, but the basic process is essentially the one so well described by Schank and Abelson.

Nevertheless, there is a third condition that we frequently observe in our juror decision-making research that seems to lie outside of the processes discussed by Schank and Abelson. Here a juror encounters a collection of new information that does not fit any simple combination of old stories. Our jurors still want to construct a cognitive model of the situation relevant to their decisions, and they still construct models in the form of stories, but we find that they rely on more elementary story construction processes than the selection and modification of old story templates. What they actually do is construct a new story from basic premises about human nature, social interaction, and other relevant world knowledge *plus* the particulars of the case they are attempting to decide (Pennington & Hastie, 1993b). Furthermore, the tools they use to construct a story include many of the quasilogical, plausible reasoning forms of the sort Schank and Abelson claim do not play a large role in everyday thinking. We also suspect that these same plausible reasoning tools are used a lot under the first two conditions when stories are applied, modified, and constructed from larger story pieces. Sometimes, Schank and Abelson reminded us of the politician whose solution to the social problems caused by teen-age pregnancy and alcohol abuse was a proposal to lower income taxes.

We do not think all comprehension involves squeezing new experiences into old templates. We do not agree with the (lousy) carpenter who once told us, "The basic rule of life is 'cut to fit, beat into place'." We think the most important point about story construction is that the fundamental goal of cognition is the construction of useful mental models of the outside world. People want to know what is happening around them. It is, nonetheless, remarkable how often the answer to this question takes the form of a story.

One of the great things about the Schank and Abelson chapter is their skillful use of stories as illustrations. Most of the stories are good ones, and our own comprehension processes will be enriched by having read them. But, there is one pair of stories that keeps reappearing in the Schank and Abelson oeuvre that we just do not get. This is, of course, the pair of stories about the overcooked steak and the too-long haircut. The steak's overcooked, you're stuck, but the haircut's too long, so you just ask the barber to keep cutting, right? This example reminds us of the circus performer who put a cork into an empty barrel, and then by blowing into another hole in the cask, blew the cork back out of the hole. As a friend said after the show, "It was a clever performance, but if the man had put his mouth to the cork hole and had blown the cask out of the bung hole, or if he had put his mouth to the cask and blown the bung out of the cork hole, or if he had put the cask to the bung hole and then blown the cork out of his mouth, it would have been much more interesting." But that's another story. . . .

REFERENCES

Abelson, R. P., Aronson, E., McGuire, W. J., Newcomb, T. M., Rosenberg, M. J., & Tannenbaum, P. H. (1968). *Theories of cognitive consistency: A sourcebook.* Chicago: Rand McNally.

Pennington, N., & Hastie, R. (1993a). A theory of explanation-based decision making. In G. Klein, J. Orasanu, R. Calderwood, and C. E. Zsambok (Eds.), *Decision making in action: Models and methods* (pp. 188–204). Norwood, NJ: Ablex.

Pennington, N., & Hastie, R. (1993b). Reasoning in explanation-based decision making. *Cognition, 49,* 123–163.

Riesbeck, C. K., & Schank, R. C. (1989). *Inside case-based reasoning.* Hillsdale, NJ: Lawrence Erlbaum Associates.

Schank, R. C. (1982). *Dynamic memory.* London: Cambridge University Press.

Schank, R. C. (1986). *Explanation patterns: Understanding mechanically and creatively.* Hillsdale, NJ: Lawrence Erlbaum Associates.

7

Stories Are Fundamental to Meaning and Memory: For Social Creatures, Could It Be Otherwise?

Stephen John Read
Lynn Carol Miller
University of Southern California

We applaud Schank and Abelson's focus on stories and their placement of them at the center of human cognitive processing. They argue that stories are highly functional, and they provide a number of compelling examples of this functionality. In our commentary, we focus on *why* stories are so functional and *why* people seem to use them so much. Our answer to these questions is somewhat different from that of Schank and Abelson. We propose that stories are so functional because social interaction is central for human beings, and stories are fundamentally about social interaction.

Historically, cognitive psychology and Artificial Intelligence (AI) have focused on knowledge of the physical world. With the notable exception of Schank and Abelson and their students, researchers in this tradition have placed knowledge of physical objects at the center of the cognitive system. Questions about the representation of this physical knowledge and how it is used have been central. In contrast, social knowledge has often been treated as peripheral, and derivative of object knowledge. The implicit research agenda was clear: First, understand the simpler case of how physical objects are represented, then simply transfer that knowledge to more complicated and messier social concepts.

This ordering of priorities, we argue, is precisely backward. For human beings, social knowledge is at the center of the cognitive system, and knowledge of physical objects is understood in terms of their relation to the social. From this perspective we see that stories are central to the human cognitive system because they capture the essence of social interaction, the structure of human action. We first elaborate this argument. Then, we discuss the role of stories in conversations and why the complexity of social interaction drove the development of stories and human evolution.

WHY SOCIAL KNOWLEDGE IS CENTRAL

As many have noted, human beings are highly social creatures, perhaps the most social of all animals. (Certainly our social relations are the most complex.) Most of our life takes place in interaction with others. We work in groups; we spend time with friends; we get married and have children; we go to school and learn in groups. Less positively, we fight wars, join gangs, sell and do drugs, and abuse our spouses and children. Social interaction is central to our most positive and our most negative experiences as human beings. It is hard to think of an aspect of everyday human behavior that does not involve the actual (or sometimes imagined) presence of other people. For all of this, a knowledge of human action is central.

The fundamental role of social interaction in psychological processes has been increasingly recognized in a wide range of areas in psychology, from developmental psychology to cognitive psychology and cognitive science. Although developmental psychologists have long been interested in social development, there has been a growing realization that social interaction plays a central role in cognitive development (e.g., Wozniak & Fisher, 1993). It is in the interaction between child and caretaker, and later with other children and adults, that the child learns to think about and negotiate the world. Social concepts, such as goals and intentionality, are readily learned by very young children and ascribed to objects that move "by themselves" (Gelman, 1990; Premack, 1990). This is true even for physical objects, such as cars or the sun, that appear to have self-generated motion; only over time does the child learn that this is not the case. This work suggests that readiness for inferring social intentionality is built in, and the child learns only with difficulty that such concepts do not apply to everything that moves seemingly "by itself."

Recently, developmental psychologists have become increasingly interested in children's theory of mind (Astington, Harris, & Olson, 1988; Whiten, 1991). Some authors have argued that the ability to take the perspective of the other, to recognize that other people are conscious, intentional actors like oneself is a fundamental part of being human. Without that awareness, one is unable to function as a social creature. For instance, several theorists (e.g., Frith, 1989; Leslie, 1991) have argued that the inability to take the perspective of others, the lack of recognition of others as intentional actors is at the root of *autism*. According to this position, the behavior of autistics is disordered precisely because they are unable to treat other people as social actors.

Researchers in cognitive science have also evinced a growing recognition that social interaction plays a major role in learning and the development of expertise, for example, in their increasing focus on situated action (e.g., Lave & Wenger, 1991; Suchman, 1987). Much of this work teaches us that true expertise is only developed through interaction with those who are more expert. Another impetus for cognitive science's growing interest in social interaction are the recent attempts to build interacting robots and more effective human–computer interfaces. Researchers have discovered that in the attempt to develop interacting agents that can successfully coordinate action, social concepts about an agent's model of the "state of mind" of the other agent are tremendously useful. Similar observations have been made in work on creating more useful and adaptive interfaces between humans and computers. Finally, there are indications that cognitive psychologists are beginning to realize that social categories and concepts are different in important ways from the more physically based categories that have been typically studied in cognitive psychology (e.g., Barsalou, 1991, 1992).

UNDERSTANDING THE PHYSICAL BY REFERENCE TO THE SOCIAL

Although interaction with others is central to human beings, we must also successfully interact with a physical world. However, even during interaction with the physical world, human action is central. Knowledge of the physical world is almost always taken with reference to human concerns. Rosch and her colleagues (Rosch, 1978; Rosch & Mervis, 1975) and others have demonstrated that the functional uses of objects play a central role in their representation. Barsalou (1985, 1991) in his work on conceptual representation and planning has made the case that the way objects relate to human goals is a central aspect of their representation. Furthermore, from an ecological approach to perception (Gibson, 1979) or social perception (Baron, 1988; McArthur & Baron, 1983; Zebrowitz, 1990), we see that a central part of the perception of an object is about what it *affords* for interaction. Recent work suggests that this "readiness" to infer functionality is with us from infancy. For example, Brown (1990) found that very young children (e.g., as young as 18 months) categorize objects on the basis of their functional properties (e.g., the object's hooked end could pull) but not on the basis of their nonfunctional properties (e.g., color). Brown's work increases the possibility that categorization on the basis of objects' functional properties may have deep roots in our ancestral past (Tooby & Cosmides, 1992). Why would categorizing objects this way be so adaptive? Because understanding functional properties of objects is central; it enables the development of successful plans. These plans are crucial to achieving everyday human goals and to continued survival.

WHY STORIES ARE CENTRAL

Schank and Abelson argue that stories are so central because of the functional role they play. For example, a major part of their argument is that stories are functional because they are useful memory structures. Stories are an efficient way to organize and store information, and they are also an efficient way to find it later when it is needed. Although this is undoubtedly true, we believe that Schank and Abelson are looking only at the surface, at a symptom of something else. The importance of stories has other, deeper roots. Stories serve important social goals. Historically, they enabled humans to gossip—far from a trivial activity. Gossip, it is argued, enabled the group to identify particular individuals and their deeds and misdeeds. It, thereby, enhanced group cohesiveness (Dunbar, 1992) and conformity to group norms and values regarding cooperation and principles of social exchange (Tooby & Cosmides, 1992). Stories also enabled individuals within a group to learn from the mistakes of others—even those who had died generations earlier—rather than via individual trial and error. In this way adaptive tales about both real and fictional human figures were undoubtedly central to the development of culture and human life as we know it. We argue that the major reason stories are so important is because they are fundamentally about human action. They provide a way to think about and describe social interaction, which is central to human concerns.

Nevertheless, granted that stories are efficient memory structures, the question remains why? One obvious answer is that stories form a richly connected network, with the numerous links providing numerous potential retrieval routes. Further, a story may provide many indices to the objects and events that are part of the story. But this only pushes the question back one level. Why are the concepts in a story so richly connected? Why are there so many possible retrieval routes? Why do stories provide so many indices to memory? We suggest that concepts in a story are so richly connected because they are made up of a number of social concepts that have rich and detailed representations. These representations are so rich and detailed because social concepts are so central to human functioning. People use these concepts all the time. In a very real sense, adult humans are social "experts" with twenty or more years of experience. Moreover, as much research has shown (Chi, Glaser, & Farr, 1988), one outstanding characteristic of experts is the rich and detailed representations of objects in their domain of expertise.

Further, successful social interaction requires that we plan our own behavior and understand the plans of others. Reminding helps us to do this. In fact, understanding the plans of others is frequently critical to making our own plans. A useful memory system should be reminded of the things that allow the individual to function and survive. Given the centrality of social interaction, one of the most useful things to be reminded of are the actions of oneself and other people.

Capturing the Essence of Social Interaction

We would like to suggest a further reason why stories are effective memory structures: The indices to stories are attributes, such as human goals, that are of tremendous intrinsic interest to human beings. Stories are about what happens to goals. In what other ways could one adequately capture the structure of human interaction?

Wants and needs are not only among the first concepts children communicate (Gelman, 1990). Concepts involving wants are also among the handful of universal concepts some linguists view as linguistic universals—primes common across all human cultures (Wierzbicka, 1992). Critical components of stories beyond basic "want" concepts also appear to be universal ones. Wierzbicka (1992) argued that these primes include the following: I, you, someone, something, this, say, want, don't want, feel, and think. Additional candidates she is currently investigating are these: know, where, good, when, can, like, the same, kind of, after, do, happen, bad, all, because, if, and two.

As Wierzbicka argued, her proposed list of hypothetical semantic primitives is not simply a list, "but a mini-language, with its own grammatical categories and its own syntax. Thus, the elements 'I', 'you', 'someone', and 'something' form something like a nominal class; the elements 'this' and 'the same' (or 'other') can be regarded as an analogue of determiners; 'good' and 'bad' as an analogue of adjectives: 'think', 'say', 'want', and 'know' as an analogue of verbs; and so on" (p. 10). From these primes, more complex concepts, specific to particular cultures, may be formed. (For a related attempt to identify a set of conceptual primitives, see Schank & Abelson, 1977.) Furthermore, in this mini-language, simple clauses can be formed, including, as Wierzbicka (1992) pointed out, the following:

I want this,
you do this,
this happened,
this person did something bad, and
something bad happened because of this.

These simple clauses capture important elements of story structure and argue that stories are universally basic to conversation and meaning making. This cross-cultural work and the developmental work described earlier suggest that, in many respects, humans appear to have a readiness, from the beginning of life, to hear and understand stories.

Stories as Event Structures

Sometimes Schank and Abelson talk as if stories take mundane events and somehow transform them into something different. However, we do not believe that stories transform events into something else. The structure of stories is the structure of human action. A number of psychologists (e.g., Miller, Galanter, & Pribram, 1960), starting at least with Roger Barker and his colleagues (Barker, 1963; Barker & Wright, 1955), have argued that human action has a structure consisting of chains of episodes, where the episodes consist of the actors' goals, the reasons for those goals, the plans enacted to achieve those goals, and the outcomes of those plans, for example, what happens to the actors' goals. Perhaps, not surprisingly, work on text comprehension has identified a similar structure for stories and narratives (Mandler, 1978; Mandler & Johnson, 1977; Rumelhart, 1977; Schank & Abelson, 1977; Stein & Glenn, 1979). Thus, from this point of view stories are basically idealized, cleaned-up *event structures*.

Stories in Ideology and the Transmission of Cultural Values

Schank and Abelson, relying on the work of Roseman (1993), note that various ideologies have morality plays at their core. They talk about good guys and bad guys, and tell us how the good guys can triumph over the bad guys: For example, left wing Democrats lay the troubles of the world at the feet of fat, greedy capitalists, and right wing Republicans rant about secular humanists or "limousine liberals." Upon reflection it is not surprising that this should be so. Again, we are talking about human action and the competition between different groups about goals, identity, and how to live. Further, ideology is about how people should be treated and how typically scarce resources are to be allocated. To the extent that people disagree about these values, there will be conflicts over goals.

Values may differ not only within cultures, but between them. Moreover, values may shift as humans adjust to differing environmental and other social conditions. Still, people tell stories, different stories, but stories whose purpose may be to make important values salient for local survival. For example, anthropologists (e.g., Cashdan, 1980) have argued that when food availability is variable, as among the !Kung San, individuals are more apt to share, and the value of sharing is emphasized, not only in prescriptions (one should share), but in the stories about persons (and descriptions of persons) who do not (e.g., he was really stingy). Across cultures, telling stories—whether involving basic structures or more culture-specific concepts—are the stuff of cultural values and cultural transmission (D'Andrade & Strauss, 1992; Fisher, 1987; Turner, 1980; White, 1980). It is easy to speculate that stories are ancient, as old as words.

Social Concepts As Stories

Stories are so embedded in social interaction that even concepts not considered to be themselves "stories" can be thought of as containing implicit, abbreviated stories. Schank and Abelson (this volume, chap. 1) make a similar point when they refer to situational concepts such as "betrayal, " "undermining my confidence," or "ordering me around" as concepts that summarize and index stories. Although we agree with Schank and Abelson that not every word or phrase indexes a story, we would argue that humans may have developed many complex social concepts precisely because they are economical "stand-ins" for full stories. These complex social concepts (referring to traits, emotions, and roles, as well as situations)—so much a part of natural everyday conversation—afford efficient communication while implicating the critical elemental units (e.g., goals, plans, resources, and so forth) of social stories.

To illustrate this, let us consider trait concepts. Miller and Read (1991) have argued that many trait terms serve as economical units for implicit storylike structures. For example, a revengeful person is someone ("y") who has perceived (probably on multiple occasions) that another person or group ("x") hurt them, and has the resources at some later point to hurt x in return, and does so. Similarly, a person might be described as "lazy." The implicit story here might go something like this: A person, ("x") doesn't do what he should do, but x could do the behavior if x wanted to. Others respond negatively to x, because x's behavior directly or indirectly causes them harm (e.g., not achieving goals because of x's failure, having to make up for x's lack of effort). Because concepts economically capture the stories, our language isn't explicitly a series of stories inside of stories[1].

Social concepts referring to traits (e.g., lazy, vindictive, manipulative, spoiled, helpful, generous, etc.) are apt to implicitly involve—among other things—a consideration of actor goals, relationships among social actors, behaviors, and consequences of behaviors. Thus, we typically refer to a person as lazy if that person consistently does not do what he or she should do (meet the demands of a job or social role), or avoids enacting the appropriate behaviors although the person has the capability to do so. On the other hand, we typically refer to a person as generous when he or she wants to give to others and does so at a level above and beyond what is typically expected. Furthermore when the !Kung San (Cashdan, 1980; Tooby & Cosmides, 1992), mentioned earlier, refer to individuals as stingy, they are implicitly telling a story about that person ("x" had extra food he didn't need; others needed the food; "x" wanted to keep the food; "x" kept the food; "x" is bad). Only when we question another's choice of trait adjectives—or abbreviated stories—do we typically ask for the "full story," as in when we ask, "Why do you think Sally is manipulative?" or say, "Oh, don't you remember the time. . . ." Stories are units of goal configurations, behavior, and consequences. The most typical ones in a given culture are abbreviated and indexed via common social concepts (e.g, stingy for the aforementioned !Kung San), precisely because they are so common and culturally important for the transmission of particular contextualized values; these concepts help to economize their communication.

We have stories for a variety of social concepts, not just for traits. For example, Read and Miller (1993) argued that to consider whether a person assumed the role of "rapist" means determining whether an individual filled a number of conceptually relevant slots in a particular way. For example, a rapist is someone who wanted to have sex with another, maneuvered to achieve this goal (e.g., pursued strategies and used resources towards this end), and committed the rape despite adequate reason to believe that the victim did not want to have sex. Furthermore, in American culture, jurists may be more apt to assign this role to a defendant if they believe that the victim was innocent (i.e., did not "put herself at risk" for the rape, either via suggestive clothing, being in a "pick up joint" such as a bar or night club, or going off with a stranger alone), did not engage in any behavior that would suggest sexual interest to a reasonable person (i.e., wasn't flirtatious, didn't allow other forms of intimacy then or earlier in this relationship), physically resisted the rapist

---

[1]This is a fascinating theme that served as the basis for an alternative science fiction world in one episode of *Star Trek: The Next Generation*. The captain of the starship, *Enterprise*, encounters a foreign culture in which concepts are represented not via single words, but rather via stories of culture-specific tales. For example, the concept of conflict is communicated by telling the story of a specific historical conflict between two leaders. Jean Luc Picard must learn this cumbersome way of communicating using stories—inside of stories—in order to avoid conflict between his ship and the members of this new world.

(preferably resulting in evidence of such resistance), and was considerably weaker than the rapist (i.e., the aggressor was capable of forcing the victim against her will). Furthermore, conviction would be more likely to the extent that few if any behavioral sequences typically associated with sexual scripts involved in consensual sex were present. For example, in a Texas rape case, a defendant may not have been indicted initially because the victim (who was attacked by the man who had broken into her home) suggested that the defendant wear a condom, a request that might have been associated with "normal" consensual sexual scripts, or perhaps—in the minds of jurors in Texas—even with sexual scripts in which the woman is experienced (not naive or innocent).

A "full story," that would perhaps be most likely to lead someone in this culture to believe that this role, rapist, should be assigned might look like this: This man ("y") wanted to have sex with this woman ("x"). She did not want to have sex with him. She was naive and innocent (had minimal experience with men who might try to take advantage of her), exhibited strict religious adherence to an injunction against sex before marriage, and did not by her actions or attire suggest that she was interested in having sex with him (adding further weight to her being unlikely to have sex voluntarily). He was very powerful. He maneuvered her into a secluded, private place against her wishes and, despite her screams and struggles that resulted in severe bodily injury, he overpowered her.

We can also consider a more "typical" role, such as teacher. What do we mean by a teacher? A teacher is someone who (presumably) wants to play an instrumental role in bringing about learning (for a pupil). A good teacher has the motivation, plans, skills, and knowledge to effectively and routinely engage the pupil to achieve these goals, and does so. One cannot be a teacher, however, in isolation. To be a teacher, one must have a willing student with compatible goals. Note that both of the social concepts discussed require the presence of others (e.g., victim, teacher).

Miller, Cody, and McLaughlin (1994) argued that the "deep structures" of such social concepts as situations, traits, roles, and emotions have a remarkable overlap: Goal based and relational concepts appear central to each class of social concepts and to story-making in general. For instance, consider the concept of situation as a location. Although we may at first think about the physical attributes of such a situation, upon reflection it is clear that what constitutes the core of our concepts of most situations is the kinds of human actions that are enacted within them.

Critical to the concept of a particular physical situation is an understanding of the different kinds of human action that are typically and appropriately performed in that context. For instance, when we think of a church, we largely define it by the human actions that are performed within it: mass, marriages, baptisms, and funerals. Church as a concept would be largely meaningless separate from those actions. Similarly, restaurants are largely defined by the social interactions that occur within them.

However, situations can also be construed in more psychological terms that transcend physical locations (Miller, Cody, & McLaughlin, 1994). For example, we can think of situations as challenging, threatening, inspiring, dangerous, or conflict-ridden. All these adjectives may themselves implicate stories about the goals, resources, and interpersonal relationships of individuals in those "situations." For example, a challenging situation is one in which an individual assesses that they have the resources to effectively enact plans to achieve the desired goals: There may be physical and relational obstacles to goal achievement, but the individual perceives that he or she has the resources to overcome these. In many respects, although personologists and social psychologists often act like we can, we cannot draw a fine line between social concepts used to refer to persons and those used to refer to situations: the knowledge structures that underlie them are intertwined and interconnected. Although the focal point of the story may differ, these social concepts all tell stories about persons and what happens to them. Such concepts are the stuff of everyday conversations.

STORIES IN CONVERSATION

Although we readily admit that stories are the stuff of conversation, the question remains, why? If the most interesting thing to people is other people, why wouldn't we spend most of our time talking about them? And, how would we talk about people and their interactions other than with stories?

Another way to approach this question is to think about the reasons why people engage in conversation. We converse in order to understand the world, exchange information, persuade, cooperate, deal with problems, and plan for the future. Other human beings are a central focus in each of these domains: We wish to understand other people and their social interactions; we need to deal with problems involving others; and other people are at the heart of many of our plans for the future. If this is so, then we need to talk about the actions of ourselves and other people, and as we have argued previously, the most natural way to talk about people is in terms of stories. For instance, to understand others and their interactions, we need to understand their goals and plans, and how these goals and plans interact with the goals and plans of others. Further, we need to understand why people come to have the goals they do, and we need to understand what happens to their goals. The same issues arise when we attempt to solve social problems. Problems in social interaction typically involve conflicts over goals and plans. To deal with these conflicts, we must understand what underlies them.

In fact, there is a growing literature that focuses on the accounts people offer of the events that happen to them (Antaki, 1988; Harvey, Orbuch, & Weber, 1992; McLaughlin, Cody, & Read, 1992). Many researchers argue that people tell stories because stories help us understand what happened. They do so in several ways: They provide a structure for what happened; they allow us to relate the event to other similar events; and, if possible, they enable us to apply lessons learned in earlier contexts to the present event.

HOW THE HUMAN GOT ITS STORY: THE
EVOLUTIONARY SIGNIFICANCE OF STORIES

Why are stories so central to memory, and why are they more accessible and easier to deal with than "purer" kinds of knowledge, such as mathematics or formal logic? Stories are directly and unavoidably related to what we do every day. They are about the stuff of everyday social interaction. Moreover, the ability to successfully interact with other human beings is central to human survival. Thus, it should be no surprise that we are so good with stories. They are what we need (and needed) to survive. It is only in recent evolutionary history that more formal kinds of knowledge, such as formal logic or mathematics, have had any real implications for survival. A knowledge of human action is far more important and functional than are various kinds of "pure" knowledge, such as logic or mathematics.

We have been arguing that stories are so important because of the centrality of the social in human cognition. At this point we would like to make a stronger point. Stories may be the only possible way to deal with the enormous complexity of human social interaction. The social interaction of humans is considerably more complex than that of any other animal, including other primates.

Numerous scholars (e.g., Barkow, 1989; Byrne & Whiten, 1988; Carrithers, 1991; Dunbar, 1992; Jolly, 1969; Humphrey, 1976; Kummer, 1982) have proposed that human intelligence developed primarily to deal with the complexities of social interaction. Carrithers (1991), following Humphrey (1976) and Byrne and Whiten (1988), has argued that the ability to manage ever more complex forms of social interaction would have been of adaptive advantage for our ancestors, and would have been selected for evolutionarily. He says, "An increasing capacity to live in groups, to vary the organization of these groups, and to create ever-more complex forms of cooperation within them would, for many reasons, have been to the advantage of members of our species" (p. 313).

Furthermore, Dunbar (1992) noted that among primates, humans maintain the largest social groups. Moreover, he argued that as primate group size grew, so too did the ability to process complex information. He also argued that "there is a species specific upper limit to group size which is set by purely cognitive constraints: animals cannot maintain the cohesion and integrity of groups larger than a size set by the information processing capacity of their neocortex . . . the neocortical constraint seems to be on the number of relationships that an animal can keep track of in a complex, continuously changing social world" (p. 681). Dunbar argues that, unlike other primates who maintain social cohesion and bonding via grooming behaviors, humans, in order to maintain the larger social groups advantageous to survival, could not simply groom: The time constraints of socially interacting with all group members would have been prohibitive. Instead, he argues, humans developed language as an alternative, time-efficient, bonding mechanism. In support of this contention, Dunbar (1992) found that gossip about relationships and personal experiences constituted as much 60% of human conversational time.

Carrithers also noted two things that seem to distinguish human social interaction from the social interaction of other animals, and that seem responsible for its greater complexity. First, human social interaction often has a very long time line. We care not just about the immediate moment, but often about how events unfold over a span of time, from minutes and hours up to lifetimes or generations. Second, humans engage in a wide array of social relationships. Consider, for example, our numerous kin relationships: parent, uncle or aunt, child, nephew, and so forth. Beyond familial roles, there is an even greater assortment of human roles, most of them creations of our social structures, that individuals often concurrently assume. Human role complexity far outstrips that of the typical member of any nonhuman primate troupes. Further, consider the variety of goals and the ways in which humans have managed to transform even biologically given goals, such as needs for food and sex, into new forms. Think also about what happens when individuals interact and attempt to negotiate among all these different roles, relations, and goals.

This point of view suggests that the cognitive system should tend to specialize on those processes and forms of representation that are most effective in managing social interaction with others. Similarly, Tooby and Cosmides (1992) argued that the need for complex representations or mental models of others' goals was necessary to keep track of individual members of the group and their tendencies to cooperate or to lie and cheat. Beyond the limit of our typical human group sizes, however, we humans have difficulty maintaining individualized representations, raising the fascinating possibility that we characterize "out-group" members in stereotypical ways (Dunbar, 1992) because of cognitive constraints.

Carrithers (1991) argued that human beings have developed a unique capacity among primates that allows them to negotiate among these complexities and effectively manage social interaction. He said:

It is this capacity which I want to designate as narrativity, a capacity to cognize not merely immediate relations between oneself and another, but many-sided human interactions carried out over a considerable period. We might say: humans understand *characters,* which embody the understanding of rights, obligations, expectations, propensities and intentions in oneself and many different others; and *plots,* which show the consequences and evaluations of a multifarious flow of actions. Narrativity, that is, consists not merely in telling stories, but of understanding complex nets of deeds and attitudes. Another way to put this would be to say that human beings perceive any current action within a larger temporal envelope, and within that envelope they perceive any given actions, not as a response to the immediate circumstances, or current mental state of an interlocutor or of oneself, but as part of an unfolding story. But characters with their relationships are also set in a flow of events, a plot, with its sense of plans, situations, acts and outcomes. Plots embody what a character or characters did to, or about, or with some other character or characters, for what reasons, and what followed on from that. To comprehend a plot is therefore to have some notion of the temporal dimension of social complexity. This complexity arises from a distinctly human form of causality in which people do things because of what others think and because of how others' places thereby change with respect to their own. By means of stories humans cognize not just thoughts and not just situations, but the metamorphosis of thoughts and situations in a flow of action. (pp. 310–311)

In short, it is because of the social, and the need to effectively manage social interactions, that we developed stories—stories made for the cognitively complex humans that we are. It is our stories that make us human.

REFERENCES

Antaki, C. (1988). *Analysing everyday explanations: A casebook of methods.* Beverly Hills, CA: Sage.

Astington, J. W., Harris, P. W., & Olson, D. R. (1988). *Developing theories of mind.* Cambridge, England: Cambridge University Press.

Baron, R. M. (1988). An ecological framework for establishing a dual-mode theory of social knowing. In D. Bar-Tal & A. W. Kruglanski (Eds.), *The social psychology of knowledge.* (pp. 48–82). Cambridge, England: Cambridge University Press.

Barker, R. G. (1963). (Ed.), *The stream of behavior.* New York: Appleton-Century-Crofts.

Barker, R. G., & Wright, H. (1955). *Midwest and its children.* Evanston, IL: Row Peterson.

Barkow, J. H. (1989). *Darwin, sex, and status: Biological approaches to mind and culture.* Toronto: University of Toronto Press.

Barsalou, L. W. (1985). Ideals, central tendency, and frequency of instantiation as determinants of graded structures in categories. *Journal of Experimental Psychology: Learning, Memory, and Cognition, 11,* 629–654.

Barsalou, L. W. (1991). Deriving categories to achieve goals. In G. H. Bower (Ed.), *The psychology of learning and motivation: Advances in research and theory* (Vol. 27, pp. 1–64). New York: Academic Press.

Barsalou, L. W. (1992). *Cognitive Psychology: An overview for cognitive scientists.* Hillsdale, NJ: Lawrence Erlbaum Associates.

Brown, A. (1990). Domain-specific principles affect learning and transfer in children. *Cognitive Science, 14,* 107–133.

Byrne, R. W., & Whiten, A. (1988). *Machiavellian intelligence: Social expertise and the evolution of intellect in monkeys, apes and humans.* Oxford: Oxford University Press.

Carrithers, M. (1991). Narrativity: Mindreading and making societies. In A. Whiten (Ed.), *Natural theories of mind: evolution, development, and simulation of everyday mindreading.* (pp. 305–317). Oxford, England: Basil Blackwell.

Cashdan, E. (1980). Egalitarianism among hunters and gathers. *American Anthropologist, 82,* 116–120.

Chi, M. T. H., Glaser, R., & Farr, M. J. (1988). *The nature of expertise.* Hillsdale, NJ: Lawrence Erlbaum Associates.

D'Andrade, R., & Strauss, C. (1992). *Human motives and cultural models.* Cambridge, England: Cambridge University Press.

Dunbar, R. I. M. (1993). Co-evolution of neocortex size, group size and language in humans. *Behavioral and Brain Sciences, 16,* 681–735.

Fisher, W. R. (1987). *Human communication as narration: Toward a philosophy of reason, value, and action.* Columbia, SC: University of South Carolina Press.

Frith, U. (1989). *Autism: Explaining the enigma.* Oxford, England: Basil Blackwell.

Gelman, R. (1990). First principles organize attention to and learning about relevant data: Number and the animate-inanimate distinction as examples. *Cognitive Science, 14,* 79–106.

Gibson, J. J. (1979). *The ecological approach to visual perception.* Boston: Houghton Mifflin.

Harvey, J. H., Orbuch, T. L., & Weber, A. L. (1992). *Attributions, accounts and close relationships.* New York: Springer-Verlag.

Humphrey, N. K. (1976). The social function of intellect. In P. P. G. Bateson, and R. A. Hinde (Eds.), *Growing Points in Ethology*. Cambridge, England: Cambridge University Press.

Jolly, A. (1969). Lemur social behaviour and primate intelligence. *Science, 153*, 501–506.

Kummer, H. (1982). Social knowledge in free-ranging primates. In D. Griffen (Ed.), *Animal Mind— Human Mind* (pp. 113–130). Berlin: Springer-Verlag.

Lave, J., & Wenger, E. (1991). *Situated learning: Legitimate peripheral participation*. Cambridge, England: Cambridge University Press.

Leslie, A. M. (1991). The theory of mind impairment in autism: Evidence for a modular mechanism of development. In A. Whiten (Ed.), *Natural theories of mind: evolution, development, and simulation of everyday mindreading*. (pp. 63–78). Oxford, England: Basil Blackwell.

McArthur, L. Z., & Baron, R. M. (1983). Toward an ecological theory of social perception. *Psychological Review, 90*, 215–247.

Mandler, J. M. (1978). A code in the node: The use of a story schema in retrieval. *Discourse Processes, 1*, 14–35.

Mandler, J. M., & Johnson, N. S. (1977). Remembrance of things parsed: Story structure and recall. *Cognitive Psychology, 9*, 111–151.

McLaughlin, M. L., Cody, M. J., & Read, S. J. (1992). *Explaining one's self to others: Reason-giving in a social context*. Hillsdale, NJ: Lawrence Erlbaum Associates.

Miller, G. A., Galanter, E., & Pribram, K. (1960). *Plans and the structure of behavior*. New York: Holt, Rinehart, & Winston.

Miller, L. C., Cody, M. J., & McLaughlin, M. L. (1994). Situations and goals as fundamental constructs in interpersonal communication research. In M. Knapp (Ed.), *Handbook of Interpersonal Communication* (pp. 162–198). Newberry Park, CA: Sage Publications.

Miller, L.C., & Read, S. J. (1991). On the coherence of mental models of persons and relationships: A knowledge structure approach. In G. J. O. Fletcher & F. Fincham (Eds.), *Cognition in close relationships*. (pp. 69–99). Hillsdale, NJ: Lawrence Erlbaum Associates.

Premack, D. (1990). The infant's theory of self-propelled objects. *Cognition, 36*, 1–16.

Read, S. J., & Miller, L. C. (1993). Rapist or "regular guy": Explanatory coherence in the construction of mental models of others. *Personality and Social Psychology Bulletin, 19*, 526–540.

Rosch, E. (1978). Principles of categorization. In E. Rosch & B. Lloyd (Eds.), *Cognition and Categorization*. Hillsdale, NJ: Lawrence Erlbaum Associates.

Rosch, E., & Mervis, C. B. (1975). Family resemblances: Studies in the internal structure of categories. *Cognitive Psychology, 7*, 573–605.

Roseman, I. J. (1993). The psychology of strongly held beliefs: Theories of ideological structure and individual attachment. In R. C. Schank & E. J. Langer (Eds.), *Beliefs, reasoning, and decision making: Psycho-logic in honor of Bob Abelson*. Hillsdale, NJ: Lawrence Erlbaum Associates.

Rumelhart, D. E. (1977). Understanding and summarizing brief stories. In D. LaBerge & J. Samuels (Eds.), *Basic processes in reading and comprehension* (pp. 265–303). Hillsdale, NJ: Lawrence Erlbaum Associates.

Schank, R. C., & Abelson, R. P. (1977). *Scripts, plans, goals, and understanding*. Hillsdale, NJ: Lawrence Erlbaum Associates.

Stein, N. L., & Glenn, C. G. (1979). An analysis of story comprehension in elementary school children. In R. O. Freedle (Ed.), *New directions in discourse processing* (Vol. 2, pp. 83–107). Norwood, NJ: Ablex.

Suchman, L. A. (1987). *Plans and situated actions: The problem of human-machine communication*. Cambridge, England: Cambridge University Press.

Tooby, J. & Cosmides, L. (1992). The psychological foundations of culture. In J. H. Barkow, L. Cosmides, & J. Tooby (Eds.), *The Adapted Mind: Evolutionary Psychology and the Generation of Culture*. New York: Oxford University Press.

Turner, V. (1980). Social dramas and stories about them. *Critical Inquiry, 7*, 141–168.

White, H. (1980). The value of narrativity in the representation of reality. *Critical Inquiry, 7*, 5–27.

Whiten, A. (Ed.). (1991). *Natural theories of mind: Evolution, development and simulation of everyday mindreading.* Oxford, England: Basil Blackwell.

Whiten, A., & Byrne, R. W. (1988). The Machiavellian intelligence hypothesis. In R. Byrne & A. Whiten (Eds.), *Machiavellian Intelligence* (pp. 1–9). Oxford: Oxford University Press.

Wierzbicka, A. (1992). *Semantics, culture, and cognition: Universal human concepts in culture-specific configurations.* New York: Oxford University Press.

Wozniak, R. H., & Fischer, K. W. (1993). *Development in context: Acting and thinking in specific environments.* Hillsdale, NJ: Lawrence Erlbaum Associates.

Zebrowitz, L. A. (1990). *Social Perception.* Pacific Grove, CA: Brooks/Cole.

8

Stories About Stories

David C. Rubin
Duke University

We must be wary of the possibility that knowledge in one domain may be organized according to principles different from knowledge in another. Perhaps there is no single set of rules and relations for constructing all potential knowledge bases at will. A desire for generality and elegance might inspire a theorist to seek a "universal" knowledge system. But if you try to imagine the simultaneous storage of knowledge about how to solve partial differential equations . . . how to write song lyrics, and how to get fed when you are hungry, you will begin to glimpse the nature of the problems. (Schank & Abelson, 1977, p. 3)

There are two modes of cognitive functioning, two modes of thought, each providing distinctive ways of ordering experience, of constructing reality. . . . Efforts to reduce one mode to the other or to ignore one at the expense of the other inevitably fail to capture the rich diversity of thought. . . . A good story and a well-formed argument are different natural kinds. (Bruner, 1986, p. 11)

Bruner is an optimist. There are two modes of thought, but two are not enough. Schank and Abelson were right in 1977; all knowledge cannot be reduced to one system, even if that system is stories. Before pursuing this thesis, I need to briefly describe Bruner's claim for different natural kinds. According to Bruner, a good story is not a good argument. A good story convinces you of its lifelikeness, believability, or verisimilitude. A good argument convinces you of its truth. A good argument has consistency and noncontradiction. It is either conclusive or not. Whereas a good argument provides universal truth conditions, a good story makes particular connections among particular events. It endows experience with meaning. It locates action in time and place.

In *Knowledge and Memory: The Real Story,* Schank and Abelson do well what they have done well in the past (Schank & Abelson, 1977); they paint in broad strokes a bold theory that addresses important issues. This strength carries with it this weakness: Earlier, often more cautious, attempts at the same issues are often ignored, both when they are congruent and, more importantly, when they might lead to modifications. The elegance of *The Real Story* is that for the genre of scientific papers, the presentation is remarkably consistent with the theory. *The Real Story* claims a privileged position for stories at the same time it makes use of the narrative style of stories. In Bruner's terms the target article usually does not argue a consistent point, it tells a story. Carefully selected anecdotes and experiments are skillfully mixed into a convincing, believable narrative. As the authors note, very strong claims are changed into strong claims and back to very strong claims with little attempt to carry a set of unchanging claims through to their logical conclusion for experimental results. If Bruner's dichotomy is accepted, this distinction in style between a story and a well-formed argument is not trivial. Use of the narrative mode takes *The Real Story* out of one realm of discourse and puts it into another. It affects what is evidence, what are the goals, and what makes a good paper. Similar tensions exist in much of psychology (Bruner, 1990). Should psychological explanation be more like explanation in history (White, 1981) or explanation in physics? I return to this point at the end of the commentary in dealing with the broader issue of what is needed to do science. For now I will examine *The Real Story* more narrowly as a psychological theory.

STORY IMPERIALISM AND TALKING HEADS

The three central claims of the target article are the following:

1. Virtually all human knowledge is based on stories constructed around past experiences.
2. New experiences are interpreted in terms of old stories.
3. The content of story memories depends on whether and how they are told to others, and these reconstituted memories form the basis of the individual's "remembered self." (p. 1)

As the authors note, these claims change a bit over the course of their article, but they remain the central claims. Thus, there is a claim for a schema theory (Alba & Hasher, 1983; Brewer & Nakamura, 1984; Rubin, 1995), but one in which stories are the only form of schema. As I have done in the past (Hyman & Rubin, 1990; Rubin & Kontis, 1983; Rubin, Stoltzfus, & Wall, 1991; Rubin, Wallace, & Houston, 1993), I provide evidence against the claim that stories (and meaning more generally construed) are the only basis for representation, and thus for such schema-driven behavior. However, first let us examine how stories get to be so important to *The Real Story* in the first place.

In order to privilege the status of stories, the target article strips away the physical world, leaving us two people using the oral–aural mode of communication, but not interacting with the rest of the world in any way. The situation the reader is asked to imagine is someone telling someone else a story in a social situation devoid of things and physical tasks. There is no context, no objects to manipulate, no work to accomplish, and no written document or other artifacts to construct. One can imagine two professors professing, or the context-free, disembodied talking heads of de Saussure (de Saussure, 1966; Harris, 1987; Smith, 1994). There is nothing left to do but talk. In this talking-heads model, "Two fundamental problems stand out: How do people map natural language strings into a representation of their meaning? How do people encode thoughts into natural language strings?" (Schank & Abelson, 1977, p. 7). That is, for the talking heads, the problem is how to transfer meaning over a verbal channel. If one were to imagine two people building a house, fixing a car, or programming a computer together, then there would still be language strings and stories to encode and decode, but there would be more. There would be a world to be understood, to be manipulated, and to serve as cues; and there would be goals to be met involving the immediate physical environment, not just representations (Norman, 1988; Zhang & Norman, 1994). Stories would help, but so would perceptual and motor representations. Stories would remind (i.e., cue) the people of other stories, but so would the configuration of objects and motor movements. This would be true, even if for a period the people involved were asked only to talk to each other. *The Real Story* is not the first to make this context-freeing move. A standard move in establishing linguistics as a separate field was to strip away all context leaving disembodied language as the isolated, reified object of study (e.g., Chomsky, 1965; de Saussure, 1966).

There are two areas of research in which I am involved, autobiographical memory and oral traditions, that also use the oral–aural mode of transmission, and that also usually strip away the physical world. For these areas of research, stories are the central organizing mechanism, but even in these areas other forms of organization play important roles. I will examine these two areas in turn to demonstrate ways of lessening *The Real Story*'s story imperialism.

AUTOBIOGRAPHICAL MEMORY

Stories are central to *autobiographical memory,* and considerations of narrative structure pervade the area of research. *The Real Story*'s claim that "the content of story memories depends on whether and how they are told to others, and these reconstituted memories form the basis of the individual's "remembered self" (p. 1) is a common one in the literature. For example, in discussing especially vivid, or flashbulb, memories, Brown and Kulik (1977) noted that reports of such memories tend to have several canonical categories such as the place, ongoing event, informant, affect on others, own affect, and aftermath. In discussing this, Neisser (1982) noted that these may not be properties of flashbulb memories at all, but rather properties of the narrative genre used to report any news. Thus these autobiographical memories are shaped by "how they are told to others." Similarly, in trying to account for the vividness of such memories, Rubin and Kozin (1984) made the claim that all memories start out as clear vivid memories, but then most fade. The ones that remain are the ones that "are told to others," rehearsed, or otherwise practiced, and they are shaped by "how they are told to others." The idea that the way memories "are told to others" shapes their final form extends to even the most mundane autobiographical memories. For instance, Barsalou (1988) asked people to recall events from their previous summer in the order in which they came to mind. The structures Barsalou formulated to describe and explain his data, which were based in part on Schank and Abelson's work (1977; Schank, 1982), could be considered either as properties of a memory system or as properties of the narrative structure used to describe those memories to another.

Many other researchers, also not mentioned in *The Real Story,* considered narrative structure central to the understanding of autobiographical memory. Some come from a psychoanalytic framework (Schafer, 1981; Spence, 1982). Others, such as Robinson (1981), are early attempts by cognitive psychologists to integrate theories of narrative from linguistics and folklore into psychology. More recently, Barclay (1986; Barclay & Smith, 1992) examined the schematic nature of autobiographical memory and the way it relates to the local and general culture in which the individual is located, leading to the "conversational nature of autobiographical remembering" (Barclay & Smith, 1992, p. 82). Fitzgerald (1986, 1988, 1992) used concepts like "narrative thought" and "self narratives" to account for autobiographical memory and the way it changes over the lifespan and with mood shifts. Freeman (1993) tied narrative to autobiographical memory in a more humanistic approach, and on the more applied side, Wagenaar, van Koppen, and Crombag (1993) documented the all too central role of a good story in the legal system. In addition to the pioneering work of Nelson (1993) cited in *The Real Story,* there has been detailed analysis of the narrative structure of autobiographical memory as observed in social situations, especially in the social situation of parents teaching their children the narrative conventions used in telling, and therefore in having, autobiographical memories (Fivush & Reese, 1992; Miller, Potts, Fung, Hoogstra, & Mintz, 1990; Miller & Sperry, 1988). Thus, autobiographical memory research provides abundant support for some of the claims of *The Real Story,* but not for the claim that stories are the only form of representation.

To see that other forms of representation are needed to describe autobiographical memory narratives, consider Brewer's (1986, 1992) definition of autobiographical memory based on the psychological and philosophical literature, and on his own phenomenological reports. What is being called autobiographical memory here and in *The Real Story,* Brewer defines as *personal memories.* Here are the main points of his definition:

> A personal memory is a recollection of a particular episode from an individual's past. It frequently appears to be a "reliving" of the individual's phenomenal experience during that earlier moment. The contents almost always include reports of visual imagery, with less frequent occurrences of other forms of imagery. . . . A personal memory is accompanied by a belief that the remembered episode was personally experienced by the self. . . . Finally, personal memories are typically accompanied by a belief that they are a veridical record of the originally experienced episode. This does not mean that they are, in fact, veridical. (Brewer, 1986, pp. 34–35)

The Real Story stresses the narrative structure of autobiographical memories, which Brewer does not deny. However, Brewer adds another form of representation, *imagery*. This imagery and the accompanying sense of reliving is a distinguishing feature of autobiographical memories, or personal memories in Brewer's terms. My autobiographical memory of writing this commentary involves an image of me, at home, correcting the text. I have no image or autobiographical memory of reading Schank and Abelson (1977), but I know that I did read the book. Imagery shows up as a characteristic of other researchers' ideas about autobiographical memory, such as that seen in work on flashbulb memories (Winograd & Neisser, 1992). It would be hard to build the self that *The Real Story* wants to build without images. Yet this form of representation is not reducible to a story. It is a different natural kind.

Imagery is a central feature (as close to a defining feature as one can get) of what most people mean by the term autobiographical memory. The argument is that *The Real Story* is incomplete. After reviewing the next domain of knowledge, I will argue that this is not a minor omission, but one that will repeat and will require a basic change in the conceptualization of cognitive processes outlined in *The Real Story*.

ORAL TRADITIONS

Oral traditions are different from the stories on which *The Real Story* focused, but epics and ballads are real stories nonetheless. In this discussion oral traditions are used to show a different variety of recall. First, like autobiographical memories but unlike stories in *The Real Story,* oral traditions depend on more than gist. Second, in oral traditions, compared with *The Real Story,* all structures unfold more strictly in the telling rather than in being able to be fully activated or addressed when cued by an index or a reminder. As with autobiographical memory, there are points of agreement with *The Real Story,* but again not with its emphasis on using only stories.

Oral traditions, such as children's counting-out rhymes, jump rope rhymes, folk ballads, and oral epic, depend on human memory for their preservation. If a tradition is to survive, it must be stored in one person's memory and then communicated to another person who can also store and retell it. All this must occur over many generations. That is, the transmission of oral traditions must yield results very different from those obtained by the standard rumor procedure noted in *The Real Story,* or else the traditions would change radically or die out. Individual pieces change little over long periods, but they do change from telling to telling. A verbatim text is not being transmitted, but rather, the theme, imagery, and poetics are transmitted along with some specific words. Oral traditions have developed forms of organization and strategies to decrease the changes that human memory imposes on the more casual transmission of verbal material. These forms make use of the many strengths and avoid the weaknesses of human memory (Rubin, 1995).

Counting-out rhymes are the most widely known genre I have studied, and the most common of these rhymes is *Eenie meenie*. The variant recalled most frequently by Duke undergraduates is the following:

Eenie, meenie, miney, mo,
Catch a tiger by the toe.
If he hollers, let him go.
Eenie, meenie, miney, mo.

This rhyme in this form has remained stable for over a century. I found only one permanent change, although many variants exist now and many existed a hundred years ago, and although an individual on retelling may vary unconstrained words such as *its* toe, *his* toe, and *the* toe (Rubin, 1995). *Tiger* is the permanent change in the rhyme, the original word being expunged by social forces outside the genre starting about the time of World War II. Thus, this piece from an oral tradition remained remarkably stable, and the systematic change that did occur fit the meaning constraint of having an animate object with feet and the rhythmic constraint of a two-syllable word with stress on the first syllable. Moreover, in my data collection and search of the folklore records, many substitutions that fit these two constraints were tried in the 1950s through 1980s (e.g., *fellow, monkey, doggie,* but not the one-syllable word *dog*), but *tiger,* the one collectively settled on, increased the sound pattern repetition by also alliterating with *toe*. A better poetic substitute is hard to find. It is hard to see how writing or other external memory aids could have played a large role in keeping the piece stable in the memory of English-speaking children worldwide. Moreover, both the rhythm and the sound pattern of the poetic devices of the genre are sophisticated (Kelly & Rubin, 1988). It is also hard to see how an analysis of the story alone could describe the rhyme or its stability.

Counting-out rhymes were used as an example because of their familiarity. One could dismiss counting-out rhymes as child's play, but other oral traditions, such as epic and religious traditions, are important in maintaining the store of a society's knowledge when written means are not available (Havelock, 1978), as has been the case through most of our evolution. That is, oral traditions were once stories used instead of, not in addition to, a written storage of knowledge.

The claim of multiple mechanisms made for counting-out rhymes holds for other traditions. In epic poetry, at least the South Slavic epic for which a large database exists, the plot, the rhythm, the general cast of characters available to fill roles, the formulaic descriptions of characters and places, and other aspects of the genre and the individual epics are stable, but the exact words sung are not (Lord, 1960, 1991; Rubin, 1995). Epics have elaborate, local narrative structure, including scripts (Schank & Abelson, 1977) that have been studied extensively in Homeric epic (Reece, 1993; Rubin, 1995). Homeric epic has a strict metrical structure that severely limits the locations that any given word can occupy in a line, and South Slavic epic, which has weaker metrical constraints, has more sound pattern repetition.

For counting-out rhymes the meaning and sound pattern are important. For most adult genres, such as epic, imagery also plays an important role. Most genres of oral traditions consist of concrete, easy-to-image, words and ideas. This is also true of counting-out rhymes to the extent that this genre contains meaningful words of any kind. The clearest observation that oral traditions avoid the abstract, and that the abstract only enters when writing is present to lessen the demands on memory, are made by Havelock (1963, 1978) in his discussions of Homeric epic and the Greek written literature that followed it.

Oral traditions, for the most part, consist of a series of actions carried out by agents whose roles and appearances are well-known by the singers and listeners. In epic, the agents are usually heroes or gods. Heroes and gods are easy to image: They are "larger than life," attention is paid to the details of their dress and stature, and they each have unique features that make them easy to place and to distinguish in an image. Heroes and gods can substitute for abstract concepts that cannot be easily imaged; that is, they each have a characteristic that they personify. As Havelock noted, having a Pantheon of gods has mnemonic advantages over monotheism. Characters, or character types, in other oral traditions often serve a mnemonic role similar to that of the Greek heroes and gods. Each character has an expected image and an expected role to play that exemplifies some more abstract, not easily imageable, concept. Moreover, Havelock notes that the images of the actions cue one another in recall. Thus, the image of Zeus throwing thunderbolts can invoke the image of Apollo shooting arrows.

Humanists, such as Havelock, have noted that oral traditions contain the concrete rather than the abstract. If imagery is divided into two components, object and spatial, then oral traditions are also highly spatial. There are graphic scenes, but most of the lines involve movement and location rather than description, and much of the description that does exist is in the form of "formulas" or "common-places." It may be no accident that epic heroes are always on the move; invoking a highly developed spatial memory system increases memorability. If all the actions occurred at one place, more confusions and interference might occur. Moreover, individual images are better for spatial relations than for sequencing, but by using a series of images tied to a path that passes through a known sequence of places, the order of events can be made more stable. In ballads, each stanza is at one location or point of view, and after each stanza or two, the location changes. There are no one scene epics; travel is the rule. The Odyssey is an odyssey.

Observations of oral traditions in the wild, and integration of the psychological literature in an attempt to understand why memory works so well, leads to a theory of serial recall in which narrative structure by itself is not enough. First, items are recalled to the degree that cues uniquely identify them from among all other items in memory on the basis of different forms of organization. Second, different forms of organization have different properties as memory structures and as cues. Third, recall of text is serial: Items already recalled can cue what remains to be recalled. Because different kinds of organization are involved in cuing, some using sound pattern, both the sound and the gist need to be recalled for effective cuing, not just the gist (Rubin, 1995).

Consider the basic types of organization present in oral traditions: narrative theme, associative meaning, spatial and object imagery, sound pattern repetition, rhythm, and music. They are good candidates for different natural kinds, and all play different roles in increasing the stability of recall. They are different forms of organization. Moreover, they are different processes. For instance, associative meaning acts more quickly than imagery (Paivio, 1971) and more slowly than rhyme. Similarly, rhyme cues are more broad than meaning cues, and act differently, depending on whether the retrieval cue was present at learning (Nelson, 1981; Nelson, Schreiber, & McEvoy, 1992).

As *The Real Story* noted, the process of recall is much like the process of construction. However, in contrast to *The Real Story,* the full meaning of a story does not reveal itself until the tale is told. In summary, oral traditions are stories that have been important to cultures. They can be understood by using the theories, methods, and findings of cognitive psychology, but not by the limited processes and organization argued for in *The Real Story.*

NATURAL KINDS

The reason for stressing the different kinds of organization seen in autobiographical memory and in oral traditions and their different roles in recall is to demonstrate the need for different natural kinds in cognition. We cannot consider all types of cues or organizations as equivalent. Our knowledge gained from behavioral studies, and more recently from cognitive neuroscience, which places our standard behavioral distinctions into different brain systems, will not permit such equivalence. Thus, from clinical cases, and more recently from brain-mapping techniques, we know that there are separate neural substrates or pathways for at least various aspects of language (Caplan, 1988), attention (Posner & Petersen, 1990), music (Joseph, 1988; Peretz & Morais, 1988; Samson & Zatorre, 1991), imagery (Farah, 1988; Tippett, 1992), and within visual imagery, both object and spatial imagery (Farah, Hammond, Levine, & Calvanio, 1988). At a gross level, these divisions often match the classical divisions of literary devices just given, such as theme, object and spatial imagery, rhyme, and rhythm. At a detailed level, theories based on behavior do not always match those based on neural structures, but it is clear that there will be more than one natural kind. More than narrative is needed for an adequate description of either autobiographical memory or oral traditions. Even casual storytelling among friends probably needs to consider imagery and poetics (Chafe, 1990; Tannen, 1987, 1989).

The Real Story ends with the claim that "cognitive and social psychology, in studying knowledge structures, memory processes, and text comprehension, have in our view lost sight of the forest by concentrating on the cellulose in the trees" (p. 82). But this is just not so. Whole areas of study, such as autobiographical memory and the intersection of cognitive psychology with folklore and studies of literature, integrate storytelling with concerns of knowledge structures and memory processes. I have tried to include just a small part of these vigorous research programs here, and only in the idiosyncratic way in which it related to my personal story. Moreover, current leaders of cognitive psychology, such as Bruner (1986, 1990) and Neisser (1982, 1993; Neisser & Fivush, 1994; Neisser & Winograd, 1988; Winograd & Neisser, 1992) have made the study of narrative and the way it shapes our behavior a central part of their psychological inquiry. Although these efforts are also not cited or included in *The Real Story,* they are central to it. We who have been working on similar problems from similar perspectives welcome *The Real Story*'s enthusiasm. We will continue to try not to lose sight of the forest by concentrating on the cellulose. We hope the real real story will not lose sight of the deserts and oceans and plains by concentrating on the forest.

BROADER IMPLICATIONS AND SELF-CONSUMING ARTIFACTS

There is a larger issue at stake. Bruner's dichotomy and my multiple mechanisms could be used to privilege different forms of representation for different purposes. If people only tell stories, then scientists only tell stories, but most of us want our scientific work to be more than stories. If people only tell stories, then Schank and Abelson and all the commentators in this volume have told each other stories, and there is no reason to expect to find a way to decide among them, or reach consensus on them, anymore than there is a way to decide among, or reach consensus on, the stories of the Iranian airliner used as examples in *The Real Story.* The different theoretical positions, individual histories, and current motives of the storytellers that fill these pages will prevent any such convergence. If people only tell stories, then there is no real story.

Science can be viewed as a special form of discourse done by real people with histories, motives, and favorite stories. However, at its minimum it is a form of discourse fashioned with agreed-upon ways of arriving at a consensus. Moreover, the various forms of consensus found in the past have regularly been the most useful ones on which to base technologies. As Bruner notes in the quote that begins this chapter, the form of such discourse is not the form of a story. From my reading of history, to do science we need at least Bruner's natural kind of a well-formed argument, imagery (Arnheim, 1969), and a written mode of communication (Have-lock, 1978; Rubin, 1995). We need more than stories.

REFERENCES

Alba, J. W., & Hasher, L. (1983). Is memory schematic? *Psychological Bulletin, 93,* 203–231.

Arnheim, R. (1969). *Visual thinking.* Berkeley: University of California Press.

Barclay, C. R. (1986). Schematization of autobiographical memory. In D. C. Rubin (Ed.), *Autobiographical memory* (pp. 82–99). Cambridge, England: Cambridge University Press.

Barclay, C. R., & Smith, T. S. (1992). Autobiographical remembering: Creating personal culture. In M. A. Conway, D. C. Rubin, H. Spinnler & W. A. Wagenaar (Eds.), *Theoretical perspectives on autobiographical memory* (pp. 75–97). Dordrecht: Kluwer Academic Publishers.

Barsalou, L. W. (1988). The content and organization of autobiographical memories. In U. Neisser & E. Winograd (Eds.), *Remembering reconsidered: Ecological and traditional approaches to the study of memory* (pp. 193–243). Cambridge, England: Cambridge University Press.

Brewer, W. F. (1986). What is autobiographical memory? In D. C. Rubin (Ed.), *Autobiographical memory* (pp. 25–49). Cambridge, England: Cambridge University Press.

Brewer, W. F. (1992). Phenomenal experience in laboratory and autobiographical memory tasks. In M. A. Conway, D. C. Rubin, H. Spinnler & W. A. Wagenaar (Eds.), *Theoretical perspectives on autobiographical memory* (pp. 31–51). Dordrecht: Kluwer Academic Publishers.

Brewer, W. F., & Nakamura, G. V. (1984). The nature and function of schemas. In R. S. Wyer Jr. & T. K. Srull (Eds.), *Handbook of social cognition* (Vol 1, pp. 119–160). Hillsdale, NJ: Lawrence Erlbaum Associates.

Brown, R., & Kulik, J. (1977). Flashbulb memories. *Cognition, 5,* 73–99.

Bruner, J. (1986). *Actual minds, possible worlds.* Cambridge, MA: Harvard University Press.

Bruner, J. (1990). *Acts of meaning.* Cambridge, MA: Harvard University Press.

Caplan, D. (1988). The biological basis for language In F. J. Newmeyer (Ed.), *Linguistics: The Cambridge survey: Vol. 3, Language: Psychological and biological aspects* (pp. 237–255). Cambridge, England: Cambridge University Press.

Chafe, W. (1990). Some things that narratives tell us about the mind. In B. K. Britton & A. D. Pellegrini (Eds.), *Narrative Thought and Narrative Language* (pp. 79–98). Hillsdale, NJ: Lawrence Erlbaum Associates.

Chomsky, N. (1965). *Aspects of the theory of syntax.* Cambridge, MA: MIT Press.

de Saussure, F. (1966). *Course in general linguistic* (C. Bally & A. Sechehaye, Eds. and W. Baskin, Trans.). New York: McGraw-Hill.

Farah, M. J. (1988). Is visual imagery really visual? Overlooked evidence from neuropsychology. *Psychological Review, 95,* 307–317.

Farah, M. J., Hammond, K. M., Levine, D. N., & Calvanio, R. (1988). Visual and spatial mental imagery: Dissociable systems of representation. *Cognitive Psychology, 20,* 439–462.

Fitzgerald, J. M. (1986). Autobiographical memory: A developmental perspective. In D. C. Rubin (Ed.), *Autobiographical memory* (pp. 122–133). Cambridge, England: Cambridge University Press.

Fitzgerald, J. M. (1988). Vivid memories and the reminiscence phenomenon: The role of a self narrative. *Human Development, 31,* 261–273.

Fitzgerald, J. M. (1992). Autobiographical memory and conceptualizations of the self. In M. A. Conway, D. C. Rubin, H. Spinnler & W. A. Wagenaar (Eds.), *Theoretical perspectives on autobiographical memory* (pp. 99–114). Dordrecht: Kluwer Academic Publishers.

Fivush, R., & Reese, E. (1992). The social construction of autobiographical memory. In M. A. Conway, D. C. Rubin, H. Spinnler & W. A. Wagenaar (Eds.), *Theoretical perspectives on autobiographical memory* (pp. 115–132). Dordrecht: Kluwer Academic Publishers.

Freeman, M. (1993). *Rewriting the self: History, memory, narrative.* London: Routledge.

Harris, R. (1987). *The language machine.* London: Duckworth.

Havelock, E. A. (1963). *Preface to Plato.* Cambridge, MA: Harvard University Press.

Havelock, E. A. (1978). *The Greek concept of justice: From its shadow in Homer to its substance in Plato.* Cambridge, MA: Harvard University Press.

Hyman, I. E., Jr., & Rubin, D. C. (1990). Memorabeatlia: A naturalistic study of long-term memory. *Memory and Cognition, 18,* 205–214.

Joseph, R. (1988). The right cerebral hemisphere: Emotion, music, visual-spatial skills, body-image, dreams, and awareness. *Journal of Clinical Psychology, 44,* 630–673.

Kelly, M. H., & Rubin, D. C. (1988). Natural rhythmic patterns in English verse: Evidence from child counting-out rhymes. *Journal of Memory and Language, 27,* 718–740.

Lord, A. B. (1960). *The singer of tales.* Cambridge, MA: Harvard University Press.

Lord, A. B. (1991). *Epic singers and oral tradition.* Ithaca, NY: Cornell University Press.

Miller, P. J., Potts, R., Fung, H., Hoogstra, L., & Mintz, J. (1990). Narrative practices and the social construction of self in childhood. *American Ethnologist, 17,* 292–311.

Miller, P. J., & Sperry, L. L. (1988). Early talk about the past: The origins of conversational stories of personal experiences. *Journal of Child Language, 15,* 293–315.

Neisser, U. (1982). Snapshots or benchmarks. In U. Neisser (Ed.), *Memory observed.* San Francisco: Freeman.

Neisser, U. (Ed.) (1993). *The perceived self: Ecological and interpersonal sources of self knowledge.* Cambridge, England: Cambridge University Press.

Neisser, U., & Fivush, R. (Eds.) (1994). *The remembering self: Construction and accuracy in the self-narrative.* Cambridge, England: Cambridge University Press.

Neisser, U., & Winograd, E. (Eds.) (1988). *Remembering reconsidered: Ecological and traditional approaches to the study of memory.* Cambridge, England: Cambridge University Press.

Nelson, D. L. (1981). Many are called but few are chosen: The influence of context on the effects of category size. In G. H. Bower (Ed.), *The psychology of learning and motivation* (Vol. 15, pp. 129–162). New York: Academic Press.

Nelson, D. L., Schreiber, T. A., & McEvoy, C. L. (1992). Processing implicit and explicit representations. *Psychological Review, 99,* 322–348.

Nelson, K. (1993). The psychological and social origins of autobiographical memory. *Psychological Science, 4,* 7–14.

Norman, D. A. (1988). *The psychology of everyday things.* New York: Basic Books.

Paivio, A. (1971). *Imagery and verbal processes.* New York: Holt, Rinehart & Winston.

Peretz, I., & Morais, J. (1988). Determinants of laterality for music: Towards an information processing account. In K. Hugdahl (Ed.), *Handbook of dichotic listening: Theory, methods and research* (pp. 323–358). New York: Wiley.

Posner, M. I., & Petersen, S. E. (1990). The attention system of the human brain. *Annual Review of Neuroscience, 13,* 25–25.

Reece, S. (1993). *The stranger's welcome: Oral theory and the aesthetics of the Homeric hospitality scene.* Ann Arbor: The University of Michigan Press.

Robinson, J. A. (1981). Personal narratives reconsidered. *Journal of American Folklore, 94,* 58–85.

Rubin, D. C. (1995). *Memory in oral traditions: The cognitive psychology of epic, ballads, and counting-out rhymes.* New York: Oxford University Press.

Rubin, D. C., & Kontis, T. C. (1983). A schema for common cents. *Memory & Cognition, 11,* 335–341.

Rubin, D. C., & Kozin, M. (1984). Vivid memories. *Cognition, 16,* 81–95.

Rubin, D. C., Stolzfus, E. R., & Wall, K. L. (1991). The abstraction of form in semantic categories. *Memory and Cognition, 19,* 1–7.

Rubin, D. C., Wallace, W. T., & Houston, B. C. (1993). The beginnings of expertise for ballads. *Cognitive Science, 17,* 435–462.

Samson, S., & Zatorre, R. J. (1991). Recognition memory for text and melody of songs after unilateral temporal lobe lesion: Evidence for dual encoding. *Journal of Experimental Psychology: Learning, Memory, and Cognition, 17,* 793–804.

Schafer, R. (1981). Narration in the psychoanalytic dialogue. In W. J. T. Mitchell (Ed.), *On narrative* (pp. 25–49). Chicago: University of Chicago Press.

Schank, R. C. (1982). *Dynamic memory: A theory of reminding and learning in computers and people.* Cambridge, England: Cambridge University Press.

Schank, R. C., & Abelson, R. P. (1977). *Scripts, plans, goals, and understanding.* Hillsdale, NJ: Lawrence Erlbaum Associates.

Smith, B. H. (1994). *Doing without meaning.* Unpublished manuscript. Durham: Duke University.

Spence, D. P. (1982). *Narrative truth and historical truth: Meaning and interpretation in psychoanalysis.* New York: Norton.

Tannen D. (1987). Repetition in conversation: Toward a poetics of talk. *Language, 63,* 574–605.

Tannen, D. (1989). *Talking voices: Repetition, dialogue, and imagery in conversational discourse.* New York: Cambridge University Press.

Tippett, L. J. (1992). The generation of visual images: A review of neuropsychological research and theory. *Psychological Bulletin, 112,* 415–432.

Wagenaar, W. A., van Koppen, P. J., & Crombag, H. F. M. (1993). *Anchored narratives: The psychology of criminal evidence.* Hemel Hempstead, England: Harvester Wheatsheaf.

White, H. (1981). The value of narrativity in the representation of reality. In W. J. T. Mitchell (Ed.), *On narrative* (pp. 1–23). Chicago: University of Chicago Press.

Winograd, E., & Neisser, U. (Eds.) (1992). *Affect and accuracy in recall: Studies of "flashbulb" memories.* New York: Cambridge University Press.

Zhang, J., & Norman, D. A. (1994). Representations in distributed cognitive tasks. *Cognitive Science, 18,* 87–122.

9

Representation and Narrative: A Commentary on Schank and Abelson's "Knowledge and Memory"

Linda M. Scott
University of Illinois, Urbana-Champaign

When I was invited to comment upon Schank and Abelson's theory of storytelling, I accepted with a mixture of interest and apprehension. Because my own background is literary and arts theory, I was intrigued by the use of a notion of "story" to model human cognition. At the same time, I had the concerns experienced by anyone writing "across disciplines," which ranged from worries about transferring terminology to not knowing where the bodies are buried. I mention all this now, of course, as a frame for my commentary, and ask my readers to allow some leeway to a person offering a viewpoint that glances off the issue from a slightly different angle.

Schank and Abelson are grappling with an idea that has appealed intuitively to anthropologists, literary critics, and historians for some time: that there is some-thing basic, something profoundly and essentially human about the narrative, that stories are somehow intimately related to the way humans *think*. As I studied this piece, however, I felt a nagging sense of absence in spite of the extraordinary breadth and level of detail provided by the authors. I was concerned by a certain lack of elegance in their theory of the narrative process, and disturbed by what I perceived as a tendency to reduce or exclude evidence that did not fit neatly into a notion of "story." These are the two concerns I would like to address in my comments.

NOTIONS OF KNOWLEDGE, METAPHORS OF MIND

Schank and Abelson argue that stories are the template for all human knowledge and thought. They position their argument against previous ideas, in which knowl-edge has been characterized as a lexicon of terms or thought as a system of rules.

Their position against these two models is based most often on either the co-occurrence of facts (or beliefs) with stories or the lack of "usefulness" of rule systems, like grammar, as a topic of conversation. Their idea of the social realm is largely limited to verbal dialogue, their notions of knowledge specifically linguistic, and their definition of intelligence focused almost exclusively upon verbal articulation. There are brief mentions of numeric knowledge, which Schank and Abelson admit is not accommodated by their model. However, other types of knowledge or skills—musical ability, spatial conceptualization, cognitive motor coordination (as in dance, sports, sculpture)—are not mentioned at all.

It was puzzling to me that the competing models of the mind here were presented as all-or-nothing propositions, including the storytelling proposal. The importance of stories, something I wholeheartedly support, does not necessarily imply the unimportance of semantics or logic. Why the metaphors must be so totalizing is unclear to me. It would seem that a complete model of human cognition must account for storytelling, abstract thinking, artistic creation, *and* the manipulation of complex sets of terms and rules, because human beings do all these things (and only humans do any of them). Both the linguistic and the nonlinguistic must ultimately be accommodated, as well as the narrative and non-narrative. The final model will not only have to account for the minimum with which communication can be achieved, as Schank and Abelson imply, but must have the capacity to encompass the most innovative statement, the most complex discourse. Human tasks and artifacts run a broad spectrum: whatever mental model we finally devise will have to explain zip-lock bags as well as stories.

I would like to suggest an alternative view, in which storytelling can be understood in terms of a larger, more flexible mental system. Central to my argument is a focus on storytelling as an *act of representation*. Although I recognize that the term "representation" will not be unknown to a readership of psychologists, I believe that the concept I use here differs from previous usage and looks more closely at an earlier step in the process of storytelling than has been done before. Obviously, my notion of representation is rooted in the humanities (sign theory, symbolic anthropology, history of literacy, rhetoric), rather than in the cognition literature, so I ask once more that my readers be charitable.

I first show how the notion of representation helps theorize storytelling as a communicative action. Then I explain how adding this step to the model might streamline the processes suggested by these authors and help open their proposal out into other acts of cognition and expression. Finally, I talk about the way storytelling, when we think of it as a form of representation, can be understood not only as an act of communication, but also as a basic mental heuristic and a symptom of a wide-ranging social system.

REPRESENTATION: THE PARAMETERS

An act of representation is the process by which an experience or an idea is translated into symbolic form. Representations can be made in a variety of symbol systems: speech, writing, pictures, numbers, music, pantomime, and so on. The basis for representation is usually just an agreement or *convention,* that such-and-such will stand for thus-and-so. In converting a problem into algebra, for example, one often begins by saying something like, "Let x = years in school," which states the basis for the representation. In a similar fashion, the mathematical system itself is based on conventions whereby we all "agree" that certain marks (for example, < or +) will always stand for certain mathematical relationships or processes, and that others will stand for certain quantities. Similarly, in writing, we agree that "b" stands for a certain speech sound. Within any symbolic system, there are rules of combination and manipulation, too. You cannot divide by zero. You cannot use "am" as a verb for "you." Learning any one of these symbolic systems requires internalizing a vast and complex set of agreements. Yet most people have some facility in several symbol systems.

In spite of the vastness, complexity, and variety of human symbol systems, all acts of representation operate under constraints. Three of these constraints are always present, regardless of the system, the medium, or the topic.

First, the Act of Representation Is Always Reductive

Think of all that exists in one moment of experience: colors, textures, sounds, scents, movement, emotion. When we recount a life event, we necessarily reduce this full-bodied experience into the relatively flat dimension of words. I can try to describe my grandmother's favorite fragrance to you, for example, but I will be fundamentally limited by the translation of scent to symbol. How, then, can I possibly recreate a truly complete story of the time she caught me skipping church, when her perfume was so much a part of her authoritative presence? In the translation from experience to symbol, something is always drastically reduced; thus, any experience is only partially "used" in a single act of representation. Exactly what is reduced or excluded will depend, in the first instance, upon the symbol system being used, since each system has its own peculiar limits and its own special strengths.

Any Act of Representation Reflects a Selective Intentionality

Even within the parameters of a single symbol system, we are faced with a further necessity to select and reduce. We must always choose *what* to represent and *how* to represent it. If I take a photograph of my child's face, I have excluded the back of her head. If I photograph her in sunlight, I have not shown how she looks in shadow. No single representation can include all aspects of the object to be represented, nor all the ways the same object can be represented. If I draw Bill Clinton in an exaggerated cartoon style rather than in the grand manner of presidential portraits, my choice reflects my intentions toward my topic: to poke fun at the President, rather than to honor him. Thus, the intentionality of the person doing the representing guides the selection of what is represented and how. No representation is free of intentionality because all representation is selective.

Any Representation Is Limited by the Material Conditions of Its Production

Time limits, page restrictions, budget considerations, tools available—all these practical considerations have an impact upon the final representation. One limiting condition always present is the expertise, skill, and personality of the person crafting the representation. A great mathematician will write a more elegant formula than a high school student. A shy person will likely not tell a joke as well as a gregarious one. Most of us are better at using some symbolic forms than others: Perhaps we are better at math than at public speaking, or we write letters better than we draw pictures.

CONVENTIONS OF GENRE

Within each symbol system, there are several types of representational forms, often called *genres,* each of which have characteristic features, structures, and purposes. In writing, for example, there are essays and poems. In pictures, there are cartoons and landscapes. One of the reasons that narrative is so intriguing is that it seems to occur as a genre in several different symbol systems. There are narrative pictures, symphonies, and dances. I would even argue that the following is a simple narrative in numeric form:

    1990 12,000
    1991 13,000
    1992 14,000
    1993 15,000.

We can see here the basic structure of a narrative: the representation of a selected chronology of events. To understand *what* happened, of course, we would need to know what these numbers stand for. Even so, we see four summations of some event(s), taken at presumably meaningful intervals to demonstrate a particular phenomenon occurring in time. Not everything that happened in these years is represented (nor can it be); not every step in the process between measurements is included. Selectivity is at work.

A narrative is not a replication of an experience occurring in time, but a crafted account of something happening. A film clip of a car driving down the street, although it happens in time, is not a story. To be recognizable as a story, a representation must conform to the conventions (structures, features) of the narrative genre. Thus, just as there are sometimes stories for rules, there are also rules for stories. Although there is somewhat more "play" in the rules for stories than in the rules for algebraic equations, narrative is nevertheless a rule-governed form. On the basis of the features determined by narrative convention, stories become distinguishable from other genres. The same is true of sonnets, portraits, or polkas.

A NARRATIVE ALGORITHM

An act of representation, then, is molded by the formal constraints of symbol and genre, by intention, and by circumstantial limitations. In conceptualizing the relationships between these factors coming together in a particular story, the following mathematical metaphor may be helpful:

$$\frac{(n_v x + i)}{c} = s$$

Where
n_v = a narrative in verbal form
x = the experience
i = the intentionality
c = circumstantial limitations
s = the story told

The definitive transformation here is that the experience is to be converted into a verbal narrative. This formal stipulation not only requires translating experience into words, but also structuring the telling to conform to narrative conventions.

The remaining terms, which were also identified by Schank and Abelson, are endemic to representation generally, not just to stories. Intentionality is what puts a certain slant on the story by the manner of its telling: the choice of events, words, tone, and gestures. In my metaphorical formula, I represented this "slant" on the story as if it were analogous to the slope of a straight line. All lines have some slope, even if the slope is zero. Similarly, all stories have some "slant," even if they seem "straightforward." In order to speak, you must choose some words over others and speak with some tone of voice. The slant of a story (and the slope of a line) are necessary outcomes of that selectivity which cannot be avoided in an act of representation. Finally, the entire story will be reduced or amplified by the circumstances: the time allowed, the skill of the teller, the setting. Hence, the effect of circumstances is represented as analogous to division.

Notice that the story produced is the output, as it were, whereas the unnarrativized experience is one input. I think this slight change gives us a model that is more elegant, as well as broader in scope. Let me suggest what I think we have gained.

PRACTICAL ADVANTAGES

In Schank and Abelson's model, the mind automatically stores and retrieves experience *in the form of a story,* because, as a machine for telling stories, that is the form of information it is equipped to process. Events are automatically narrativized when received. The stories created are retrieved and reused as needed. Any piece of the experience that is not used as a story is soon forgotten or "dumped," as is any story that is not frequently told.

Schank and Abelson argue that the mind will always choose to retrieve and play back the same story rather than revise or create a new one. In actuality, however, the stories we tell of an experience, although they are often very, very similar, are never exactly replicated. We do not (and probably cannot) replay our stories with the kind of consistency that a VCR replays a video. We change the vocabulary slightly or speed it up a little bit or lose our train of thought—or do any number of things that cause each telling to differ in some small way from all those that went before it. The difference may not be meaningful. We may think of it as still "the same" story, but in actuality there *are* differences. We need a model to account for output that is often functionally similar and practically the same, but is, in fact, infinitesimally differentiated.

If we think of storytelling as being more like software than hardware, we can still account for the tendency to tell the story many times in "the same" way: it is a small step from a formula to the formulaic. A fairly narrow band of variables will result in running the routine in a way that tends to yield minimally differentiated results. As long as nothing significant changes in our motives for telling the story or the circumstances under which we tell it, we will tell a story that, while it may vary in minor ways, is each time substantially the same. We can think of the effort as, quite literally, routinized.

We also need to account for stories written anew in drastically different ways. If, after a while, we can only revise the stories we have already told, then there is actually no mechanism for "adding back" information from the original experience. When people face a life-changing event—a divorce, a death, a career change—they often revise the way they tell the stories about persons and decisions in their past. These revisions often include adding back material that has not been told (or even thought about) in a very long time, sometimes material that has never been told before at all. To account for these major revisions, we would need to be able to retrieve the experience itself, not merely revise one of the extant stories. Within the algorithm I have proposed, each story of an experience can still vary in endless ways. Each variation in output can also be traced to a change in some particular variable that relates to a new external condition.

OTHER FORMS AND OTHER USES

In Schank and Abelson's model, we are left with no way to account for non-narrative, nonlinguistic mental activity, and no reason or means to retain experience for purposes other than storytelling. By rethinking storytelling as a software routine that designs a particular sort of representation, however, we create a space to conceptualize other forms of representation, while leaving experience available for other uses.

Look again at our formula for representing a story. Instead of the variable for "verbal narrative," for example, we might insert one for another genre, such as poems or caricatures, or for a narrative in a different form, such as a drawing or a dance. Instead of an "x" for experience, we might have a variable to represent an idea or a desire. Intended impact and circumstantial limitations would always be in the formula, but they might be manifest in different ways: the choice of one musical style versus another or a limit to black-and-white versus color. With this added flexibility in the independent variables, the final output could now range from a blueprint to a sermon. If we elaborated this formula a little bit, we could probably even accommodate representations that include multiple symbolic forms, such as charts, checks, ads, and popular songs.

If the representation routine is only one of the mind's processes, then we might theorize new algorithms for other kinds of processes: quantifications, comparisons, deductions. Abstractions or observations generated in one part of the mind can be brought to the representation routine and made into a form that can be communicated. Thus, we could explain Schank and Abelson's observation that facts are often found in stories.

If the experience is stored as data and not as a story, other aspects of the event remain available for different processes and uses. Schank and Abelson argue that all experience is a kind of story. This statement seems intuitively persuasive on its face. The temporal dimension of experience is something we tend to notice consciously. Experience, however, is also spatial, a fact we tend to overlook, even in life. We take in from the space around us all kinds of information used for non-narrative, nonlinguistic tasks. I may not include a description of my dentist's office in the story of my root canal, for example. If asked, I might not be able to tell you what his wallpaper looks like. That does not mean I'm not using that information or that it is "lost." When I go to my dentist's office, I know I have been there before because I recognize (remember) the space. If you and I are choosing wallpapers for a new house and you comment that one sample "looks like it belongs in a dentist's office," I will know what you mean. I will know because of all the accumulated experience I have with dentists' offices that I have probably never bothered to verbalize. If you ask me for directions to my dentist's office, I may tell you a story (as Schank and Abelson suggest), but I might just as likely draw you a map. Then, too, I might verbalize the location in spatial terms: "It's on Park Street, two blocks west of First, between Travis and Wright." I am able to do these things because I have a geographical knowledge of the area, and I have learned to represent spatial information in both pictorial and verbal symbols.

Using our past experiences of space, we perform tasks, make predictions, and avoid danger. In these actions, we also employ nonlinguistic symbol systems (responding to traffic lights) and engage in non-narrative cognitive processes (choosing colors of paint). If we assume, as Schank and Abelson suggest, that all we do and all we remember is encoded into a verbal story—and that everything else is useless or lost—we omit a substantial part of human experience as well as other forms of thinking that are just as characteristically human as the narrative.

RULES, ROTE, AND REPRESENTATION

Schank and Abelson argue that learning is accomplished by stories, that factual knowledge is actually a kind of narrative, and that rules are meaningful only insofar as they are associated with tales. Yet the representational systems that make verbal stories possible are often learned in a rote fashion, as are many of the rules for using them.

It is axiomatic in linguistics that the connection between a word and its referent is utterly arbitrary (e.g. conventional). Consequently, we learn most words by rote. Of course, there is a story of origin behind the meaning for nearly every word, but we don't learn any of those until long after we have mastered language well enough to understand a concept like "etymology." We teach babies the words for things by pointing to objects and repeating the words for them over and over. Babies certainly learn these words in the context of temporal experience (which is not a story), yet many different experiences with the word are usually required before the baby learns it. The rules for combining words (grammar) appear to be learned by imitation. The simplest sentence is a complex achievement. Not until grammar and vocabulary are somewhat developed, however, can the child grasp a story.

Because the narrative conventions of our culture are distinctively literate, we should look also at writing. The alphabet is learned by rote. By repetition of the letter and the sound, as well as by repeatedly coupling letters with pictures, we teach children alphabetic writing. The logic of combination that characterizes phonetic writing is hardly obvious or natural: Other forms of writing, like cuneiform, were in existence for thousands of years before the Greeks invented the alphabetic system around 750 B.C. Furthermore, spelling rules are fraught with exceptions that must be learned on a case-by-case basis, often with the aid of mnemonic devices based on rhyme or rhythm, not story ("i" before "e" except after "c"). Schank and Abelson reduce the importance of linguistic rule systems by saying that communication is possible with a minimum of grammar. Still, *some* grammar is required, and, therefore, must be theorized. Moreover, in order to understand the human mind, we must be able to account for very complex statements, as well as for sets of rules other than grammar with which humans communicate and think.

Stories play a profound role in negotiating and maintaining the social world, a fact that Schank and Abelson have also emphasized. These authors suggest several times, however, that basic representational terms and rules are not social constructs (or at least not very important ones), since they are seldom discussed in a social setting. In considering which form of knowledge is more socially integrated and important to interaction, let's return once more to the basis for representation: conventional agreements. Speech and writing exist only because we can agree that "s" sounds like a snake or that "cat" refers to a certain furry, four-legged animal. We can invent all sorts of narratives for "reasoning out" such conventions, but in the end the link is arbitrary. Storytelling itself rests on a huge body of interrelated social conventions.

Knowledge of facts or conventions borrowed from nonlinguistic systems are often necessary to the comprehension of a story. To understand a story about dinosaurs, I must know what a dinosaur is. Yet, obviously, I can have no actual experience with these creatures. Consequently, my "knowing what a dinosaur is" necessarily rests on my previous exposure to verbal statements of fact (of the "A whale is a mammal" variety), other symbolic artifacts like pictures of what a dinosaur might have looked like, and mathematical concepts (numbers that can help me imagine the size of a dinosaur or how long ago it lived). It doesn't seem reasonable to insist that these bits of information depend on being encapsulated in this story, since the story just as surely depends on this information.

Trying to privilege the story as the single form of "real" knowledge unnecessarily underestimates the significance of other kinds of knowledge, rule-based thought, and methods of learning. Let me emphasize that I am not arguing for a model that is totalized as a dictionary or a grammar. Such systems are also inadequate for this task. Grammar and vocabulary alone cannot explain poetry, stories, or rhetoric, as has become clear from the failure of structuralism in literary theory. We need to explain and interrelate rules, facts, concepts, and fictions without privileging any one at the expense of the others.

LIVING WITH STORIES

Thus far, I have represented narrative as a process "done to" experience in order to represent an event to someone else. Does that mean, then, that a story doesn't exist until it is told? I don't think so. I believe, with Schank and Abelson, that we "narrativize" our own experiences. I think this often happens regardless of whether a story is actually told in speech or writing. Instead of thinking of the narrative as a template through which all experience must pass or be forgotten, however, I prefer to think of it as *one* of the mental tools with which we craft experience into a form we can use.

When we experience an event, one of the things we are likely to do, it appears to me, is to "make sense" of it by fitting it into our current notion of what our "life story" is. What we do with a given event in order to absorb it will be a function of how we can "slant" it so as to make it "fit in" (the intended impact) and of the circumstances under which we must work with it (our age, our emotional state, our health). This process would be basically the same as the narrative algorithm, but instead of being an act of interpersonal communication, this narrativizing is an interpretive act upon reality. Just because a narrativizing function is performed, however, doesn't mean that other functions are not performed, or that unnarrativized information is not stored. Perception is not necessarily identical to narration.

What about the stories we hear of other people's lives? These, after all, come to us already packaged as stories. Perhaps we can use our narrative algorithm to begin modeling the listener's process. Here it is again:

$$\frac{n_v x + i}{c} = s$$

Where
n_v = a narrative in verbal form
x = the experience
i = the intentionality
c = circumstantial limitations
s = the story told

This time, try solving for "x." First, you account for the circumstances ("I didn't hear the whole story because we were interrupted by the train, but he did tell me that . . ."). Think of this action as multiplying both sides by "c." Now we have $n_vx + i = sc$. Next, you situate the story by inferring an intention. We might describe this as discounting for the interests of the speaker ("I could tell he was just trying to get me to sleep with him"). Subtract the intended effect from both sides. This will give us $n_vx = sc - i$. Finally, you interpret the story as a representation of experience. This step involves knowing the culture's narrative conventions, as well as understanding the language. Consequently, we divide both sides by n_v, which leaves $x = (sc - i)/n_v$. What remains is knowledge of the experience (x) that is filtered through a (reduced, slanted, limited) representation.

It's not as tidy as it seems, of course. Schank and Abelson rightly point out that different readers hear the same story differently. They attribute the difference to individual memories or life stories. Theirs is an observation shared by reader–response critics in literary theory. Those critics would add, however, that the reader also interprets the story in accordance with his or her *motives* for listening. Therefore, we still need to address the reasons for listening to the story.

Schank and Abelson argue that we attend to the stories of others only until we can match them up with past experiences (stories) of our own. Furthermore, like the remainders of our own experiences, those parts of others' stories that do not fit with ours are either not heard at all or are quickly forgotten. To some extent this may be true, but it also leaves out a great deal. When we are faced with new situations, we often recall the stories and experiences of others to help guide us about what to do. When I grieved the death of my father, for example, I thought a lot about what my Dad had said about grieving *his* father. During my mourning, friends who had lost a parent volunteered their stories, and I listened to them closely, looking for "a way to think about" my father's death. Stories are more than data we make, match, and store. They are, as Kenneth Burke (1973) said long ago, "equipment for living" (p. 293). All sorts of motivations may cause us to attend closely to a story quite different from our own. Stories have many uses and many pleasures.

Schank and Abelson model much of their theory of the mind on the premise that people are cognitively lazy, that they avoid mental processing whenever possible. This stance makes sense, perhaps, if we are talking about cognitive tasks that most people find difficult or unpleasant, such as predicting the statistical probabilities in a game of roulette, or preparing your federal income tax return. When it comes to stories, however, this premise flies in the face of the facts. People often enjoy processing stories and seek out opportunities to do so. If they did not, there would be no market for literature nor ticket sales for movies. What is reading a novel or watching a film, if not a voluntary act of processing a story? Virtually all of prime time television is fictional narrative; if people don't enjoy stories, what makes a couch potato? Surely, we do not seek out only those books or films that match our own experiences. Who among us has lived *Jurassic Park* or *Schindler's List?*

Whatever parallels may exist between our lives and these stories seem minor compared to their meaningful differences.

A mental processing theory based on an efficient, but slothful, store-revise-retrieve loop seems unlikely to account for highly imaginative stories. Spinning a fiction is a purposive act of invention. No doubt Schank and Abelson would argue that even a fiction makes use of the known, of stories already heard, and I would agree. Nevertheless, the will to create stories about imaginary people, impossible situations, fantastic places, and outrageous events seems a remote possibility in a world where humans avoid thinking beyond their own personal experience.

When we go to the movies or watch TV, we sometimes take away stories we can use in life or characters we can emulate, but we also take away ideas, historical lessons, moral values, and other messages that may not directly relate to our lives. (I have learned, for example, that Klingons should be approached with shields up and phasers ready.) When we collect around the celluloid campfire, we learn about our past, we imagine our future, we forge collective connections, we negotiate values—and learn new conventions of representation.

MAKING SENSE

Consider that we now have an organism which takes in experience and feeds it into a variety of cognitive processes and mental files, so it can be used in various ways for negotiating the future environment. At this point, the narrative routine is part of a larger system of software engaged with an overall task we might call "making sense" of the environment. This is a good place to find ourselves, since it connects up nicely with the way both anthropologists and perceptual psychologists talk about human interaction with the world. For an anthropologist, "culture" is essentially a learned system that makes the environment intelligible and uses past experience to extrapolate future action. Symbol systems would be one of the primary components of any culture. For a perceptual psychologist, our perceptions are focused, refined, and guided via a process that includes not only physical development, but social direction and experience with symbolic artifacts.

Our symbol systems and representations, by helping us make sense of the world, in turn have an impact on how we experience it, as well as how we behave in it. This is not just a matter of theory. The introduction of writing, for example, has an identifiable effect upon what and how a culture thinks. All sorts of mental analyses and cognitive activities are found in literate cultures that simply do not exist in preliterate societies. The manner in which a culture represents the world can also be shown to produce a bias in the way its members perceive experience. To the extent that representational systems affect the way we make sense of the environment, our very perceptions and thoughts are based on a complex web of social agreements. This is what cultural critics mean by the somewhat overwhelming phrase, "the social construction of reality."

If reality itself is largely (some would say entirely) mediated by symbols, then it becomes difficult to accept the idea that humans avoid symbolic processing as a matter of course. Human beings are distinguished from other life forms by many things, but one of the most distinctive characteristics is their *propensity* to use symbols. This is not simply to say that humans *can* use symbols, but that they do, they will, they *must* use them. In this light, human thinking is a multi-faceted, highly sophisticated, simultaneous, and even celebratory manipulation of symbol and experience.

CONCLUSION

Schank and Abelson have taken an important leap of the imagination to propose that the human mind is a storyteller. Stories appear in many forms, throughout historical time and in every culture of the world. Narrative predates writing, mathematics, and formal logic. There is no question that narrative is one of the primary forms of human thought and expression. Any theory of human cognition would be incomplete without it. I am only concerned here that the story not be privileged at the expense of the image, the song, the gesture, and the tool, all of which can lay equal claim to centrality, and that the door to conceptualizing other forms of cognition be left open. Schank and Abelson's enthusiasm for narrative reveals the curiosity and excitement of discovery that is so characteristic of human inquiry; the lust for understanding is, in many ways, what is best about us as a species. Their proposal promises to put research on a path that is, in the fullest sense of the word, humane. This is a path certain to be rewarding.

ACKNOWLEDGMENT

The author wishes to thank Thomas C. O'Guinn for his help in developing this commentary.

REFERENCE

Burke, K. (1973). Literature as equipment for living. In *The philosophy of literary form* (p. 293). *Berkeley: University of California Press.*

10

Personal Storytelling In Everyday Life: Social and Cultural Perspectives

Peggy J. Miller
University of Illinois at Urbana-Champaign

Schank and Abelson argue that we remember by telling stories of our experiences. They say, "Storytelling is not something we just happen to do, it is something we virtually have to do if we want to remember anything at all." (p. 33) This is a very strong and sweeping claim, and it immediately raises for me reservations about the "anything at all," for I assume that there are aspects of the world, such as spatial configurations, that we remember by other means. However, I find highly plausible the more limited claim that telling stories of personal experience plays a fundamental role in human memory and self-construction.

Much of the evidence that I find persuasive to this claim—and the problems that I have with other parts of the authors' argument—arises from traditions of inquiry that, oddly enough, are not primarily concerned with memory. They speak instead to the use of personal storytelling in everyday life and to the nature of personal storytelling as a social and cultural phenomenon; thus, they are relevant to the functional and contextual arguments that Schank and Abelson make. Schank and Abelson say that memory is affected by the social context in which stories are told, and that stories are constructed according to culturally shared norms of coherence. However, if remembering *is* a matter of telling stories, they have greatly underestimated the extent to which memory is constituted by social and cultural processes. My argument, then, is that the position that Schank and Abelson take—that remembering is a matter of telling stories—requires that they engage the social and cultural dimensions of storytelling in a much more thoroughgoing fashion.

THE PERVASIVENESS OF PERSONAL STORYTELLING

If telling stories of one's past experiences plays a privileged role in remembering, we would expect it to be widely distributed across social groups. And, indeed, the

177

anthropological and folklore literatures suggest that this type of narrative activity is a probable cultural universal (Miller & Moore, 1989). In the United States, personal storytelling can be heard at the dinner table (Ochs, Smith, & Taylor, 1989; Polanyi, 1985), the corner bar (Leary, 1976), and the therapist's office (Nye, 1994). It flourishes in working-class communities where listeners are often riveted by artful performances (Bauman, 1986; Labov & Waletzky, 1967; Miller, 1994) and in a wide variety of ethnic groups, including western Apache (Basso, 1984), African-American (e.g. Heath, 1983; Labov, 1972), and native Hawaiian (Watson, 1973; Watson-Gegeo & Boggs, 1977).

In addition to its wide range geographically, culturally, and socioeconomically, personal storytelling is not confined to adults. Personal storytelling occurs in high school corridors (Shuman, 1986), kindergarten classrooms (Michaels, 1991) and streets where preadolescents gather after school (Goodwin, 1990). Perhaps most surprising, the developmental roots of personal storytelling run deep. It is now well established that children begin to recount past experiences in conversation during the second and third years of life (e.g. Engel, 1986; Fivush, Gray, & Fromhoff, 1987; McCabe & Peterson, 1991; Nelson, 1989; Sachs, 1983; Snow, 1990). Again, the evidence extends to children from diverse cultural and socioeconomic groups (e.g., Eisenberg, 1985; Heath, 1983; Miller & Sperry, 1988; Miller, Potts, Fung, Hoogstra, & Mintz, 1990; Sperry & Sperry, 1993). By two years of age children have already stepped into the narrative practices of family and community, thereby laying claim to some of the most powerful interpretive tools of their culture (Bruner, 1990).

Moreover, the small number of studies that have examined personal storytelling in the context of everyday family interaction suggest that young children's home environments are densely populated with stories. In four working-class families, personal stories occurred at average rates that ranged from four to twelve per hour (Miller, 1994). In a sample of culturally diverse children, youngsters and caregivers co-narrated stories of the child's personal experience at a median rate of 2.4 per hour for 2½-year-olds and 4.7 per hour for 5-year-olds (Miller, Mintz, Hoogstra, Fung, & Potts, 1992).

All of this suggests that personal storytelling is a pervasive and robust part of social life, thereby lending credibility to Schank and Abelson's claim that telling and retelling past experiences in ordinary talk serves an important function in human memory. Without even considering the stories that we tell to ourselves privately in mental conversations, there is a lot of storytelling going on. At the same time, because personal storytelling is embedded in social life, it is inherently variable, and thus it becomes necessary to talk of *varieties* of personal storytelling, and, by implication, varieties of remembering.

SOCIOCULTURAL VARIABILITY IN PERSONAL STORYTELLING

When people are observed actually telling stories to one another under everyday conditions, it becomes clear that sociocultural variation exists along a host of dimensions that far exceed those mentioned by Schank and Abelson in their section on social context. These include, for example, norms of reportability (i.e., what counts as a storyworthy event), the means and norms for conveying the point or significance of the story, the degree of self-aggrandizement versus self-denigration, and whether the narrator is required to stick close to the literal truth or allowed to fictionally embellish (Miller & Moore, 1989).

Norms of reportability and evaluation are relevant to specific points that Schank and Abelson make. For example, in discussing the social context of storytelling, they note that speakers have to select appropriate stories to tell, depending on characteristics of the listener. Although this is undoubtedly true, there are culture-specific norms of reportability that constrain such choices from the outset, and which are closely related to local values and frameworks for interpreting experience. In South Baltimore, a working-class Euro-American community, experiences of anger, aggression, and violence are highly reportable—often inspiring dramatic narrative performances—and caregivers do not censor such stories in deference to children (Miller & Moore, 1989; Miller & Sperry, 1987). Even stories of fights, shootings, wife beatings, and child abuse were told in the presence of young children, 'a practice that is consistent with the mothers' childrearing goal of "toughening" the child and promoting a clear grasp of the harsh realities of life.

Many of the stories that the children heard their mothers tell were stories in which the mother described herself as speaking up, talking back, or otherwise defending herself in response to being wronged. When mothers told stories about their young children in the child's presence, they invoked experiences in which the child behaved similarly (Miller, Potts, Fung, Hoogstra, & Mintz, 1990). One mother told the following story about her 23-month-old daughter, "Johnny told her the other night, he says to her, 'Isn't your mother a creep?' And he kept telling her all these things and she says, 'Na huh.' She says, 'YOU are Daddy, YOU'RE the creep. . . .' That's what she told him. He like to come off that chair. . . ." By repeatedly telling stories about this kind of experience rather than others, caregivers conveyed to young children which of their experiences were reportable—those in which they effectively asserted themselves. By creating particular renditions of what happened, they showed what the component events were, how the events were related, and what was important about them.

Another illustration of culture-specific norms of reportability and evaluation comes from a comparison of personal storytelling in middle-class Chinese families in Taipei and middle-class Euro-American families in Chicago (Miller, Fung, & Mintz, in press). One focus of this study was on co-narrated stories. These were stories of the child's past experience that were told jointly by the child and one or more family members. Although 2½-year-olds in both cultural cases regularly co-narrated their past experiences with family members and narrative practices were similar along several dimensions, a striking difference emerged in norms of reportability. Chinese youngsters and their caregivers were much more likely than their American counterparts to tell stories about young children's past transgressions and to structure their narrations so as to establish the child's misdeed as the point of the story. In the following Chinese example, Didi's mother prompts him to narrate a misdeed that occurred when he accompanied his mother to his older sister's music lesson. As narrated from the mother's perspective, Didi (2½-years-old) cried and made a scene when the teacher did not give him a sticker (a reward distributed only to members of the class), causing his mother to lose face.

Mother:	(looks at child) Eh, eh you that day with Mama, with younger sister (pats sister's back), with older sister went to the music class. Was that fun?
Child:	It was fun.
Mother:	What didn't the teacher give you?
Child:	Didn't, didn't give me a sticker.
Mother:	Didn't give you a sticker. Then you, then what did you do?
Child:	I then cried.
Sister:	Cried loudly, "Waah! Waah! Waah!"
Mother:	You, you then cried? Yeah, you constantly went: "Waah didn't, (gestures wiping eyes, makes staccato gesture of fists away from body) why didn't you give me a sticker [whined]? Why didn't you give me a sticker [whined]," didn't you?
Child:	(looks up from book, gazes at mother, smiles, and looks down at book again)
Sister:	Yes, "Why didn't you give me a sticker?" (claps hand)
Mother:	(looks at sister and smiles) Sticker (sighs) Ai, you made Mama lose face. That, that, I wanted to dig my head into the ground. Right? (smiles, shakes head, smiles again)
Child:	(points to picture book and says something unintelligible)
Sister:	Almost wanted to faint. Mommy almost began to faint.

This co-narration continues through 59 more turns, and a few minutes later it is told a second time. There is nothing comparable to this in our corpus of middle-class Euro-American co-narrations. To greatly oversimplify, American co-narrators seem to be operating with an implicitly evaluative, overtly self-affirming interpretive framework instead of the explicitly evaluative, overtly self-critical framework that is at work in the Chinese stories.

These studies show that from a very early age, children from different sociocultural groups participate routinely, day-by-day, in narrative practices that differ qualitatively and quantitatively in norms of reportability and evaluation. Every co-narrated story provides the child with another opportunity to hear which of her past experiences are reportable and to construct with significant others a culture-specific interpretation of her own experience. Interpretive frameworks are thus redundantly instantiated in personally relevant terms. It seems reasonable to suppose that the different ways in which past experience gets collaboratively carved out and structured for the purposes of personal storytelling will be reflected in patterns of remembering. (see Fivush, 1993, for a similar argument with emphasis on gender variation in co-constructed stories and Nelson, 1993, for discussion of the social origins of autobiographical memory and its relation to childhood amnesia.)

Moreover, it is important to emphasize that there are many other dimensions of variation in personal storytelling, and that these encompass not only which past events get talked about and how they are interpreted, but who gets to do the narrating and how narrations are socially coordinated. For example, oral narrative traditions vary in interactive style. Scollon and Scollon (1981) contrasted the unilateral narrative style of many oral traditions with the highly negotiated nature of Athabaskan performances in which the audience, in effect, tells the story. Even in more unilateral styles, listeners have a definite, though more limited, role to play in structuring the story. Responsibility for telling the tale lies with the narrator, yet the performance remains sensitive to interlocutor response and to the social discourse in which it is embedded (Kirshenblatt-Gimblett, 1975).

One of the most fascinating dimensions of variation in the narration as a social event concerns the distribution of storytelling rights. Often the protagonist of a personal story and the narrator are one and the same. That is, the narrator tells a story about his or her past experience. However, this is not necessarily the case. In the Chinese example, Didi's experience at the music class is narrated by his mother, who takes the lead, and his older sister, whose contributions support the mother's account. Didi's role as "author" of his own experience is thereby limited. Asymmetries in storytelling rights among narrating participants, often reflecting and legitimating asymmetries in power and status, are not unique to the Chinese, nor to the parent-child relationship, but pervade the everyday practice of personal storytelling (Goffman, 1981; Ochs & Taylor, 1992; Shuman, 1986). The implication is that remembered events, as they get narrated and renarrated, will be shaped in systematic ways by the interests of the narrating participants who are inevitably socially positioned relative to one another. We might expect, then, that as Didi participates repeatedly in co-narrating his past experience with mother and sister, he will come to remember not only "their" version of what happened that day at older sister's music lesson, but also the judging voices of mother and sister as they narrated what happened.

THE DYNAMICS OF PERSONAL STORYTELLING

However, the situation is actually more complicated than this because when mother does actually renarrate the event a few minutes later—this time with Didi as witness rather than co-narrator and the researcher as addressee—she adds details that were omitted before. Specifically, she brings in Didi's perspective on the past event, saying that he felt excluded when all the other children got stickers and he did not. This underscores a point related to Schank and Abelson's functional view of memory. When stories are examined in use, it becomes apparent that change is inherent in personal storytelling both in the sense that people recurrently tell stories about different past experiences, and in the sense that particular past experiences are narrated repeatedly (Miller, 1994).

Microlevel analyses of the "natural history" of stories—that is, of multiple retellings of the "same" story—indicate that the nature and direction of change is systematically related to the larger events and social processes in which the retellings are situated. For example, Shuman (1986) describes how adolescent girls' stories of minor offenses are structured differently, depending on which phase of the peer dispute process they are embedded in—the beginning of the dispute, the height of the dispute, or after the dispute has been resolved. Nye (1994) describes a similar pattern with respect to how personal stories change across the phases of psychoanalysis. Wolf and Heath (1992) document children's prolonged engagement with and transformation of particular stories within the context of ongoing narrative practices in the family. Miller, Hoogstra, Mintz, Fung, and Williams (1993) describe a similar case in which a young child reconfigured the story plot and resolved affectively charged conflicts through successive retellings in an interpersonal context in which he was granted considerable latitude as author.

These studies challenge Schank and Abelson's claim that subsequent iterations of a story will leave out or emphasize the same information and underscore the extent to which changes in personal storytelling are socially constructed. What, if anything, Didi will remember—a week later, a year later, or ten years later—about the incident at older sister's music lesson will depend on the subsequent history of narrations by himself and his family.

In sum, my argument is that the literature on how personal storytelling is actually practiced in everyday life is highly relevant to the position developed by Schank and Abelson. This literature shows that in a wide variety of sociocultural groups, people participate with one another in complex and shifting networks of narrative practices that are characterized by systematic variability and crosscutting redundancy. In any given group, particular frameworks of evaluation and interpretation are instantiated again and again in stories of personal experience, while at the same time narrators are constantly customizing their narrations in terms of here-and-now social contingencies. Thus, remembering in the service of personal storytelling appears to be highly dynamic and reconstructive in the Bartlett (1932) sense, but the reconstructive work is culturally situated and socially distributed. Moreover, it is important to emphasize—in support of Schank and Abelson's functional view— that narrators are not necessarily engaged in remembering for the sake of remembering. They are creating stylish performances, projecting intelligible selves, solving interpersonal problems, reintegrating distressing past experiences, or doing any number of other things. A comprehensive model of human memory needs to take account of how these culturally organized activities shape the way we remember.

REFERENCES

Bartlett, F. C. (1932). *Remembering*. Cambridge, England: Cambridge University Press.
Basso, K. H. (1984). Stalking with stories: Names, places, and moral narratives among the Western Apache. In E. M. Bruner and S. Plattner (Eds.), *Text, play and story: The construction and reconstruction of self and society* (pp. 19–55). Washington, DC: American Ethnological Society.

Bauman, R. (1986). *Story, performance, and event: Contextual studies of oral narrative.* New York: Cambridge University Press.

Bruner, J. (1990). *Acts of meaning.* Cambridge, MA: Harvard University Press.

Eisenberg, A. R. (1985). Learning to describe past experiences in conversation. *Discourse Processes, 8,* 177–204.

Engel, S. (1986). *Learning to reminisce: A developmental study of how young children talk about the past.* Unpublished doctoral dissertation, The City University of New York.

Fivush, R. (1993). Emotional content of parent-child conversations about the past. In C. A. Nelson (Ed.), *Memory and affect in development: The Minnesota Symposia on Child Psychology.* Vol. 26. (pp. 39–77). Hillsdale, NJ: Lawrence Erlbaum Associates.

Fivush, R., Gray, J. T., & Fromhoff, F. A. (1987). Two-year-olds talk about the past. *Cognitive Development, 2,* 393–410.

Goffman, E. (1981). *Forms of talk.* Philadelphia: University of Pennsylvania Press.

Goodwin, M. H. (1990). *He-said-she-said: Talk as social organization among black children.* Bloomington, IN: Indiana University Press.

Heath, S. B. (1983). *Ways with words: Language, life and work in communities and classrooms.* New York: Cambridge University Press.

Kirshenblatt-Gimblett, B. (1975). A parable in context: A social interactional analysis of story-telling performance. In D. Ben-Amos and K. S. Goldstein (Eds.), *Folklore: Performance and communication,* (pp. 105–130). The Hague: Mouton.

Labov, W. (1972). *Language in the inner city.* Philadelphia: Univeristy of Pennsylvania Press.

Labov, W., & Waletzky, J. (1967). Narrative analysis: Oral versions of personal experience. In J. Helm (Ed.), *Essays in the verbal and visual arts* (pp. 12–44). Seattle: University of Washington Press.

Leary, J. P. (1976). Fists and foul mouths: Fights and fight stories in contemporary rural American bars. *Journal of American Folklore, 89,* 27–39.

McCabe, A., & Peterson, A. (1991). *Developing narrative structure.* Hillsdale, NJ: Lawrence Erlbaum Associates.

Michaels, S. (1991). The dismantling of narrative. In A. McCabe & C. Peterson (Eds.), *Developing narrative structure* (pp. 303–351). Hillsdale, NJ: Lawrence Erlbaum Associates.

Miller, P. J. (1994). Narrative practices: Their role in socialization and self-construction. In U. Neisser & R. Fivush (Eds.), *The remembering self: Construction and accuracy in the self-narrative* (pp. 158–179). New York: Cambridge University Press.

Miller, P. J., Fung, H., & Mintz, J. (in press). Self construction through narrative practices: A Chinese and American comparison of early socialization. *Ethos.*

Miller, P. J., Hoogstra, L., Mintz, J., Fung, H., & Williams, K. (1993). Troubles in the garden and how they get resolved: The history of a story in one child's life. In C. A. Nelson (Ed.), *Memory and affect in development: The Minnesota Symposia on Child Psychology.* Vol. 26. (pp. 87–114) Hillsdale, NJ: Lawrence Erlbaum Associates.

Miller, P. J., Mintz, J., Hoogstra, L., Fung, H., & Potts, R. (1992). The narrated self: Young children's construction of self in relation to others in conversational stories of personal experience. *Merrill-Palmer Quarterly, 38,* 45–67.

Miller, P. J., & Moore, B. (1989). Narrative conjunctions of caregiver and child: A comparative perspective on socialization through stories. *Ethos, 17,* 43–64.

Miller, P. J., Potts, R., Fung, H., Hoogstra, L., & Mintz, J. (1990). Narrative practices and the social construction of self in childhood. *American Ethnologist, 17*(2), 292–311.

Miller, P. J. & Sperry, L. (1987). The socialization of anger and aggression. *Merrill-Palmer Quarterly, 33,* 1–31.

Miller, P. J. & Sperry, L. (1988). Early talk about the past: The origins of conversational stories of personal experience. *Journal of Child Language, 15,* 293–315.

Nelson, K. (Ed.). (1989). *Narratives from the crib.* Cambridge, MA: Harvard University Press.

Nelson, K. (1993). The psychological and social origins of autobiographical memory. *Psychological Sciences, 4,* 7–14.

Nye, C. H. (1994). Narrative interaction and the development of client autonomy in clinical practice. *Clinical Social Work Journal, 22,* 43–57.

Ochs, E., Smith, R., & Taylor, C. (1989). Detective stories at dinnertime: Problem-solving through co-narration. *Cultural Dynamics, 2,* 238–257.

Ochs, E., & Taylor, C. (1992). Family narrative as political activity. *Discourse and Society, 3,* 301–340.

Polanyi, L. (1985) *Telling the American story.* Norwood, NJ: Ablex.

Sachs, J. (1983). Talking about the there and then: The emergence of displaced reference in parent-child discourse. In K. E. Nelson (Ed.), *Children's language.* Vol. 4. (pp. 1–28). New York: Gardner Press.

Scollon, R., & Scollon, S. B. K. (1981). *Narrative, literacy and face in interethnic communication.* Norwood, NJ: Ablex.

Shuman, A. (1986). *Storytelling rights: The uses of oral and written texts by urban adolescents.* New York: Cambridge University Press.

Snow, C. E. (1990). Building memories: The ontogeny of autobiography. In D. Cicchetti and M. Beeghly (Eds.), *The self in transition: Infancy to childhood,* (pp. 213–242). Chicago: The University of Chicago Press.

Sperry, L. L., & Sperry, D. E. (1993). African-American toddlers' portrayals of self in past and fantasy narratives. Paper presented at the biennial meeting of the Society for Research in Child Development, New Orleans, March.

Watson, K. A. (1973). A rhetorical and sociolinguistic model for the analysis of narrative. *American Anthropologist, 75,* 243–264.

Watson-Gegeo, K. A. & Boggs, S. T. (1977). From verbal play to talk story: The role of routines in speech events among Hawaiian children. In S. Ervin-Tripp & C. Mitchell-Kernan (Eds.), *Child Discourse,* (pp.67–90). New York: Academic Press.

Wolf, S. A. & Heath, S. B. (1992). *The braid of literature: Children's worlds of reading.* Cambridge, MA: Harvard University Press.

11

Stories in Memory:
Developmental Issues

Katherine Nelson
City University of New York Graduate Center

There is much to agree with in Schank and Abelson's story. From the developmental perspective, their proposals cohere with recent research with children, but also leave open many questions and avenues of research. I first identify some of the claims that seem to have important implications for developmental theories, then flesh out some of the propositions and evidence from my own research, summarized in the target article. In the end I voice reservations about some of the holes in the argument as presented.

ISSUES RELEVANT TO DEVELOPMENT

Following are some of the propositions put forth by Schank and Abelson that I think are important to developmental issues.

Knowledge (and memory) is functional, acquired to facilitate everyday activities. "Memory is looking for knowledge that tells it something about the nature of the world in general" (p. 38–39). I agree that this is an idea that is often lost sight of in the effort to construct scientific, efficient knowledge storage systems, such as taxonomic hierarchies, which are particularly inappropriate when attributed to the heads of young children. Understanding the world one lives in and one's place in the world is first and foremost in most people's—and certainly children's—lives. This complex body of knowledge is foreground for children and background for adults, thus, from the adult perspective, easily dismissed or overlooked.

Reporting significant happenings for self and others in language is key to knowledge acquisition in myriad ways. We use language to try to comprehend what is going on and to tell things to other people. But what about those without language (infants and toddlers, young deaf children, autistic individuals)? How do comprehension and memory function for them? These are questions that need attention. Because such individuals manifestly do learn and comprehend much that goes on around them, it is tempting for theorists to believe that language and its narrative products are useful tools, but that they do not change cognition in any important way. Schank and Abelson's thesis (and that of others noted herein) argue otherwise.

Schank and Abelson believe that stories make memories coherent for language users. The content of story memories, they claim, depends on whether and how they are told to others, and these reconstituted memories then form the basis of the remembered self. Shared story memories within particular social groups define particular social selves, which may either bolster or compete with individual remembered selves. The self is constructed through the stories that one tells others and oneself, providing an edited self-history conforming to the accepted social stories of one's cultural group. Thus self concepts are to a significant degree social–cultural products.

Stories in memory get there through experience, through hearing others' stories, and through composing them. Stories derived from these sources become more real when they are told. It is noteworthy that the sneaky effects of social uses of language on perceptions of reality are seen as pervasive throughout the Schank and Abelson paper, lending it a strong Whorfian flavor, intended or not.

An important proposal is that comprehension is a process of matching what one hears with what one knows, or matching others' stories with those in memory. Different memories of individuals imply differential understanding. This proposition holds in spades for children whose story stocks are small and idiosyncratic from the adult's point of view. It also presents a huge theoretical problem not addressed by Schank and Abelson: Where do the first stories come from? The authors do concern themselves with the fate of "real" memories. As they have previously laid out, experiences of a similar kind lead to updating and to loss of specific detail through merging into scripts, into dynamic disconnection of parts, or both. Story construction stops the process of dynamic disconnection and provides coherence; in this process the original episodic memory is lost and the story takes its place.

SPECIFIC DEVELOPMENTAL IMPLICATIONS

I have already indicated that the importance of stories in memory, knowledge acquisition, and social life as outlined by Schank and Abelson poses significant problems for theories of development, social and cognitive. The implications are actually far more profound than most contemporary developmental psychologists seem willing to confront. These implications suggest that mature social–cognitive functioning depends upon the capacity for telling and understanding extended narratives about people in the world. This suggestion runs counter to the current developmental (and cognitive science) zeitgeist that views the functioning of the human mind as uniform in process from birth to death. Indeed, it is common today to be confronted with claims that infants have theories about the world; if theories, then surely stories as well.

However, in the Schank and Abelson scheme, it is the *telling* of the story, to self or to others, that makes the coherent memory. Such telling requires a degree of language competence that is not usually found in children under the age of three years. My study of narratives produced by the child Emily (Nelson, 1989) indicated that she began to construct coherent stories of her life at about two years, but her language skills were very precocious, and her stories also gained in elaboration, coherence and complexity over the succeeding year.

These considerations indicate that there is a marked discontinuity in social and cognitive functioning from the pre-story to the storytelling stage of development. Indeed, research indicates that there are marked changes in cognitive and communicative functioning between the ages of three and five years, changes that are plausibly related to emerging narrative skills. Such changes include what developmentalists (and philosophers) call "theory of mind"—the idea that children become able to attribute to others beliefs different from their own and from current real states of affairs (see Astington, 1993; Astington, Harris, & Olson, 1988; Whiten, 1991). Related developments during this age-range include a new focus on explanations for anomalous or puzzling facts, states, or events, and, as my own research has explored, the establishment of autobiographical memory (see discussion in the following section). Moreover, there is now extensive evidence from studies of parent–child talk that during this age–range children begin to listen to the stories of others, to tell their own stories, and to co-construct stories in the present and about the past (Fivush & Hudson, 1990). Further, it is during this time that children's memories are most vulnerable to the accounts of others about shared experiences (Ceci & Bruck, 1993). The conclusion seems clear: Mental functioning changes strikingly when storytelling becomes part of one's mental and social life.

These claims open up huge areas of unexplored territory for developmental psychologists, many of which are related to the unanswered questions that Schank and Abelson raise. What is the nature of event memory that is not a story? What part does imagery play? What is the relation of stories or scripts to "raw" memory for an experience? Does this change with development? How malleable is memory? Does telling a story alter a memory, as Schank and Abelson imply? If so, are there identifiable principles that determine how memory is altered, or does telling fix a memory-story?

Is there a difference between telling others and telling oneself? Based on the data from the study of Emily's narratives, I have suggested that telling oneself has a different function for young children (e.g., understanding) than telling others, or listening to others, or co-constructing an account with others, the latter having the functions of sharing experience with socially significant people and establishing close relationships.

An important aspect for the child is that when telling involves another, the opportunity for comparing one's own version of a story with the other's version is opened up. On the one hand, this opportunity makes it possible for others' views of the matter to intrude into one's memory, but it also enables comparison and reflections on one's own experience from others' perspectives. In contrast, telling oneself does not have this social validating possibility.

Where do skeletal stories come from? Unless one assumes some kind of universal Jungian human story form, it appears that skeletal forms must come from hearing versions of these types many times. Young children are unlikely to have many, if any, of these types stored in memory. Folk tales (e.g. "The Three Little Pigs," "Cinderella") provide children in Western societies with the beginnings of these forms, and no doubt specific familial, religious, and cultural tales universally invoke familiar story skeletons over time. However, the accrual of relevant story structures must take a great deal of social developmental time.

By Schank and Abelson's account, comprehension of another's stories by a child must be very effortful and error-prone, because children lack a good store of skeletal stories. Indeed, most stories must seem anomalous to the young child, bearing little similarity to the child's small number of known stories. Perhaps then, storing stories in early childhood takes place through different, more effortful and constructive, processes than the story fitting processes that Schank and Abelson outline for adults.

Relatedly, research shows that preschool children are very poor at constructing stories when asked to do so. Children younger than six years are likely to produce scripts or simple variations on scripts (Hudson & Shapiro, 1991; Nelson, 1986). Presumably they lack the cultural formats or skeletal stories that would enable them to plot a story. Again, however, this suggests a major discontinuity between the younger child compared to older children and adults if stories are as important to mental and social functioning as Schank and Abelson claim, and as some developmental research also implies.

SOCIAL INVENTION OF AUTOBIOGRAPHICAL MEMORY

Schank and Abelson included a précis of my recent theoretical account of the origins of autobiographical memory. I have no quarrel with their outline of my position (Nelson, 1993a; Nelson, 1993b), and, therefore, I do not need to take space to outline it in detail. However, I can expand a bit here on the evidence behind it. In brief, the claim is that children have event memories—generic and scriptlike as well as specific and episodic—from infancy, but that their memories do not become systematized as autobiographical until sometime in the late preschool and early school years. Experience with sharing memories with others leads to a new function of memory, a self-history that is differentiated from, but partially defined by, those with whom one's experiences and memories are shared.

Research with young children documenting different styles of shared memory talk indicates that parents (possibly unwittingly) teach children how to organize their remembered accounts of an experience. During the preschool years, children learn to narrativize, that is, to make coherent wholes of the fragments of their memories (Hudson, 1990). Of great interest is that mothers (and presumably fathers) differ in the degree to which they model and support coherent whole narrative structures, rather than emphasize the parts of an experience. This has been found both for experiencing present events (Tessler & Nelson, 1994) and for remembering past events (Engel, 1986; Fivush & Hamond, 1990). In both cases, it has been shown that children's structuring of memory parallels mothers' (or caretakers' generally), and that the narrative format produces more complete memories. Of particular importance is the demonstration in a longitudinal study (Reese, Haden, & Fivush, 1994) that over the years from three to five, children with elaborating (narrative) mothers remember significantly more memories in greater detail at the later age than do children whose mothers focus on separate isolated parts of the experience.

A corollary to the proposal that children learn to talk with others about their memories is that children in cultures where such talk is de-emphasized would have fewer and later autobiographical memories from childhood. This proposition was tested by Mullen (1994) with adults of North American and Asian family backgrounds (Korean and Chinese). Asian students had significantly later first memories than their Causasian counterparts in several studies, confirming the hypothesis. Mullen also found that Korean mothers talked less with their preschool children about their memories in narrative formats than do American mothers.

My proposal suggests that the experience of sharing memories in narrative form has the following multiple potential effects:

It provides a verbal label for the memory (perhaps equivalent to Schank and Abelson's index).

It restructures the memory into a coherent whole narrative, as Schank and Abelson also propose, such that the ensuing story becomes the memory.

It provides a rehearsal, or more powerfully, a reinstatement, of the episode remembered, so that its retention over time is ensured.

It provides a social and cultural validation and value to the personal experience, pointing up the social–cultural significance of its different parts.

Over time, it provides a self-history, an autobiography, that serves as a storehouse of self-knowledge from which one may extract self-descriptive traits, differentiating oneself from others.

RESERVATIONS

Schank and Abelson admit to many unanswered questions in their account, and invite the profession to address them. It is a bit surprising, therefore, that they have not noticed some of the recent attempts to do just that. For example, Bruner's (1986, 1990) theory of narrative and paradigmatic thinking differentiated between stories and the list structures so favored in traditional cognitive psychology. According to Bruner, narrative is a primary means of making meanings. However, it is not the only way. Even very young children often delight in sorting their possessions into groups and subgroups, solving puzzles, playing rule-governed games, painting pictures, and playing with language in rhymes and songs. Thinking, speaking, knowing and remembering are not *only* storytelling. Thus, Schank and Abelson's claim seems a bit too audacious and all-encompassing.

In a similar proposal, Donald (1991), discussing the evolution of the modern mind, spoke of narrative as the "natural product" of language, but he views it as only one component of the hybrid mind-system, with theoretical constructions as a later, more abstract development. Moreover, many other social scientists have in recent years begun to emphasize the narrative component of human experience, in contrast to the abstract structures of scientific theory.

In short, Schank and Abelson are not the only ones who have noticed that a lot of thinking, talking and remembering goes on in story form. Yet not everyone is as convinced as they that stories account for most of what matters, even in the social knowledge domain. Beyond the overreach, many commentators will no doubt note that there is little in the way of hard data or even hard analysis to back up their story. Some of the bothersome holes that seem papered over include such questions as these: What is a memory that is not a story? Is it only a fragment that gets distributed into generic knowledge schemes? What about the imagic memories often reported in discussions of "flashbulb" memories? What is an index? Sometimes Schank and Abelson speak as though an index is a label, and suggest that there are multiple indexes for any story. In other places, the index seems to be a memory itself. Do the same comprehension processes (e.g., matching one's stored schemas to what one hears) apply to nonstory forms as to stories? How does one acquire new forms?

Finally, I feel compelled to ask if they really mean statements like the following: "It is in the storytelling process that the memory gets formed" (p. 34), and "What we fail to tell gets forgotten (although it can be reconstructed)" (p. 34) . What seems missing here is an overall view of memory and memory processes that would show how different kinds of memory interact, form, and drop out. One of the intriguing findings from research with young children is that children tell different parts of their memory to different people at different times, and that they may tell a more complete story two years after the event than in the months immediately following it (Fivush & Hamond, 1990). Perhaps the memory system of young (2- to 4-year-old) children is different from that of adults (as indeed the memory account summarized above indicates). However, a better integration of the story memory account with alternative modes of organization in memory would shore up the weaknesses in the present theory.

These are quibbles with the account as presented. On the whole, I think the account is right and accords with my developmental model very well indeed, as Schank and Abelson have discussed. The strong form of the claims made are provocative and will no doubt, thereby, help to fill the holes that presently exist in psychology's treatment of the role that stories play in our social and cognitive lives and thoughts.

REFERENCES

Astington, J. W. (1993). *The Child's Discovery of the Mind.* Cambridge, MA: Harvard University Press.
Astington, J. W., Harris, P. L., & Olson, D. (Eds.). (1988). *Developing Theories of Mind.* Cambridge, England: Cambridge University Press.

Bruner, J. S. (1986). *Actual minds, possible worlds.* Cambridge, MA: Harvard University Press.

Bruner, J. S. (1990). *Acts of meaning.* Cambridge, MA: Harvard University Press.

Ceci, S. J., & Bruck, M. (1993). Suggestibility of the child witness: A historical review and synthesis. *Psychological Bulletin, 113,* 403–439.

Donald, M. (1991). *Origins of the modern mind.* Cambridge, MA: Harvard University Press.

Engel, S. (1986). *Learning to reminisce: A developmental study of how young children talk about the past.* Unpublished doctoral dissertation, City University of New York Graduate Center.

Fivush, R., & Hamond, N. R. (1990). Autobiographical memory across the preschool years: Toward reconceptualizing childhood amnesia. In R. Fivush, & J. A. Hudson (Ed.), *Knowing and remembering in young children* (pp. 223–248). New York: Cambridge University Press.

Fivush, R., & Hudson, J. A. (1990). *Knowing and remembering in young children.* New York: Cambridge University Press.

Hudson, J. A. (1990). The emergence of autobiographic memory in mother-child conversation. In R. Fivush, & J. A. Hudson (Ed.), *Knowing and Remembering in Young Children* (pp. 166–196). New York: Cambridge University Press.

Hudson, J. A., & Shapiro, L. R. (1991). From knowing to telling: The development of children's scripts, stories, and personal narratives. In A. McCabe, & C. Peterson (Ed.), *Developing Narrative Structure* (pp. 89–136). Hillsdale, NJ: Lawrence Erlbaum Associates.

Mullen, M. K. (1994). Earliest recollections of childhood: A demographic analysis. *Cognition, 52,* 55–79.

Nelson, K. (1986). *Event knowledge: Structure and function in development.* Hillsdale, NJ: Lawrence Erlbaum Associates.

Nelson, K. (Ed.). (1989). *Narratives from the crib.* Cambridge, MA: Harvard University Press.

Nelson, K. (1993a). The psychological and social origins of autobiographical memory. *Psychological Science, 4,* 1–8.

Nelson, K. (1993b). Towards a theory of the development of autobiographical memory. In A. Collins, M. Conway, S. Gathercole, & P. Morris (Ed.), *Theories of memory.* Hillsdale, NJ: Lawrence Erlbaum Associates.

Reese, E., Haden, C. A. & Fivush, R. (1993). Mother-child conversations about the past: Relationships of style and memory over time. *Cognitive Development, 8,* 403–430.

Tessler, M., & Nelson, K. (1994). Making memories: The influence of joint encoding on later recall. *Conciousness and Cognition, 3,*

Whiten, A. (Ed.). (1991). *Natural theories of mind: Evolution, development and simulation of everyday mindreading* . London: Basil Blackwood.

12

Memory for Events in Close Relationships: Applying Schank and Abelson's Story Skeleton Model

John G. Holmes
Sandra L. Murray
University of Waterloo

The term "storytelling" has a delightful double meaning. On the one hand, it implies recounting experiences in a coherent narrative format with the perspective of an audience in mind. On the other hand, it can also connote a certain slippage from the realities of the episodes it supposedly portrays, if not a wholesale bending of the facts to create a "good story." Indeed, this latter theme is perhaps as apparent in Schank and Abelson's chapter as the former one. They suggest that life's exigencies are such that the natural complexities of our realities are not easily contained in a story format. "This means, in effect, that one has to lie. We must leave out the details that don't fit, and invent some that make things work better" (p. 34).

Schank and Abelson develop the provocative view that these leveling and sharpening aspects of storytelling are critical in determining memory for events: The "laundered version" of experiences, as represented in the story skeleton, is largely what is remembered. Almost everything else is reconstructed. "We lose the original and keep the copy," eventually believing the story we have told. The authors base this argument on a functionalist view of social cognition, suggesting that knowledge is often structured in a story format to facilitate adaptations to everyday situations, and to aid efficient storage in memory of interconnected experiences. The dictates of cognitive economy are such that individuals typically "enter a situation wanting to tell a certain kind of story." As a result, old stories shape the meaning of new situations. Given this perspective, the chapter focuses heavily on assimilative processes and on the role of the structure of existing stories in shaping interpretations of events.

In this commentary we argue that although these themes are an integral part of the story, they fail to capture some important aspects of the process of narrative construction. Individuals don't tell stories about all of the events in their lives. Instead, storytelling is often triggered by efforts to give meaning to negative events. Because such events are typically neither anticipated nor desired, they may not be easily assimilated into old stories. In fact, individuals face an interesting conundrum in creating stories about events with aspects they would rather forget. Namely, will the cognitive activity that is devoted to them have the ironic effect of only making them more memorable (cf. Srull & Wyer, 1989), or can individuals tell their stories in ways that dull the recollection of intrusive elements? We believe that individuals often adjust to disappointing realities by accommodating them in revised or even original stories, stories that seem to turn apparent disappointments into trivial exceptions or even somewhat positive experiences. Thus, we contend that the process of story reconstruction and change deserves more attention than it receives in Schank and Abelson's short discussion of "anomalies."

Certain types of stories are likely to handle this accommodative function, whereas others are likely to handle the assimilative function. In making this argument, we are suggesting that the authors do not distinguish between different types of narratives. We argue that stories are organized in a hierarchical fashion, ordered in terms of the degree to which they support significant beliefs and values. Higher-order or *master stories* serve as templates for editing experiences, as the authors describe in their depiction of old favorites. On the other hand, lower-order stories that are less central to individuals' goals act as a first line of defense in terms of dealing with the often troubling circumstances that require storytelling. Put another way, we believe that some stories are constructed or revised in a more on-line fashion that accommodates or reacts to the dictates of reality. The functions of such stories and their properties may be quite different from those that describe stories central to a person's beliefs. We argue that lower-level stories often have the goal of adjusting realities so that they can more easily be incorporated into the master stories.

In a broader sense, we are suggesting that storytelling is a process located at the intersection of motivation and cognition. The leveling and sharpening aspects of storytelling are ideally suited to individuals' goals of "seeing what they want to see," and ultimately, "remembering what they want to remember." Our comments will focus on the process of motivated construal, particularly in the domain of close relationships. We argue that narrative form provides considerable cognitive advantages in terms of helping individuals sustain important relationship beliefs.

SOME STORIES ARE MORE IMPORTANT THAN OTHERS

Beliefs about specific relationships, like beliefs about the self, have been depicted as organized in a hierarchical manner (Baldwin, 1992; Brickman, 1987; Gergen & Gergen, 1988; Holmes, 1981). Certain beliefs are broad in scope and essentially summarize individuals' attitudes toward a relationship. These might include conclusions about the partner being the "right person," someone who is worthy of love and trust. Such prototypical beliefs would index vivid exemplars or master stories that supported and justified the conclusions. As Schank and Abelson note, the beliefs and stories are essentially packaged together.

Various theorists have argued that individuals are strongly motivated to tell such good stories about partners to support unequivocal conclusions about their relationships. This sense of closure or conviction fosters feelings of security in the face of the considerable risks experienced in close relationships (e.g., Bowlby, 1977; Holmes, 1991) and justifies continuing commitments (e.g., Abelson, 1959; Johnson & Rusbult, 1989). Of course, not all individuals are able to feel confident telling good stories. Individuals with more ambivalent feelings may entertain a story with a skeleton summarizing their current concerns with their relationship, one that competes with a story summarizing their hopes.

Midlevel stories are less inclusive and portray generic experiences within more limited domains. For instance, Kelley (1979; 1992) has suggested that there are only a limited number of prototypical situations that individuals confront in their interactions. Thus their stories are likely to focus on the particular *types* of situations seen as formative in their relationships. For instance, individuals will learn the consequences of being an assertive person in circumstances requiring initiative, and of being vulnerable in situations where they are depending on their partner's willingness to respond to their needs. Such beliefs might be stored in several locations depending on the consistency of experience across relationship domains. For example, a person might separately index stories about counting on her partner in the household and affectional domains.

Such learning templates would seem to have a narrative, sequential structure: They link types of situations, the stage, to particular performances that are contingent on each other. They essentially resemble generic "scripts" (Schank & Abelson, 1977). Indeed, relationship knowledge has been posited to be stored in such "if-then" production sequences that describe self in-relation-to other in certain situations (Baldwin, 1992; Kihlstrom & Cantor, 1983). For instance, a story might feature a plot developing from the stem, "If I try to depend on my husband to do his share of household duties without reminding him, then. . . ." Memories of such sequences must preserve the connections among events if they are to facilitate behavioral adaptation in relationships. Research using lexical decision tasks suggests that the if-then units are accessed as a whole, and that retrieval is facilitated when the unit is consistent with higher-level relationship beliefs such as trust or distrust (Baldwin, Fehr, Keedian, Seidel, & Thompson, 1993).

Finally, micronarratives are more limited in scope, focusing on either specific events or narrow categories of experience (Gergen & Gergen, 1988). These types of limited accounts have been seen as a promising tool for examining subjective interpretations and construals of experiences. The narrative form permits investigators to explore the spontaneous cognitive structure of individuals' representations in ways that are not easily captured by scaled response formats (e.g.,

Baumeister, Stillwell, & Wotman, 1990; Harvey, Flanary, & Morgan, 1988; Murray & Holmes, 1994; Ross & Holmberg, 1990).

Schank and Abelson acknowledge such a possible hierarchy of stories when they discuss how old stories are selected in terms of their similarity to new circumstances. They suggest that new situations and old stories can be examined for common elements at the level of plans, goals, or even themes that drive those goals. They also concede that individuals form stories from a definite point of view, and that the master story will dominate other stories that might be vying for attention. It is to this latter issue that we now turn.

SOME STORIES ARE MORE FLEXIBLE THAN OTHERS

We are proposing that micronarratives, and to a certain extent, midlevel stories, provide the interface with the ongoing realities of relationships: They are the repositories of updated information. These stories can be more easily modified because they have fewer associations with other stories, and because they are more flexible in terms of the demands of good narrative form than broadly thematic stories. The malleability of lower-level stories gives individuals the ability to develop a good story to suit the occasion, absorbing new or even inconsistent information, while doing so in a way that renders the realities more palatable in terms of their implications for the relationship. At times these efforts at editing experience through creative storytelling may not be fully successful. For instance, a narrative about a partner's transgression may have implications for perceptions of an attribute that is seen as important in other stories. As we explore, however, revisions in lower-level stories typically need not contaminate stories that are dear to a person's heart. This is because storytelling at these lower levels is often controlled, in a top-down manner, by the more imperial macrolevel stories that individuals are strongly motivated to maintain. The stories that index significant beliefs will strongly shape the accessibility of story skeletons at lower levels. Thus, whereas micronarratives must sometimes be revised or constructed on-line to incorporate information that does not easily fit old stories at that level, the storytelling process will typically be designed to absorb the anomalies without disturbing more significant beliefs. Micronarratives and midlevel stories exist in the service of maintaining individuals' convictions.

Convictions about relationships, however, can be eroded, as individuals' experiences all too painfully attest. Like a house of cards, good stories may unravel as the substories and plots that once supported them start to point to alternative, less positive story lines. Holmes and Rempel (1989) characterized individuals who entertain a pessimistic story that competes for attention with a more optimistic one as being uncertain or ambivalent. Uncertainty is considered to be an aversive state that individuals will be motivated to reduce by searching for the "real story." Once individuals start to test hypotheses about their relationships, there is a basic change in the nature of information processing.

Whereas individuals with a sense of conviction in their master story seek to select micronarratives that help sustain their attitudes wherever possible, individuals with competing stories are more likely to treat new information as potentially diagnostic, and to let the story unfold with fewer a priori restrictions. Thus, new or revised narratives are more likely to contaminate their hopeful master story. The purpose of storytelling shifts from attitude-maintenance to attitude-formation and the testing of alternative story lines. Framed in terms of Kruglanski's (1989) lay epistemic theory of knowledge, individuals' primary motivation may shift from the need for specific closure to a fear of invalidity.

Because several master stories are competing for dominance in uncertain individuals, the *context* of storytelling may have a greater influence on the story that emerges, priming one skeleton or another. Holmes and Rempel (1989) suggested that uncertain individuals' concerns with vulnerability are easily primed by salient negative information. If the pessimistic skeleton is accessed, the result may be a risk-averse orientation to protect themselves from a further dashing of their hopes. Thus, uncertain individuals' approach in selecting appropriate micronarratives may not simply be a more bottom-up or inferential one, but a cautious one guided partly by a relatively accessible pessimistic master story.

For instance, Holmes and Rempel asked married individuals to vividly recall an episode from their marriage and to tell the story into a tape recorder. Some participants recalled a time when their partner had responded positively to important needs, whereas others recalled a time when their partner had disappointed them and let them down. In recounting events in a *subsequent* interaction with their partners, uncertain individuals who were primed with the negative memory depicted the interaction far more negatively than did comparable individuals in a control group. In contrast, trusting individuals described the interaction more *positively* after being primed with the negative memory, compared to trusting individuals in a control group or in the condition where they had recalled a positive memory. The latter result is consistent with the notion that threatening negative information triggered the positive master story of trusting individuals, who then used the accessible story skeleton to guide the construction of their micronarrative.

NEGATIVE EVENTS AS A SPUR TO STORYTELLING

Taylor (1991) has suggested that negative events are particularly likely to mobilize cognitive activity, as a consequence of individuals' adaptive efforts to evaluate and react to potential threats. Researchers in the close relationships area have made a similar point, arguing that events that disrupt plans and goals prompt a meaning analysis that focuses on a causal understanding of the situation (Berscheid, 1983; Holtzworth-Munroe & Jacobson, 1985). Indeed, most of the stories given as examples by Schank and Abelson involve negative events. Even their stories involving relationships center on individuals' explanations for the dissolution of their marriages. Not surprisingly, these stories have a heavy emphasis on self-justification, as individuals struggle to make sense of a very significant event.

The research of Harvey and his colleagues (e.g., Harvey, Weber, Galvin, Huszti, & Garnick, 1986) on individuals' *accounts* of their divorces supports this emphasis on causal explanations as a major component of storytelling. Indeed, research on significant negative life events has focused on individuals' need to find meaning in such circumstances as a way of reestablishing a sense of control and dealing with their shattered assumptions (e.g., Janoff-Bulman, 1989; Silver & Wortman, 1980).

Although significant negative life events are especially likely to trigger storytelling, individuals obviously also construct stories about more positive circumstances. Relationship sagas do not focus solely on betrayal. At any point in time, most individuals report being relatively satisfied in their marriages (cf. Brehm, 1992), and their master stories will affirm such positive conclusions. However, we argue that even under these circumstances, most storytelling is still likely to be spurred by individuals' efforts to deal with negativity in their relationships.

For happy couples, negative aspects of their relationships raise doubts and threaten the integrity of their convictions: They represent troubling loose ends that are inimical to maintaining a good story (Brickman, 1987; Murray & Holmes, 1993). Consequently, individuals will strive to reformulate their stories in ways that diffuse the meaning of the negative elements, while at the same time they edit the offending experiences to make them less threatening. Somewhat paradoxically then, we are proposing that the stories told by satisfied individuals about their relationships are particularly revealing of their concerns about their partners, although these concerns may be masked by the way they are embedded in their stories.

For less happy couples, negative experiences are likely to trigger storytelling because of individuals' self-protective concerns that such events might have larger implications for their relationship. Salient negative information about partners may prime their pessimistic story, which competes for attention with a more hopeful one, because the negative circumstances requiring storytelling have more elements in common with it. As we argued earlier, the issue of which story dominates, and which provides coloration, is likely to be determined by features of the context eliciting the story.

SCHANK AND ABELSON'S BASIC MODEL

Schank and Abelson propose that once a story skeleton has been developed to capture significant experiences, it will control memory for events that fall under its purview. For instance, they suggest that generic betrayal stories will guide recall of autobiographical material by providing a template for reconstructing negative elements that are consistent with its theme. In contrast, positive elements that do not fit the skeleton are less likely to be recalled. After all, caveats to a theme do not satisfy the dictates of good storytelling.

Some evidence for such a pattern was apparent in the "First Years of Marriage Project," a longitudinal study of newlyweds conducted at the University of Michigan by Joseph Veroff and his colleagues (reported in Holmberg & Holmes, 1994). In this study, newlywed couples were asked to tell the story of their relationships.

Two years later the couples were asked to retell the stories about their relationship history. Thus, for the early stages of their relationships (courtship, wedding and honeymoon period), individuals' memories for the same events were available, collected two years apart. Half the couples in the memory study were selected on the basis of their showing a significant decline in their marital well-being during this period; the other half were matched in terms of initial satisfaction, and remained stable in well-being over the two years. Coders rated the stories for affective content and statements of ambivalent feelings about the period being described (e.g., expressed desires for independence rather than intimacy).

The results indicated that husbands whose current story skeleton was negative recalled the courtship and newlywed period as much more negative than they had two years before. Both husbands and wives in this declining satisfaction group showed a similar negative bias in their statements about ambivalent feelings. In contrast, couples in the stable satisfaction group recalled the early years as being even more positive than they had described them in their original stories.

The storytelling process for unhappy couples seems to subject them to a case of double jeopardy. Not only are they unhappy now, but positive aspects of their earlier experiences are lost to them, masked by their current story skeleton. Their current copy of the story of what their relationships were once like is only a pale shadow of the original. One can easily imagine an earnest marital therapist trying to generate a modicum of good feeling to motivate constructive change by having partners remember how they once felt for each other—and coming up cold. Indeed, the process of recounting the past might only strengthen current views and sharpen the storyline further by highlighting supposed experiences that pointed to their problems and disaffection, even then.

STORY CONSTRUCTION AND ITS IMPACT ON MEMORY

Schank and Abelson's intriguing portrayal of the impact of story skeletons on memory has much to commend in it. However, if their theory is accepted at face value, then the process of story construction itself becomes central to understanding memory. It becomes critical to specify how individuals might arrive at their laundered version of events because it is the skeleton that then controls recall. Thus, the rules that govern composition of a good story are ultimately related to propositions about what will be remembered. We believe that the implications of such rules for predictions about memory have not been sufficiently considered.

There are some obvious influences on story construction, including norms about how a story must be composed to achieve explanatory coherence, the availability of cognitive templates from old stories, individuals' goals in composing the story, and one would assume, the dictates of the realities that must be conveyed. Despite the intuitively compelling aspects of the latter premise, we will argue that objective realities typically provide little constraint on storytelling, and when they do, their effects are often insidious and delayed. If this is the case, the door is left open for the other sources of influence to play a more integral role than one might have expected.

As do all good storytellers, individuals appear to possess considerable license in constructing impressions of the partners they most want or expect to see (Murray & Holmes, 1993). That is, behavior must be interpreted and given meaning, motives for that behavior must be inferred, and most indirectly of all, impressions of a partner's personal characteristics must be constructed (e.g., Gergen, Hepburn, & Fisher, 1986; Griffin & Ross, 1991). As a result, intimates need not be bound by only one possible construal of another's virtues and faults as dictated by some stern objective reality. For instance, an individual might reconcile the threat posed by her partner's stubbornness during conflicts by interpreting it as a sign of integrity, rather than selfishness. Alternatively, she might try to excuse this fault by embellishing her partner's generally tolerant nature in her stories.

The potential for considerable flexibility in the storytelling process is readily acknowledged by Schank and Abelson. Indeed, they talk about the "art of skeleton selection," and note that "very little objective reality exists here. . . . Authors construct their own reality" (p. 52). This license in interpretation allows the possibility of working backwards (cf. Ross, 1989), of deciding on a good story and "then finding the facts that support this point of view," (p. 50) as the delightful example from the movie *Annie Hall* illustrated. Consequently, seeing particular events as an instance of a more general, preferred story causes the teller of the story to forget the differences between the particular and the general, so that the latter then controls memory of the situation (p. 50).

Just how far can the fabric of reality be stretched in these ways? And to what extent does the cognitive work involved in rendering it compatible with a favorite story affect the recall of events? That is, if a potentially incongruent event is somehow transformed into an expectancy-consistent story, what principles govern memory for what happened? In the discussion that follows, we suggest that the notion of interpretive license in the editing process has some interesting and important implications for memory.

Memory for Everyday Events in Close Relationships

Research on married individuals' attributions for events in their relationships suggests that satisfied, trusting intimates tend to make interpretations of behavior that are relationship-enhancing, that is, they create charitable micronarratives consistent with their overall positive attitudes. For instance, such individuals tag misdeeds to unstable features of situations or to relatively innocuous characteristics, thereby avoiding any unpleasant generalizations about their partners' characters (cf. Bradbury & Fincham, 1990). In terms of the Schank and Abelson model, one might think of trusting individuals as accommodating to circumstances by creating favorite stories that offer "ready-made excuses" for transgressions, or that feature relatively endearing imperfections. For example, periodic lateness by a partner might fit a storyline involving "being busy at work" or "being the type of absent-minded person who has no idea about time." Such interpretations, according to the authors, become part of the story index itself (p. 67), and are thus more easily accessed when they are needed.

To make such stories fit the circumstances, a certain degree of license may be required in editing out details of events that aren't consistent with the explanations and selectively focusing on details that support them. The consequence of this leveling and sharpening process is that it supposedly allows memory to forget the details not collected in the composition: Memory maintains the themes of the story skeleton, and perhaps not much else. If this is the case, what was once a potentially negative experience, one inconsistent with individuals' expectations and convictions, may be essentially erased from memory. Not only will troubling details be forgotten, but by relegating the event to a mundane, somewhat insignificant story, the laundered version itself may not even be remembered as an exemplar.

Storytelling in such cases would become a self-erasing process that approximates the authors' dictum of "tell it once, and never tell it again" (p. 44). Even in less extreme cases where the particular event is not forgotten but largely remembered in its edited form, storytelling may still be effective in suppressing unwanted thoughts compared to other alternatives. The issue is not only whether negative, inconsistent information is remembered more or less better than expectancy-consistent information, but whether storytelling renders negative information less memorable than unfocused efforts to merely forget what happened.

The implications of the story construction process for individuals' memory for everyday events in their marriages were examined by Holmberg and Holmes (1993). In this study, both partners completed standardized daily diary forms four days a week for a period of three weeks. On time-line forms, individuals depicted in their own words any interaction they experienced within a three-hour period that had an impact on their feelings for their partner. At the end of the time period, they were asked to describe the most significant of these events in more detail, and to provide interpretations of their partners' behavior on scaled attribution questions.

From these protocols, a positive and a negative story were selected randomly for each person. Roughly five weeks after the target day, participants were asked to recall, as accurately as possible, the detailed descriptions and attributions they had provided initially. A very brief description of the event was provided, in their own words, to key them to the particular episode. A variety of other measures was collected on the target and recall days, including individuals' feelings for their partner that day and their mood at the time of their ratings. Finally, efforts were made to index individuals' master stories or *mental models* of their relationships in terms of the trust individuals reported in their partners.

Trusting individuals' initial stories about negative events were clearly more excusing of their partners' transgressions than were the stories of less trusting, uncertain individuals. According to the ratings of trained coders, the accounts of those higher in trust diminished the significance of the event in relatively narrow stories by focusing on more specific, less global causes. In contrast, trusting individuals were more likely to interpret positive events in terms of their larger story, highlighting how their partners' actions reflected their broader virtues. Individuals' responses to scaled attribution questions were very consistent with the observers' ratings of their open-ended narratives.

For trusting individuals in this study, negative events were more incongruent with expectations than they were for uncertain individuals, whereas positive events were more congruent. Information that is inconsistent with expectations has typically been found to be more memorable, presumably because it is processed more extensively (cf. Srull & Wyer, 1989). Are trusting individuals thus saddled with clearer memories of instances where their partners fall short of expectations? Or is a negative event rendered less memorable after trusting individuals have cognitively transformed it within a narrative that is *not* inconsistent with their beliefs, as they appeared to do?

The results for measures of memory were consistent with this latter line of reasoning about a *decay hypothesis.* Each thought unit at time one was compared to an individual's protocol at time two. Trusting individuals were *less* accurate in remembering aspects of negative episodes than were uncertain individuals, whereas trusting women, but not men, were more accurate in remembering positive episodes. That is, the more individuals trusted their partners, the fewer the "hits" they attained for negative events, controlling for the total number of items to be recalled. (The lack of effect for trusting men in their recall of positive events is consistent with other research which suggests that in terms of cognitive activity about relationships, men go by the axiom, "If it ain't broke, don't fix it.")

Such differential remembering might have consequences for the way individuals evaluate past events at the time of recall. In terms of how participants remembered feeling and thinking about the event, trust was strongly related to evidence of distortions in memory. The more individuals trusted their partners, the greater their tendency to underestimate how upset they had been at the time and how much they had blamed their partner for a transgression. High trust was also associated with remembering positive events in positive ways, whereas uncertainty was associated with underestimating the good feelings and credit given to the partner initially. (Distortions in memory were also predicted, though less strongly, by variables postulated by other authors to influence memory, such as individuals' mood and their feelings for their partner at the time of recall.)

Further, this apparent tendency for individuals to use their master story about trust as a heuristic for guiding reconstruction was much more pronounced in certainty-oriented persons (Sorrentino, Holmes, Hanna, & Sharp, in press). Such individuals exhibit a chronic style of thinking that orients them to achieving cognitive clarity and avoiding ambiguity through assimilating new information into existing conclusions. They are uncomfortable when faced with new evidence that challenges their old stories, and they fail to show the normal pattern of better memory for expectancy-incongruent information that is apparent for uncertainty-oriented individuals (Driscoll, Hamilton, & Sorrentino, 1991). These correlational results are open to a variety of explanations and we present them largely to promote debate on some interesting issues.

First, the results do not fit the pattern of better recall for expectancy-incongruent events. Many of the results showing that pattern were obtained in laboratory paradigms where clear behavioral descriptions were quite patently inconsistent with the general impressions provided of a target person (e.g., Hastie & Kumar,

1979). Perhaps in many circumstances, individuals have far more flexibility in interpreting the meaning of behavior than they had in such studies. Further, in contrast to those studies, individuals typically have a story that they would prefer to tell about an episode, for both cognitive and motivational reasons.

What rules best describe memory when an apparently incongruent event has been transformed in the process of story construction into a less offensive version? Does editing and reframing then result in convenient memory such that the event now functions like a congruent element, facilitating forgetting? In other words, why remember an event that is just one more exemplar of an old story or a new but mundane one? Schank and Abelson's emphasis on story construction and our perspective on interpretive license suggest that more attention be given to this issue of how the construal process affects principles of memory.

Second, the present results suggest that the selection of story skeletons for depicting events is controlled in a top-down fashion by individuals' master stories about their relationships. For instance, trusting individuals clearly constructed more charitable narratives about their partners' transgressions. But the content of these original narratives was not fully retained, in that differential memory loss and distortion occurred over and above individuals' initial construal of events. These memory effects were in a direction consistent with the more general themes and interpretations apparent in the initial stories.

Thus, as Schank and Abelson suggest, only the story skeletons may be retained—the substance—and almost everything else may involve reconstruction. We forget the differences between the particular and the general, retaining a structure that provides only some sort of base-rate accuracy. The results we observed would be consistent with this idea that memories were accentuated because leveling and sharpening occurred in a way that preserved a coherent storyline, but not the details.

Finally, we suggested earlier that individuals may have midlevel stories that permit some degree of acuity in inferring more concrete details. For instance, an individual might have a story skeleton relating to what typically happens when she and her husband have disputes about certain types of household chores. By categorizing the situation to be recalled, she might achieve the semblance of an account through stereotypic or base-rate accuracy. However, if she were happy in her relationship, she may have had fewer opportunities to compose stories about such conflicts, or may have resisted the temptation to extract broader themes from her experiences. Her narrative may have been a more extemporaneous effort to minimize the situation. As we noted earlier, micronarratives can be used to accommodate to events without disturbing more important stories. If she had not developed as coherent a story skeleton, she would be less able to generate "hits" than an uncertain individual who had a well-worn storyline. This logic is quite consistent with our findings for trusting individuals' poorer recall of negative events.

Straining to Tell a Story

Sometimes storytelling is a difficult task, in contrast to the above portrayal. Certain troubling realities have a way of stubbornly resisting the best storytelling efforts to put them to rest. For instance, newlyweds typically explain away the importance of conflicts in their relationships, but the incidence of conflict at marriage predicts declines in satisfaction several years later (Kelly, Huston, & Cate, 1985; Markman, 1981). Such results suggest that stories that are more tall tales than docudramas may catch up with individuals over time.

Our hunch is that individuals are able, in a vague sense, to monitor their own cognitive processes (e.g., Schwarz, Bless, Strack, Klumpp, Rittenauer, Schatka, & Simons, 1991), and that the experience of strain in fashioning a story functions as information about the success of the storytelling venture itself. At some point, difficulty in reframing negative actions and editing out offending details will also result in a level of cognitive activity that only makes the episodes all the more memorable (Srull & Wyer, 1989). For instance, Hamilton, Grubb, Acorn, Trolier, and Carpenter (1990) found that when an attributional task was difficult, individuals recalled more information about behavioral events and their context than when it was easy. In the Holmberg and Holmes (1994) study described previously, very serious negative behavior by a partner was actually remembered as being more negative than the way it was initially portrayed, presumably because it received more extensive cognitive processing. What recourse is left to storytellers as they confront this dilemma where their partners' negative behavior is not easily masked by existing stories?

Creating New Stories to Deal With Old Circumstances: Accommodating to Reality?

As couples' lives change and interdependence increases, some old favorites that once seemed timeless may begin to feel dated and naive. For instance, when evidence of particular faults (e.g., stubbornness) recurs, ready-made excuses that automatically tagged such misdeeds to situational factors (e.g., stress) may seem tired and lame. Storytellers come to realize that such recurrent misdeeds cannot simply be explained away, but warrant dispositional or trait inferences (e.g., Kelley, 1971). Also, new stresses, such as the changing demands posed by first parenthood, inevitably reveal weaknesses in their partners that storytellers never foresaw in the creation of their existing stories. In the rush of romantic love, for example, few intimates may contemplate eventual struggles over household chores. In the face of such challenges, many intimates appear to revise their existing tales or construct new stories to acknowledge past and present offenses but still preserve the integrity of their prevailing, positive macrolevel storylines.

Revising Old Tales: A Threat Induction Paradigm

In a recent set of studies, we developed an experimental paradigm to examine precisely how individuals accommodate their stories to incorporate their partners' chronic faults (Murray & Holmes, 1993; 1994). To do this, we created negative attributes in the laboratory by threatening what we felt were relationship truisms for dating individuals. The truisms were "conflict in relationships is bad" and "differences are bad." By arguing in favor of the opposite propositions (e.g., conflict is good), we turned partners' apparent virtues (e.g., low conflict) into faults. Comparing the perceptions of threatened individuals to the old story baseline provided by controls allowed us to observe the story-accommodation process directly.

In the first study, we threatened dating individuals' existing stories by depicting their partners' reluctance to initiate conflicts over joint interests as a significant fault. Experimental and control participants first depicted their partners as rarely initiating disagreements over joint interests. We then turned these specific instances of conflict avoidance into a fault by exposing experimental subjects to a bogus *Psychology Today* article arguing for the intimacy-promoting nature of conflict-engagement. (Control subjects read the article at the end of the study.) All subjects then described their partners' general willingness to initiate conflicts on a scaled conflict index and wrote open-ended stories about the development of intimacy in their relationships. We expected experimental subjects to dispel their doubts by transforming their stories about their partners' conflict behavior, making it appear less negative or even positive.

In the next study, we created a potential source of negativity by depicting partners' inattention to their differences as an impediment to intimacy. To establish this threat, we first asked participants to provide concrete examples of similarities and differences between themselves and their dating partners. (These examples consisted primarily of similarities.) Experimental subjects then read a bogus *Psychology Today* article that argued that partners' awareness of their differences fosters relationship intimacy. Control participants read an article on an unrelated topic. To explore how individuals transformed their similarities into stories about differences, we then gave all participants the opportunity to provide any additional details they wished to their original pool of examples, purportedly to help the experimenters better understand their meaning.

Defusing Doubts by Seeing Virtues in Faults

The results of both storytelling experiments illustrate intimates' ability to reconstruct their memories in ways that turn apparent faults in their partners into virtues. In response to the threat in Study 1, the experimental subjects who possessed the least actual evidence of conflict in their relationships were most likely to construct images of conflict-engaging partners on the scaled conflict index (when compared to controls). Threatened individuals also retold the stories about the history of their relationship in their open-ended accounts, focusing more heavily on how their partners' virtues around engaging conflicts had brought them closer together.

Threatened individuals in Study 2 also constructed virtues in apparent faults, finding evidence of their strengths around recognizing differences in the face of their overwhelming similarities. Most important, threatened individuals transformed the meaning of specific pieces of evidence. For example, in providing additional details to their original similarities, they turned these similarities into differences. Like revisionist historians, threatened individuals in both studies conveniently whitewashed the past (that contained evidence of the offending attributes) for the exigencies of the present. Presumably, the story skeletons that now captured their goals (e.g., "we really do argue" or "we really are different") were used to recruit the desired evidence from their memories. In this way, interpretive license inherent in storytelling may restore intimates' convictions by blinding them to the selectivity of their own recollections.

Defusing Doubts by Constructing "Yes, but . . ." Refutations

In some cases, denial may place too much of a strain on even the best storytellers. However, acknowledging faults need not undermine positive storylines if intimates restructure or "refence" their midlevel theories or stories in ways that defuse the meaning of imperfections. That is, individuals may strategically accommodate their personal theories about which attributes are the most important ingredients of success according to their partners' actual virtues and faults (e.g., Kunda, 1987). For example, threatened individuals in Study 2 embellished the significance of their differences by linking them to enhanced feelings of closeness, security and warmth, whereas control subjects maintained their original story lines by downplaying the significance of such differences.

Intimates' construction of "yes, but . . ." arguments that acknowledge their partners' faults while simultaneously minimizing their significance reveals these relationship-affirming theories. Individuals might keep their partners' weaknesses from tarnishing their positive stories simply by denying the significance of their partners' weaknesses (e.g., "I know he isn't that expressive, but it really doesn't matter. I love him just the way he is.") Similarly, compensatory "Yes, buts . . ." that link faults to virtues in related domains may also contain the threat posed by negativity (e.g., "He's a rather closed type of man, but that's not so important. He shows he cares in other ways," Holmes, 1991).

If individuals integrate negativity but refute its implications in their storytelling, acknowledging their partners' faults need not pose any threat to their positive stories. In Study 1, for example, threatened individuals defused concerns about their partners' conflict-avoidance around joint interests by linking this fault to their partners' greater virtues around conflict-engagement in other areas. We also found evidence for such compensatory storylines in a third study we designed to examine whether individuals can defuse concerns about their partners' faults by linking them to related, more significant virtues. Affectively consistent attitudes may even depend on the presence of such refutational "Yes, but . . ." structures (e.g., Chaiken & Yates, 1985; Holmes & Rempel, 1989).

GOOD STORIES: THE STRUCTURE OF CONFIDENCE

We suspect that confidence in an intimate partner does not allow for any important loose ends in one's stories, as evidenced in less than positive, charitable construals of a partner's attributes. Instead, a partner's positive and negative qualities may need to fit together into a unified whole or *gestalt* where the meaning of potential faults is interpreted in light of surrounding virtues (e.g., Asch, 1946; Asch & Zukier, 1984). Thus, storytelling, when it is successful, culminates in complex, cogent narratives that sustain confidence.

Such a perspective is consistent with Pennington and Hastie's (1992) story model of juror decision making. They found that factors facilitating explanatory coherence in story structures led to more confident verdicts. This hypothesized relation between confidence and cognitive structure also has strong parallels to McGuire and Papageorgis' (1961) inoculation theory of attitude stability. Just as cultural truisms are vulnerable to threat, stories that focus only on virtues may be quite fragile, whereas stories that acknowledge but counterargue faults may prove more resilient. In other words, the strategies individuals use in fending off doubts at the level of microstories may result in macrolevel narratives that are more or less likely to instill confidence over time.

For instance, if positive storylines rest on intimates' denial of disappointing realities, the microstories or ready-made excuses woven around negative behavior may unravel as evidence inconsistent with the individual's construction intrudes again and again. Also, if individuals deal with their doubts by turning faults into virtues, such blatant denial may leave them quite vulnerable to recurring evidence of negativity. Alternatively, intimates might compartmentalize faults and diminish their relevance by constructing personal theories that simply deny the significance of their partners' weaknesses. However, in stories with categories restricted to grievances, current doubts may prime past concerns without also being cushioned by a partner's virtues. As a result, individuals' illusions may be left quite vulnerable to disquieting resurgences of ambivalence (Holmes & Rempel, 1989).

Intimates may be more likely to reach a lasting sense of confidence if they weave their mid- and microlevel stories in such ways that their partners' faults actually remind them of greater virtues. Through this process of *constructive linkage,* the partner's many virtues can buffer or defuse the threats posed by apparent frailties. For individuals who tell integrated stories, positive memories may be there when they need them the most, allowing them to bite their tongues in moments of crisis and anger. For instance, a wife might be less disturbed by instances of her husband's laziness around household chores if she thinks his devotion to their children more than makes up for it.

Continued confidence in an intimate partner may rest on this type of structural integrity within individuals' stories. As we noted earlier, high-trust individuals actually evaluated their partners' behavior and motives most positively when they had just been induced to recall a situation where their partners disappointed them (Holmes & Rempel, 1989). Cushioning faults within virtues may protect intimates' positive illusions from the inevitable threats posed by renewed evidence of negativity. Therefore, intimates who see the best in one another—while still acknowledging their partners' faults—may possess the types of integrated representations most likely to be resilient over time.

A potential risk in this storytelling strategy is that instances of the fault only become more memorable while they dilute the value of the virtues. Instead, we argue that virtues in such associative networks will typically seem more special, and memorable, precisely because of their link to faults (e.g., Brickman, 1987). The virtues become central to a story skeleton in a story that was told only because the fault elicited it. Wyer and Martin (1986) describe a similar bolstering effect in memory following attributional judgments. In contrast, denying or compartmentalizing faults may require constant efforts at suppression to effectively dull intimates' concerns. Ironically though, such active efforts at suppression may only make past faults more difficult to forget, especially when new evidence of negativity surfaces (e.g., Wegner, Erber, & Zanakos, 1993).

Constructing resilient, confidence-maintaining narratives necessitates merging the demands of a particularly challenging dialectic. Intimates must sustain a delicate tension between telling the story they wish to tell and telling a story that is attuned to the reality of their partners' actual qualities. Therefore, if they are to preserve feelings of confidence, individuals may need to interpret negativity in a charitable light without stretching the fabric of their experiences to an extent that involves ignoring evidence of negativity that is likely to have an insidious effect over time.

The nature of the stories intimates construct reveals the manner in which they have resolved this dialectical tension and, by inference, the fragility of their sense of confidence. Thus, by eliciting intimates' stories, researchers may uncover whether felt confidence depends on fragile, idealized narratives that may leave individuals at risk, or on stories that more realistically integrate negativity. In this way, the very structure of the narratives individuals weave may foretell the future course of their relationships—forecasting continued confidence or eventual disillusionment when old story skeletons can no longer be stretched to fit the existing data.

REFERENCES

Abelson, R. P. (1959). Modes of resolution of belief dilemmas. *Journal of Conflict Resolution, 3,* 343–352.

Asch, S. E. (1946). Forming impressions of personality. *Journal of Abnormal and Social Psychology, 41,* 258–290.

Asch, S. E., & Zukier, H. (1984). Thinking about persons. *Journal of Personality and Social Psychology, 46,* 1230–1240.

Baldwin, M. W. (1992). Relational schemas and the processing of social information. *Psychological Bulletin, 112,* 461–484.

Baldwin, M. W., Fehr, B., Keedian, E., Seidel, M., & Thompson, D. (1993). An exploration of the relational schemata underlying attachment styles: Self-report and lexical decision approaches. *Personality and Social Psychology Bulletin, 19,* 746–754.

Baumeister, R. F., Stillwell, A., & Wotman, S. R. (1990). Victim and perpetrator accounts of interpersonal conflict: Autobiographical narratives about anger. *Journal of Personality and Social Psychology, 59,* 994–1005.

Berscheid, E. (1983). Emotion. In H. H. Kelley, E. Berscheid, A. Christensen, J. H. Harvey, T. L. Huston, G. Levinger, E. McClintock, L. A. Peplau & D. R. Peterson (Eds.), *Close relationships* (pp. 110–168). New York: Freeman.

Bowlby, J. (1977). The making and breaking of affectional bonds. *British Journal of Psychiatry, 130,* 201–210.

Bradbury, T. N., & Fincham, F. D. (1990). Attributions in marriage: Review and critique. *Psychological Bulletin, 107,* 3–33.

Brehm, S. S. (1992). *Intimate relationships.* New York, NY: McGraw-Hill.

Brickman, P. (1987). *Commitment, conflict, and caring.* Englewood Cliffs, NJ: Prentice-Hall.

Chaiken, S. & Yates, S. (1985). Affective-cognitive consistency and thought-induced polarization. *Journal of Personality and Social Psychology, 49,* 1470–1481.

Driscoll, D., Hamilton, D., & Sorrentino, R. (1991). Uncertainty orientation and recall of person-descriptive information. *Personality and Social Psychology Bulletin, 17,* 494–500.

Gergen, K. J., & Gergen, M. M. (1988). Narrative and the self as relationship. In L. Berkowitz (Ed.), *Advances in experimental social psychology,* (Vol. 21, pp. 17–56). San Diego, CA: Academic Press.

Gergen, K. J., Hepburn, A., & Fisher, D. C. (1986). Hermeneutics of personality description. *Journal of Personality and Social Psychology, 50,* 1261–1270.

Griffin, D. W., & Ross, L. (1991). Subjective construal, social inference and human misunderstanding. In M. P. Zanna (Ed.), *Advances in experimental social psychology,* (Vol. 24, pp. 319–359). New York: Academic Press.

Hamilton, D. L., Grubb, P., Acorn, D., Trolier, T., & Carpenter, S. (1990). Attribution difficulty and memory for attribution-relevant information. *Journal of Personality and Social Psychology, 59,* 891–898.

Harvey, J. H., Flanary, R., & Morgan, M. (1988). Vivid memories of vivid loves gone by. *Journal of Social and Personal Relationships, 3,* 359–373.

Harvey, J. H., Weber, A. L., Galvin, K.S., Huszti, H., & Garnick, N. (1986). Attribution in the termination of close relationships: A special focus on the account. In R. Gilmour & S. Duck (Eds.), *The emerging field of personal relationships* (pp. 189–201). Hillsdale, NJ: Lawrence Erlbaum Associates.

Hastie, R., & Kumar, P. A. (1979). Person memory: Personality traits as organizing principles in memory for behavior. *Journal of Personality and Social Psychology, 37,* 25–38.

Holmberg, D., & Holmes, J. G. (1994). Reconstruction of relationship memories: A mental models approach. In N. Schwarz and S. Sudman (Eds.), *Autobiographical memory and the validity of retrospective reports* (pp. 267–288). New York: Springer-Verlag.

Holmes, J. G. (1981). The exchange process in close relationships: Micro-behavior and macromotives. In M. J. Lerner & S. C. Lerner (Eds.), *The justice motive in social behavior* (pp. 261–284). New York: Plenum.

Holmes, J. G. (1991). Trust and the appraisal process in close relationships. In W. H. Jones and D. Perlman (Eds.), *Advances in personal relationships* (Vol. 2, pp. 57–104). London: Jessica Kingsley.

Holmes, J. G., & Rempel, J. K. (1989). Trust in close relationships. In C. Hendrick (Ed.), *Review of personality and social psychology: Close relationships* (Vol. 10, pp. 187–219). Newbury Park, CA: Sage.

Holtzworth-Munroe, A., & Jacobson, N. S. (1985). Causal attributions of marital couples: When do they search for causes? What do they conclude when they do? *Journal of Personality and Social Psychology, 48,* 1398–1412.

Janoff-Bulman, R. (1989). Assumptive worlds and the stress of traumatic events: Applications of the schema construct. *Social Cognition, 7,* 113–136.

Johnson, D. J., & Rusbult, C. E. (1989). Resisting temptation: Devaluation of alternative partners as a means of maintaining commitment in close relationships. *Journal of Personality and Social Psychology, 57,* 967–980.

Kelley, H. H. (1971). Attribution in social interaction. In E. E. Jones, D. E. Kanouse, H. H. Kelley, R. E. Nisbett, S. Valins, & B. Weiner (Eds.), *Attribution: Perceiving the causes of behavior* (pp. 1–26). Morristown, NJ: General Learning Press.

Kelley, H. H. (1979). *Personal relationships: Their structures and process.* Hillsdale, NJ: Lawrence Erlbaum Associates.

Kelley, H. H. (July, 1992). *The logic of interpersonal relations.* Paper presented at the International Society for the Study of Personal Relationships, Maine.

Kelly, C., Huston, T. L., & Cate, R. M. (1985). Premarital relationship correlates of the erosion of satisfaction in marriage. *Journal of Social and Personal Relationships, 2,* 167–178.

Kihlstrom, J. F., & Cantor, N. (1983). Mental representations of the self. In L. Berkowitz (Ed.), *Advances in experimental social psychology* (Vol. 17, pp. 1–47). San Diego, CA: Academic Press.

Kruglanski, A. W. (1989). *Lay epistemics and human knowledge: Cognitive and motivational bases.* New York, NY: Plenum Press.

Kunda, Z. (1987). Motivated inference: Self-serving generation and evaluation of causal theories. *Journal of Personality and Social Psychology, 53,* 636–647.

Markman, H. J. (1981). Prediction of marital distress: A five-year follow-up. *Journal of Consulting and Clinical Psychology, 49,* 760–762.

McGuire, W. J., & Papageorgis, D. (1961). The relative efficacy of various types of prior belief-defense in producing immunity against persuasion. *Journal of Abnormal and Social Psychology, 62,* 327–337.

Murray, S. L., & Holmes, J. G. (1994). Storytelling in close relationships: The construction of confidence. *Personality and Social Psychology Bulletin, 20,* 650–663.

Murray, S. L., & Holmes, J. G. (1993). Seeing virtues in faults: Negativity and the transformation of interpersonal narratives in close relationships. *Journal of Personality and Social Psychology, 65,* 707–722.

Pennington, N., & Hastie, R. (1992). Explaining the evidence: Testing the Story Model for juror decision making. *Journal of Personality and Social Psychology, 62,* 189–206.

Ross, M. (1989). Relation of implicit theories to the construction of personal histories. *Psychological Review, 96,* 341–357.

Ross, M., & Holmberg, D. (1990). Recounting the past: Gender differences in the recall of events in the history of a close relationship. In J. M. Olson & M. P. Zanna (Eds.), *Self-inference processes: The Ontario symposium* (Vol. 6, pp. 135–152). Hillsdale, NJ: Lawrence Erlbaum Associates.

Schank, R. C., & Abelson, R. P. (1977). *Scripts, plans, goals, and understanding.* Hillsdale, NJ: Lawrence Erlbaum Associates.

Schwarz, N., Bless, H., Strack, F., Klumpp, G., Rittenauer-Schatka, H., & Simons, A. (1991). Ease of retrieval as information: Another look at the availability heuristic. *Journal of Personality and Social Psychology, 61,* 195–202.

Silver, R. L., & Wortman, C. B. (1980). Coping with undesirable life events. In J. Garber & M. Seligman (Eds.), *Human helplessness* (pp. 279–340). New York: Academic Press.

Sorrentino, R. M., Holmes, J. G., Hanna, S. E., & Sharp, A. (in press). Uncertainty orientation and trust in close relationships: Individual differences in cognitive styles. *Journal of Personality and Social Psychology.*

Srull, T. K., & Wyer, R. S., Jr. (1989). Person memory and judgment. *Psychological Review, 96,* 58–83.

Taylor, S. E. (1991). Asymmetrical effects of positive and negative events: The mobilization-minimization hypothesis. *Psychological Bulletin, 110,* 67–85.

Wegner, D. M., Erber, R., & Zanakos, S. (1993). Ironic processes in the mental control of mood and mood-related thought. *Journal of Personality and Social Psychology, 65,* 1093–1104.

Wyer, R. S., Jr., & Martin, L. L. (1986). Person memory: The role of traits, group stereotypes, and specific behaviors in the cognitive representations of persons. *Journal of Personality and Social Psychology, 50,* 661–675.

13

Stories, Identity, and the Psychological Sense of Community

Eric Mankowski
Julian Rappaport
University of Illinois at Urbana-Champaign

At the conclusion of their chapter on knowledge and memory, in which they detail their argument that stories are the "fundamental constituents" of memory, knowledge and communication, Schank and Abelson assert that cognitive and social psychologists have "lost sight of the forest by concentrating on the cellulose in the trees." We like their story-based, functional approach, precisely because it provides a much needed alternative to overly individualistic frameworks that fail to adequately appreciate the reciprocal relationship between individual and social memory, and other related phenomenon such as personal and social identity. Here, we suggest some of the questions, settings, and methods that such a narrative psychology, based on the formulations presented by Schank and Abelson, brings to mind if we ask about that forest (social ecology) of community life and its impact on the individual trees (see also, Sarbin, 1986).

In trying to apply Schank and Abelson's theory to questions of how community and social contexts influence individual stories and storytelling, however, we note several ways in which their conceptualization could be usefully expanded. First, Schank and Abelson argue that we tell stories and remember them based on the frameworks provided by story skeletons. They present several situations that show how various story skeletons can produce a range of interpretations and retellings of an experience. Their model is excellent at describing how new experiences are fit into existing skeletal frameworks. However, Schank and Abelson do not indicate where the cultural library of story skeletons come from or how they originate. We need to ask how past understandings are revised when entirely new story skeletons are encountered and used to narrate experiences. Without answers to such questions, we will have difficulty in adequately describing how individuals change what

211

they believe about themselves, or how they learn or create something new about themselves or the world.

Schank and Abelson also present a useful account of how memory functions from the perspective of a socially based theory of knowledge. Other theorists have also described memory as a product of social interaction (Middleton & Edwards, 1990; Nelson, 1993). Schank and Abelson point out that our stories define ourselves, and hint at how the competition to tell these stories in social settings determines whether the aspects of ourselves represented by such stories are denied or reified. This social process strikes us as interesting and important, and requires further elaboration. However, this takes the application of the "knowledge as stories" metaphor into territory beyond that represented by the concept of human memory. In this regard, we suggest that the principles of storytelling can be used in understanding the relationship between personal and social identity, and the way group storytelling is involved in the creation and transformation of memories about the self.

A final way in which Schank and Abelson's framework invites examination of the relationship between individual and social forms of knowledge is through their emphasis on the creation of knowledge through social discourse. When examining storytelling at broader levels of analysis (e.g., group, community, culture), it becomes necessary to consider a variety of forms in which stories may be communicated and indexed. Schank and Abelson limit their discussion to linguistic modes of story transmission; however, the stories that impact us most deeply are often communicated in social settings through art, song, mass media and dramatic performance. These forms of stories need also to be considered.

In what follows, we expand on these three points to indicate why story is a particularly useful concept for studying memory and identity across levels of psychological analysis, and then we present several examples from our research that illustrate how the concept of human knowledge as stories can be used to explain the function of individual storytelling in a variety of social contexts.

COMMUNITY NARRATIVES AND PERSONAL STORIES

More specifically, we suggest that Schank and Abelson's functional analysis of knowledge in terms of storytelling is useful in understanding a wide range of social phenomena that might be thought of as "conversion experiences." These experiences all concern development of, and change in, personal and social identity, or how one understands "who I am, how I got this way, how I ought to be, and what may be my future." Specific examples include these: the ways in which families, ethnic groups and sometimes neighborhoods, control, socialize, and sustain individual lives; the power of organized communities such as churches and work settings to give meaning to everyday life through their public narratives; the ways in which voluntary organizations in general, and mutual help organizations in particular, enable people to accomplish both personal identity and behavioral change; and the power of art as an indexer of collective memory and national identity stories. In short, *the phenomena of identity development and change may be understood in terms of the appropriation of shared narratives into one's personal life story on the one hand, and the creation of new narratives or modification of existing narratives on the other.*[1]

The first question to ask is one of etiology: Where do the stories and story skeletons posited by Schank and Abelson to be the starting point for interpreting new knowledge come from? They do not simply appear as whole cloth out of our individual experience. Rather, they are a product of our collective (not only our personal) histories and experiences in social settings. The ecology of settings extends psychologically over time. Settings have a history and a future. They have both proximal (direct social interaction) and distal (implicit cultural and subcultural) components (e.g., see Bronfenbrenner, 1979).

Although of concern to historians, sociologists (Mumby, 1987), anthropologists (Bruner & Gorfein, 1983), and, interestingly, ethicists (e.g., see Goldberg, 1985; Hauerwas, 1983; Goldberg, 1985; McClendon 1986), there is scant knowledge from the psychological point of view as to exactly how members of community settings create their narratives, and how these narratives in turn create both meaning and social control. Also, there is not a great deal of psychological information about how social and community settings help or hinder people who seek to make changes in their personal and social identity. These sorts of questions are of theoretical concern not only to social and cognitive psychologists. They also have important implications for clinical and community psychologists, and for anyone interested in social policy and community intervention.

Schank and Abelson's idea that knowledge is created through storytelling can be used to suggest answers to the question of how members of a community know who they are. To what extent do the members know who they are by directly memorizing the beliefs, attitudes, and rules of the community (its principles), or by example (modeling), or, as Schank and Abelson would suggest, by listening to and retelling stories? Do a community's stories teach us to do more than remember precise behaviors, moral codes, or values? How do we learn what might be thought of as (in old-fashioned language) "character," that is, the ways in which "I am and ought to be"? How do the repeated and overlearned stories known to members of a community provide the compacted images that index complex behaviors, motives, beliefs, and values that make up the shared social identity of community members? How do we participate in the creation of such stories, and how can we

---

[1]We use the term "story" to refer to an individual's cognitive representation or social communication of events that are unique to that person and organized thematically and temporally. We use the term "narrative" to describe stories that are not idiosyncratic to individuals. Therefore, a narrative is a story that is common among a group of people. The narrative may also be shared by the group through social interaction, texts and other forms of communication. We define this group as a community and their shared stories as community narratives. It may also be useful to refer to "dominant cultural narratives"— those narratives that are communicated through powerful modes of mass media or through social institutions that touch the lives of most people (e.g., public schools). These cultural narratives are likely to be known by most members of the society and serve as an influential backdrop against which community narratives and personal stories are told.

change the ones's we live by? These are the sorts of questions that arise when we see people as storytellers and listeners in their natural community contexts.

LEVELS OF ANALYSIS AND THE ROLE OF STORIES

For those trying to understand the relation between communities and individuals, one of the most serious logical mistakes to be made is what has been called the ecological fallacy, or the "error of logical typing" (Watzlawick, Wakeland, & Fish, 1974). This is the notion that a community may be understood by simply adding up the individual tendencies of its members. One example is the belief that the economic behavior of a society is the sum of individual economic decisions, without consideration of the society's overarching organizational principles, policies, or narratives (about heroic entrepreneurship, or collective loyalty, for example). Another example is believing that the prevalence of violence in a given society or subculture is the result of individual decisions, without regard to social organization or community narratives about the way anger and insults are to be dealt with (often expressed in stories, songs, and the characterization of legendary heroes such as "big, bad Leroy Brown" or John Wayne).

This difficulty in logic resembles the problem of reductionism in psychology, wherein, for example, all behavior is thought to be explainable in terms of neurochemistry. Nevertheless, even while avoiding the problem of reductionism, it is reasonable to expect that at each higher level of analysis, the known facts of lower levels should not be contradicted. Thus, if communities tell stories, and these stories have no importance with respect to the individual members' knowledge, motivation, behavior, or identity development, then the fact of such communal storytelling is of little consequence for psychologists. For this reason, a cognitive psychology based on storytelling and its functions in individual memory is of keen interest to those who believe that community narratives, in fact, do have a powerful influence on the behavior of individuals (and vice versa). That this influence can be for good or for ill (think of the Waco, Texas, Branch Davidians, or the Ku Klux Klan on the one hand, and the Amish community or the Southern Christian Leadership Conference on the other) makes it very important to applied social, clinical, and community psychologists, and ultimately to policy makers.

IDENTITY AS A STORY: EXPANDING THE PSYCHOLOGICAL SIGNIFICANCE OF THE STORY METAPHOR

Stories and storytelling are useful concepts for a cognitive psychology that spans levels of analysis. Schank and Abelson focus the implications of these concepts on memory. However, memory alone is insufficient to describe a person's current experience, expectations about the future, and the relationship between knowledge about the past, present, and future. Candidates that might meet these criteria are goals (Schlenker & Weingold, 1989) and motivations (Murray, 1938). We believe, however, that neither of these concepts are as useful or comprehensive as *identity*. Identity represents self-knowledge about the past, present, and future, and the relations among these types of knowledge. Although dependent on memories of the past, identity also encompasses individuals' current concerns (Klinger, 1977) and future visions or possible selves (Markus & Nurius, 1986). In addition, identity can be conceptualized at several levels of analysis, including the individual (personal identity), and the social or group (sense of community) (see Sarason, 1974).

Finally, and most important for this analysis, identity can be understood in terms of stories. If the *self is a knowledge structure* (Kihlstrom & Klein, in press) and *knowledge is stories,* then these ideas, in combination, suggest another metaphor: that the *self is stories.* More specifically, identity is created, enacted, and maintained through storytelling. Through the organizational and integrative functions of storytelling, disparate past experiences can be understood in relation to current and future visions of reality. The resulting personal story presents one's life as if it had happened, is continuously happening, and is expected to continue to happen in a meaningful and purposeful order. This metaphorical view of identity has a precedent in McAdams' model of identity stories (1988), and in the social constructionist writings of the Gergens (e.g., Gergen, 1991; Gergen & Gergen, 1988). In its emphasis on the interaction between personal and social discourse processes in the construction of identity, this view also shares many basic premises with Harre's (1983) and Breakwell's (1986) theories of identity development. The roots of these views can be traced to Murray's (1938) work in personology, and to Erickson's (1959) views about the importance of viewing identity development through the histories or significant episodes of individuals' lives.

THE RELATION BETWEEN COMMUNITY NARRATIVES AND PERSONAL IDENTITY STORIES

Given our definitions of *personal identity* as a story that represents individuals' self-knowledge, and *social identity* as a narrative representing the knowledge of a group about itself, we can now illustrate how individuals create, enact, and maintain or change their personal identity through the appropriation, or (in Schank and Abelson's terminology) "mapping" of such narratives into their own story. This process may occur when an individual has an experience that cannot be completely understood in terms of previously stored story skeletons. Depending on the significance of the event, the failure to integrate such an experience may be perceived as a threat to identity (see Breakwell, 1983). When individuals seek out, or attempt to establish new communities, it may be that they are looking for alternative narrative frameworks within which such experiences can be integrated into a coherent and whole personal story.

Although we will highlight the influence of the group narrative on individual stories in the examples that follow, it is also important to remember that an individual's stories, particularly those of community leaders, may create and influence those of the group. Stories are created by people, and in turn, create us. These reciprocal relationships between individual stories and community narratives can be characterized as transactional (Altman & Rogoff, 1987), or dialogic (Bruner & Gorfein, 1983; Hermans, Kempen, & van Loon, 1992), meaning here that social knowledge constitutes the forms in which individual knowledge is created, while individuals also contribute to the revision of community narratives.

Schank and Abelson suggest that an audience selectively shapes what stories are told and how they are told, and that as a result, people like to tell particular stories about themselves. Furthermore, Schank and Abelson argue that those stories come to constitute the self-definition of the individuals. In the following examples, we elaborate on the dynamics of this process, showing how communities establish themselves through storytelling, how storytelling in various kinds of social groups provides story skeletons that members appropriate in developing and maintaining identities, how these normative structures for community storytelling (story skeletons) are established and enforced, and how people resolve alternative interpretations of experiences they address by competing or conflicting narratives.

The Church as a Context for Identity Stories

As previously mentioned, one place to look for the origins of new story skeletons, and to study how they become incorporated into individual identities, is the major institutions of a society. Religious settings are a particularly powerful and significant setting in this regard. Outside of their families, more people gather in churches each week than in any other setting in American society (Jacquet, 1984; Maton & Pargament, 1987). During church, people hear, read, and tell powerful narratives, and perform ritual and symbolic enactments of these narratives. The Bible, as the repository of Judeo-Christian knowledge, is filled with these narratives (Hauerwas, 1983). The narratives, like the sacred texts of other religions, have been read and told among Jews and Christians for centuries. The narratives provide answers to basic questions of human identity such as, "Who am I?", and "How should I live my life?". By communicating and enacting these narratives in public, social contexts such as churches and synagogues, group or community identity is established (e.g., "We are Christians," and "We strive to model our lives after Christ's").

Various forms of storytelling, forms that are often not linguistic, dyadic interactions, are used to persuasively communicate these narratives and to reinforce their adoption into the personal stories of participating individuals. For example, upon hearing the word "communion" in the church context, Christians may index the story of Jesus' Last Supper with his disciples. The communion may also be "told" through ritual performance, prompting participants to recall previously stored events contained in the story. In Schank and Abelson's terminology, church members understand relevant personal experiences by "mapping" them onto details of the Christian narrative that are made salient through such repeated rituals (e.g., "Oh, that's like the time when I . . ."). Through community storytelling, the Christian identity of each individual is bolstered (see Rappaport & Simkins, 1991;

Mankowski & Thomas, 1992, for further discussion of these processes; see also Vitz, 1990).

Another form of storytelling in the church is the personal confession. Confession can be viewed as a process for resolving an identity crisis that was precipitated by performing a behavior that cannot be integrated into the individual's life story, nor mapped onto the narrative of the Catholic Church. Part of the Catholic narrative, however, instructs parishioners to confess the behavior by telling the story to the priest of the church. The narrative explains that the person will be forgiven by God for confessing the sin. As a result of this storytelling, the coherence and value of the person's life and identity may be restored. This process reminds us of Schank's (1990) hypothesis that the best way to forget an experience is to tell it once and never again.

Another process in narrative-guided identity construction within religious settings is the drastic reinterpretation or revision of personal history that accompanies religious conversions (Wakefield, 1990). Conversions may often be preceded by an epiphanic experience that cannot be adequately understood in terms of previously heard stories. In some cases, this situation may be subjectively experienced as quite disturbing, unsettling, or confusing. In others, it may be experienced as a sudden sense of coherence, similar to the way Kuhn (1970) describes how scientists see data in a new way after learning of a different theory. After an epiphanic experience, individuals may seek new narratives to provide this coherence.

As Schank and Abelson indicate in their discussion of couples fighting over the details of a co-biographical story, storytelling can potentially suppress or deny another's personal identity. This can also happen at the community or group level of storytelling. Goldberg (1985) suggested that "virtually all of our rock-ribbed beliefs about our lives are grounded in some bedrock story, and consequently, our more serious convictional disputes with one another (and perhaps with one's self) frequently reflect rival narrative accounts" (p. 13).

Community and cultural narratives often fail to represent experiences that are part of an individual's personal stories; group norms may suppress or deny these stories and the aspects of identity that they represent. Without the validation of the community or culture through storytelling, these identities may be extremely difficult to experience and maintain. Individuals may attempt to seek out new narratives to support these identities. For example, when their experiences conflict with narratives of the church to which they belong, or when they have an experience that cannot be explained by, or integrated into, their personal story or the narratives of the church, people may seek out a different spiritual community. Different churches offer somewhat different versions of the same Biblical narratives.

As Schank and Abelson suggest, different versions can be created during the story construction process by adapting the narratives in a number of ways to suit the goals of the storyteller, or in this case, the church. A good contemporary example is the way in which some churches have adapted their story to meet the needs of the newly vocal gay community.

Mutual Help Groups as a Context for Identity Stories

Mutual help groups are another culturally important site in which to validate Schank and Abelson's hypothesis that stories that are told become part of one's identity and those that go untold no longer define oneself. Such groups also give us a good opportunity to analyze the role of the community narrative in this process (Humphreys & Rappaport, 1994). First, we describe the current significance of mutual help group settings in our society, and then illustrate how personal testimonies are mapped onto the narratives of these groups.

Epidemiological data suggest that at least 20% of the United States population will experience some sort of diagnosable mental disorder during their lifetime (see Weissman & Klerman, 1978). Among the many people who experience such serious problems in living as mental illness or addictions are those who find professional treatment to be either inaccessible or inadequate. Those who reject professional care have criticized it by saying that professional treatment, especially for those who are viewed as "chronic mental patients," often requires the recipients of care to accept a story about who they are that tends to put them in the role of dependent receivers of assistance, rather than active participants in their own lives and the lives of others (Chamberlin, 1979). For example, the typical story told about a person with a history of mental hospitalization is that he or she has an illness that requires learning to see oneself as sick and dependent on medication. Patients are expected to desire "independent living," despite its loneliness, and to see themselves as recipients of services with little to offer others.

In part as a reaction to the story of mental illness and addiction as told by the professional community of service providers, there are now a wide variety of self and mutual help organizations that have come into existence (Borkman, 1991; Powell, 1990). Recent estimates are that approximately 7.5 million Americans participate in self and mutual help groups as an addition or an alternative to professional care (Lieberman & Snowden, 1993). Some even suggested that self-help groups may become the major mode of assistance for most problems in living (Jacobs & Goodman, 1989). These organizations, run by the participants themselves, typically tell a story to their members that is quite different than the one they hear from mental health professionals.

Perhaps the most well-known example of a self-help organization is Alcoholics Anonymous (AA). This organization has become the model for what is known as a "twelve-step program," referring to the twelve steps toward recovery specified in the organization's literature and methods. The twelve steps are an ordered series of behaviors that may be thought of as indexes to the AA narrative. Many other mutual help groups and organizations, for all types of problems in living, including medical, psychiatric, and interpersonal problems, are based on the AA model.

Typically, twelve-step and other mutual help groups involve their members in personal storytelling sessions. Often referred to as personal testimonies, these sessions allow the members to report to each other, in a socially supportive context, the history of their lives with respect to the particular problem the group addresses. Most of these organizations also have what Antze (1976) called an "ideology" or a world view that provides the narrative context in which these stories are told. In this sense, such organizations are quite similar to any voluntary association that offers its members an explicit understanding about what it means to be a member. One of the characteristics of such organizations is that they provide for their members an alternative world view (a community narrative) to the dominant cultural story about who they are. Depending on how large or well organized the group is, it may have its narrative in written, archival form. This community narrative often involves a sense of the history of the organization, its founders or heroes, and a variety of explicit stories that convey to the members a great deal of information. From these components of the narrative, members learn how histories are constructed out of events that are similar to those having occurred in their own lives, understand how the group founders have coped with experiences that were difficult in the context of this history, and see how the founders and other longtime members are currently living.

The structure of an organization such as AA has allowed new members, as well as some researchers (Cain, 1991; Humphreys, 1992), to listen to the personal testimonies of members over time, and to compare these to the organizational story (see also Rappaport, 1993). In these cases, it is found that over time, the individual members tend to modify their personal life story to fit it into the organization's alternative community narrative. For example, Cain (1991) found that the answers to the question "Who am I?" (Kuhn & McPartland, 1954) were closely related to what she called the "AA identity" among those members who had adopted the AA story as a model for their own personal testimony; and over time the personal stories told by members become quite similar to those that appear in the AA literature.

The Cultural Debate on Masculinity as a Context for Identity Stories

Trait concepts can be viewed, in the language offered by Schank and Abelson, as highly accessible story skeletons, or as ways of "captioning" the details of a story during its communication. Masculinity and femininity can be usefully examined from this perspective as central trait concepts in the characterization of a person's identity in our culture. In particular, masculinity refers to the constellation of traits, or story indexes, that describe how men are typically socialized to behave: independently, oriented toward achievement, aggressively, toughly, rationally not emotionally, and in ways that avoid appearances of femininity and homosexuality (Good, Borst, & Wallace, 1994). These traits may index stories about how men are supposed to think, feel, and behave.

Recently, however, the challenge of the feminist movement to these broadly accepted stories and the changes in interpersonal relationships that it produced, as well as men's own critical views of this version of masculinity, have created a kind of cultural crisis in masculine identity, prompting many men to ask themselves who they are, and what they want (Graham, 1992; Shweder, 1994). Men and women alike are questioning whether the stories that define masculine ideology advocate behaviors and ways of understanding the world that are conducive to mental and physical well-being (Good, Borst, & Wallace, 1994).

In the context of this dissatisfaction and lack of personal identification with the stories guiding the construction of masculine identity, alternative accounts of masculinity have been authored from the perspectives of men's liberation (Nichols, 1975), men's spirituality (Bly, 1990), men's rights (Farrell, 1993), or profeminism (Stoltenberg, 1993) (see Shweder, 1994 for an overview). These accounts suggest, alternatively, that men should become more emotional, or focus on their grief over the abusiveness or absence of their fathers and other role models, or become more in touch with their spiritual roots, or resist the changes urged by feminists. Despite these differences, as a whole, these new stories function as resources for men in the process of reinterpreting their personal histories in terms of gender, defined differently than by dominant cultural narratives about masculinity.

According to Schank and Abelson, for a story to become part of memory, and we would add, to become part of identity, individuals must have an interested audience that will listen to it. Just as churches serve as social forums in which the stories of the Bible are made accessible to members, so too, the new masculine ideology requires a social setting in which men can gather to exchange stories based on these new narratives. Men's groups (Kauth, 1992; Shiffman, 1987; T. S. Stein, 1982; Sternbach, 1990) and manhood development programs (Watts, 1993), similar in many ways to the self-help groups in the preceding discussion, have been formed around the country to fill this function. These audiences provide alternatives to settings such as the Elk's club, sporting events, bars, and the Masonic Lodge, where stories guided by the dominant masculinity narratives have traditionally been exchanged.

Spending time in a men's group, one is likely to observe that storytelling is a common activity, part of the natural ecology of the group (e.g., see Gilbert, 1990). One kind of storytelling is the exchange of personal testimonies in which men take turns telling about key moments or turning experiences that are common to each of their lives. Another form of discourse in men's groups is the appropriation of mythic stories to interpret the conditions and events of men's lives. The myth, legend, or fairy tale contains some crucial lesson for the lives of men. Similar to the ideas of Schank and Abelson, Bly (1990) suggested that these mythic narratives are reservoirs of human knowledge where we keep ways of responding that can be adapted to new situations. These forms of storytelling characterize many men's groups as well as their efforts to develop alternative versions of masculine ideology narratives and to facilitate the incorporation of these narratives into the personal stories of individual men.

Government-Sponsored and Neighborhood Art as a Context for Identity Stories

If Schank and Abelson are correct in arguing that stories told and retold to ourselves and to others become indexed in memory (rather than experiences lost along with a variety of other everyday events), then it is no surprise that governments have learned that art can both efficiently reify the status quo and create change. If the index for a story serves as a kind of shorthand device that enables recall, or embellishment, with a great number of details that would otherwise be forgotten, then art, in its various forms (visual, performance, verbal) serves as the keeper of a society's memory, and, in turn, its identity. The more well-known the story, the more briefly it can be indexed. New stories require more detail; stories told many times can be indexed in a more symbolic shorthand. Such indexes need not be verbal. Art objects, performances, and rituals can serve as indexes for the well-known stories of a society, and are a means to teach and reinforce those stories (Lippard, 1990; O'Brien, 1990).

Government-sponsored, public display of art is one of the most obvious examples of the power of community narratives to influence the personal lives of citizens. Flags, national anthems, statues, public buildings, socialist realism, and the art of Nazi Germany are examples of governments making use of the power of art and symbols to index what they consider to be important national narratives. Governments attend to these matters because they influence the behavior of their individual citizens. Many people come to appropriate the national story into their own sense of themselves. In many places in the world, the national story may be weaker than the more traditional ethnic stories with which they compete. Events in the former Soviet Union demonstrate that historical community identities, developed over centuries of storytelling in words, music and visual images, are not easy to change. As can be seen by the tragic events in former Yugoslavia, when the national story ceases to make sense, people seek a sense of community elsewhere—in this case in ethnic narratives that have a longer and deeper history.

In the United States, where many different ethnic identities are newly relocated, nationalistic art tells us a great deal about who we are, because it reminds us of stories we learned in school about our country, its history, and its leaders. For example, the heroic painting of Washington crossing the Delaware brings to mind a complex story about the American war for independence, one that efficiently reminds us about our membership in a national community and our own responsibilities to defend, even with violence, the integrity of the community. Conversely, the new established government of Nicaragua in the early 1990's quickly set about to obliterate murals that had been commissioned by the previous government (Kunzle, 1993).

The power of art as a storyteller is that it can influence the citizens' sense of community, national identity, and behavior. Although the loss of national identity can be tragic, in the United States and Canada many people see the hegemony of a single community identity story as exclusionary. Minorities have learned that articulation of a more particular community identity (albeit in the context of a stable national identity) can have important positive psychological and social effects. For many ethnic and racial minorities, such opportunities can provide a way to gain a voice in the creation of their own identity and to rediscover and create their own memories, rather than accept the (often negative) stories about who they are that are told to and about them by others. A narrative psychology that spans levels of analysis, from individual to local community to national, can learn a great deal about the relationships between individual and social identity by conducting naturalistic research with people who are searching for their own voice through the use of local arts projects (Kimmelman, 1993; Thomas & Rappaport, in press).

CONCLUSION: POSSIBILITIES FOR METHOD AND ACTION

In concluding our commentary on, and expansion of, Schank and Abelson's provocative set of ideas, we would like to make some brief suggestions for the way hypotheses generated by thinking about the social context of individual storytelling might be tested and acted upon by interested psychologists.

In our research group (Rappaport, 1992) we have searched for ways to evaluate the general hypothesis that the narratives of a community will be similar in structure and content to the personal life stories of its longer-term members, and ways to document social processes in the setting that might be responsible for such "mapping." In order to do so, a broad range of methods and forms of data will be required.

First, it seems necessary to spend time in the setting, engaged in participant observation (Denzin, 1989; Zimmerman et al., 1991). During this time, the re-searcher can be locating possible sources of the community's narratives—rituals, commonly read texts that may describe the organization's history and beliefs—and conducting interviews with small groups of the members (Morgan, 1988) focused on aspects of the community's narrative, such as the history, purpose, vision, values, and key figures. After establishing rapport with members, interviews can be conducted with individuals about their life story (see Mishler, 1986, for a guide to conducting interviews and analyzing their transcripts from a narrative perspective). The texts obtained from the community and the individuals may then be analyzed in terms of their structure and content.

There are few agreed-upon procedures for analyzing textual material in psychology, although a variety of techniques are possible, ranging from rule-based coding systems of small semantic units (e.g., Mandler, 1984; N. L. Stein, 1982) to content analysis (Smith, 1992) to larger categories of meaning (e.g., Baumeister, Stillwell, & Wotman, 1990) to more interpretive approaches that can be validated by the community members themselves (e.g. Denzin & Lincoln, 1993; Lincoln & Guba, 1985). McAdams (1988) has developed a detailed and fairly reliable system of coding the components (characters, ideological setting, nuclear episodes), structures (complexity), and thematic contents (power and intimacy) of life stories that he has collected. A similar system may be applicable to community narratives.

Finally, a comparison of the analyses of the stories and the community narratives must be made to determine their similarity. In some cases, the methods of participant observation, investigative reporting, and others more commonly used by anthropologists and sociologists may be necessary. Audio or visual recordings of the community, or their texts, or on-line coding of the community's social interactions, rituals, and performances can be obtained and analyzed in order to demonstrate how the storytelling processes create similarity and uniformity between the individual stories and community narratives (Humphreys, 1993; Lin, 1993).

Keeping oral transmission of culture alive is vitally important to the survival of a community because, as Schank and Abelson assert, not telling our experiences means not remembering, and, therefore, not being able to use them in adapting to our changing environments. For applied psychologists who want to assist local communities and groups outside the mainstream culture to maintain their own sense of identity, such research as described here can be a vehicle that serves both the science and the community. Results from such studies can be fed back to the community to assist them in their evaluation of whether they are accomplishing their goals. Through this action, communities may consciously evaluate whether the forms of storytelling they practice contribute to achievement of their goals, and they may learn how to more consciously apply the tools of their own cultural experiences.

REFERENCES

Altman, I., & Rogoff, B. (1987). World views in psychology: Trait, interactional, organismic, and transactional perspectives. In D. Stokols & I. Altman (Eds.). *Handbook of environmental psychology* (pp. 7–40). New York: Wiley.

Antze, P. (1976). The role of ideologies in peer psychotherapy groups. *Journal of Applied Behavioral Science, 12,* 323–346.

Baumeister, R. F., Stillwell, A., & Wotman, S. R. (1990). Victim and perpetrator accounts of interpersonal conflict: Autobiographical narratives about anger. *Journal of Personality and Social Psychology, 59,* 994–1005.

Bly, R. (1990). *Iron John: A book about men.* Reading, MA: Addison-Wesley.

Borkman, T. J. (Ed.). (1991). Special Issue: Self-help groups. *American Journal of Community Psychology, 19* (whole #5).

Breakwell, G. M. (1983). *Threatened identities.* New York: Wiley.

Breakwell, G. M. (1986). *Coping with threatened identities.* New York: Methuen.

Bronfenbrenner, U. (1977). Toward an experimental ecology of human development. *American Psychologist,* (July), 513–531.

Bruner, E. M., & Gorfain, P. (1983). Dialogic narration and the paradoxes of Masada. *Text, play, and story* (pp. 56–116). Washington, DC: The American Ethnological Society.

Cain, C. (1991). Personal stories: Identity acquisition and self-understanding in Alcoholics Anonymous. *Ethos, 19*(2), 210–253.

Chamberlin, J. (1979). *On our own: Patient controlled alternatives to the mental health system.* New York: McGraw-Hill.

Denzin, N. K. (1989). *The research act: A theoretical introduction to sociological methods* (pp. 156–181). Englewood Cliffs, NJ: Prentice-Hall.

Denzin, N. K., & Lincoln, Y. S. (Eds.). (1993). *Handbook of qualitative research.* Thousand Oaks, CA: Sage.

Erickson, E. H. (1959). Identity and the life cycle: Selected papers. *Psychological Issues, 1,* 5–165.

Farrell, W. (1993). *The myth of male power: Why men are the disposable sex.* New York: Simon & Schuster.

Gergen, K. J. (1991). *The saturated self.* New York: Basic Books.

Gergen, K. J., & Gergen, M. M. (1988). Narrative and the self as a relationship. *Advances in Experimental Social Psychology, 21*, 17–56.

Gilbert, R. K. (1990). Revisiting the psychology of men: Robert Bly and the mytho-poetic movement. *Journal of Humanistic Psychology, 32*, 41–67.

Goldberg, M. (1985). *Jews and Christians: Getting our stories straight.* Nashville, TN: Abingdon Press.

Good, G. E., Borst, T. S., & Wallace, D. L. (1994). Masculinity research: A review and critique. *Applied and Preventive Psychology, 3*, 3–14.

Graham, S. R. (1992). What does a man want? *American Psychologist, 47*, 837–841.

Harre, R. (1983). *Personal being.* Oxford: Basil Blackwell.

Hauerwas, S. (1983). *The peaceable kingdom.* Notre Dame, IN: Notre Dame Press.

Hermans, H. J. M., Kempen, H. J. G., & van Loon, R. J. P. (1992). The dialogical self: Beyond individualism and rationalism. *American Psychologist, 47*, 23–33.

Humphreys, K. (1992, May). Stories and personal transformation in Alcoholics Anonymous. J. Rappaport (Chair). *Community narratives and personal stories.* Symposium presented at the annual meeting of the Midwestern Psychological Association, Chicago, IL.

Humphreys, K. (1993). *World view transformations in adult children of alcoholics mutual help group.* Unpublished doctoral dissertation, University of Illinois at Urbana-Champaign.

Humphreys, K., & Rappaport, J. (1994). Researching the effects of self-help/mutual aid organizations: Many roads, one journey. *Journal of Applied and Preventive Psychology, 3*, 217–231.

Jacobs, M. K., & Goodman, G. (1989). Psychology and self-help groups: Predictions on a partnership. *American Psychologist, 44*, 536–545.

Jacquet, C. H. (Ed.). (1984). *Yearbook of American and Canadian churches.* Nashville: Abingdon Press.

Kauth, B. (1992). *A circle of men: The original manual for men's support groups.* New York: St. Martin's Press.

Kihlstrom, J. F., & Klein, S. B. (in press). The self as a knowledge structure. In R. S. Wyer (Ed.), *Handbook of social cognition,* Vol. 8. Hillsdale, NJ: Lawrence Erlbaum Associates.

Kimmelman, M. (1993, September 26). The New York Times. p. 1 (Arts & Entertainment section).

Klinger, E. (1977). *Meaning and void: Inner experience and the incentives in people's lives.* Minneapolis, MN: University of Minnesota Press..

Kuhn, M. H., & McPartland, T. S. (1954). An empirical investigation of self-attitudes. *American Sociological Review, 19*, 68–76.

Kuhn, T. (1970). *The structure of scientific revolutions* (2nd ed.). Chicago, IL: University of Chicago Press.

Kunzle, I. (1993). The mural death squads of Nicaragua. *Z Magazine,* April, 62–66.

Lieberman, M. A., & Snowden, L. R. (1993). Problems in assessing prevalence and membership characteristics of self-help group participants. *The Journal of Applied Behavioral Science, 29*, 166–180.

Lin, A. W. (1993). *The child as a conversational partner: The creation of participation roles as cultural activity.* Doctoral dissertation, Clark University, Worcester, MA.

Lincoln, Y. S., & Guba, E. G. (1985). *Naturalistic inquiry.* Newbury Park, CA: Sage.

Lippard, L. (1990). *Mixed blessings: New art in a multicultural America.* New York: Pantheon Books.

Mankowski, E. S., & Thomas, E. (1992, May). Individual and group identity among members of a religious foundation: The role of community narrative. J. Rappaport (Chair). *Community narratives and personal stories.* Symposium presented at the annual meeting of the Midwestern Psychological Association, Chicago, IL.

Mandler, J. (1984). *Stories, scripts and themes: Aspects of schema theory.* Hillsdale, NJ: Lawrence Erlbaum Associates.

Markus, H., & Nurius, P. (1986). Possible selves. *American Psychologist, 41*, 954–969.

Maton, K. I., & Pargament, K. I. (1987). The roles of religion in prevention and promotion. *Prevention in Human Services, 5*, 161–205.

McAdams, D. P. (1988). *Power, intimacy and the life story: Personological inquiries into identity.* New York: Guilford.

McClendon, J., Jr. (1986). *Systematic theology: Ethics*. Nashville: Abingdon Press.

Middleton, D., & Edwards, E. (1990). *Collective memory*. London: Sage.

Mishler, E. G. (1986). The analysis of interview-narratives. In T. Sarbin (Ed.), *Narrative psychology: The storied nature of human conduct* (pp. 233–255). New York: Praeger.

Morgan, D. (1988). *Focus groups as qualitative research*. (Sage University Paper Series on Qualitative Research Methods, Vol. 16). Newbury Park, CA: Sage.

Mumby, D. K. (1987). The political function of narrative in organizations. *Communication Monographs, 54*, 113–125.

Murray, H. A. (1938). *Explorations in personality*. New York: Oxford University Press.

Nelson, K. (1993). The psychological and social origins of autobiographical memory. *Psychological Science, 4*(1), 7–14.

Nichols, J. (1975). *Men's liberation: A new definition of masculinity*. New York: Penguin Books.

O'Brien, M. (1990). Introduction. *Reimaging America: The arts of social change* (pp. 9–10). Philadelphia: New Society Publishers.

Powell, T. J. (Ed.). (1990). *Working with self-help*. Silver Spring, MD: NASW Press.

Rappaport, J. (1992, May). Community narratives and personal stories: An introduction to five studies of cross level relationships. J. Rappaport (Chair). *Community narratives and personal stories*. Symposium presented at the annual meeting of the Midwestern Psychological Association, Chicago, IL.

Rappaport, J. (1993). Narrative studies, personal stories, and identity transformation in the mutual help context. *Journal of Applied Behavioral Science, 29,* 239–256.

Rappaport, J., & Simkins, R. (1991). Healing and empowering through community narrative. *Prevention in Human Services, 10,* 29–50.

Sarason, S. B. (1974). *The psychological sense of community: Prospects for the Community Psychology*. San Francisco, CA: Jossey-Bass.

Sarbin, T. R. (Ed.). (1986). *Narrative psychology: The storied nature of human conduct*. New York: Praeger.

Schank, R. (1990). *Tell me a story: A new look at real and artificial memory*. New York: Scribner.

Schlenker, B. R., & Weingold, M. F. (1989). Goals and the self-identification process: Constructing desired identities. In L. A. Pervin (Ed.), *Goal concepts in personality and social psychology,* (pp. 243–290). Hillsdale, NJ: Lawrence Erlbaum Associates.

Shiffman, M. (1987). The men's movement: An exploratory investigation. In M. S. Kimmel (Ed.), *Changing men: New directions in research on men and masculinity* (pp. 295–314). Newbury Park, NJ: Sage.

Shweder, R. A. (1994, January 9). What do men want? A reading list for the male identity crisis. *New York Times Book Review,* pp. 3, 24.

Smith, C. (1992). *Motivation and personality: Handbook of thematic content analysis*. New York: Cambridge University Press.

Stein, N. L. (1982). The definition of a story. *Journal of Pragmatics, 6,* 487–507.

Stein, T. S. (1982). Men's groups. In K. Solomon & N. B. Levy (Eds.), *Men in transition: Theory and therapy* (pp. 275–307). New York: Plenum Press.

Sternbach, J. (1990). The men's seminar: An educational and support group for men. *Social Work with Groups, 13,* 23–39.

Stoltenberg, J. (1993). *The end of manhood: A book for men of conscience*. New York: Dutton.

Thomas, R.E., & Rappaport, J. (in press). Art as community narrative: A resource for social change. In M. B. Lykes, R. Liem, A. Banuazizi, & M. Morris (Eds.), *Unmasking social inequalities: Victims, voice, and resistance*. Philadelphia: Temple University Press.

Vitz, P. C. (1990). The use of stories in moral development: New psychological reasons for an old educational method. *American Psychologist, 45,* 709–720.

Wakefield, D. (1990). *The story of your life: Writing a spiritual autobiography*. Boston, MA: Beacon Press.

Watts, R. J. (1993). Community action through manhood development: A look at concepts and concerns from the frontline. *American Journal of Community Psychology, 21,* 333–359.

Watzlawick, P., Wakeland, J. H., & Fish, R. (1974). *Change: Principles of problem formation and problem resolution.* New York: Norton.

Weissman, M., & Klerman, G. (1978). Epidemiology of mental disorders. *Archives of General Psychiatry, 35,* 705–712.

Zimmerman, M., Reischl, T., Seidman, E., Rappaport, J., Toro, P., & Salem, D. (1991). Expansion strategies of a mutual help organization. *American Journal of Community Psychology, 19,* 251–279.

14

So All Knowledge Isn't Stories?

Robert P. Abelson
Yale University

Roger C. Schank
Northwestern University

The commentaries on our piece, "Knowledge and Memory: The Real Story," are remarkably gentle. We had expected more fire and brimstone à la Bill Brewer. The modal response was something like this: "Schank and Abelson (may) have overstated their case, but they have advanced a compelling position. We think that their argument can be amplified in domain X, as follows . . ." Domain X is variously specified as developmental psychology, social evolution, interpersonal relations, life stories, communal memories, cultural knowledge, and more.

In our response, we first consider the general objection to our putative overassertion, "all knowledge is stories." We then briefly comment on the separate critiques.

NON-STORY KNOWLEDGE

When doubters are exposed to claims of universality, they recruit counterexamples. The universalist has two lines of defense: reinterpreting the counterexamples to fit the generalization, or dismissing them somehow as irrelevant cases. The strong version of our claim—*all* knowledge is stories—has evoked massive disbelief: What about images? What about procedural knowledge? What about *eenie meenie miney mo?* We, too, have two alternative types of counterargument. We can try to show that a proposed item of nonstory knowledge can be interpreted as storylike, or show that it is not really an item of knowledge.

We used both of these rhetorical devices in our chapter (apparently unconvincingly), and again have that option here. Thus, in the case raised by Brewer of the shapes of state boundaries on the map of the U.S., we could make stories from

227

familiar boundaries ("the time I was in Utah, Wyoming, Arizona, and New Mexico all at once"), and pooh-pooh less familiar contours (When was the last time you had a conversation about the shape of Nebraska?).

This in turn raises the question of the role of conversation in our thesis, a role that Brewer has misconstrued. Our reliance on social interaction is not simply an arbitrary way of filtering out uncongenial examples. Conversation plays a major role in the shaping and alteration of memories. Material that is not talked about, or at least rehearsed, is not edited and integrated into the rest of memory. For all practical purposes, such material remains inert and useless. At best it might be used for a fixed purpose and then discarded, like a grocery list, a mnemonist's demonstration, or an Ebbinghaus experiment.

If our rhetorical sparring seems gratuitous, the reader should consider (as have Baumeister and Newman) the conservative epistomological history of major portions of cognitive psychology, cognitive science, artificial intelligence, and linguistics. Despite much recent work supporting story conceptions, there remain prestigious avowals that *no* knowledge is stories. Holdouts who insist on the preeminence of propositional formalisms and syntactic rules for knowledge representations have provoked us into a heavy-metal rendition of the storytelling point of view.

Ad hominem remarks are ordinarily shunned in scientific discourse, but it is appropriate, we think, to note that theorists of mind often project their own cognitive styles onto their conceptions of how other people think. Twenty years ago, a staunch opponent of the introduction of mental imagery into cognitive models turned out to be one of those relatively rare individuals who have no mental imagery. (He confessed this after refusing the use of a map and getting hopelessly lost trying to lead a group of Carnegie-Mellon symposium participants to Allen Newell's house.)

Most academics, having habits of nuanced analytic thought, tend (quite wrongly!) to presume such analytic habits exist in the general public. Models of rational decision making are correspondingly overextended. By contrast, Schank is impatient with the use of formalisms, and loves to tell stories, and Abelson is somewhat the same way.

Perhaps we *have* overstated our case. In the last analysis, however, the debate about *all* vs. *most* vs. *some* is beside the point. The heart of our proposal is concerned with the consequences for memory and knowledge of the preparation and telling of stories. The commentators all have a vital interest in these consequences. In our comments (which are in no special order), we focus for the most part on the broad mutual agenda.

COMMENTS ON THE SEPARATE CHAPTERS

Baumeister and Newman have presented the interesting idea that propositional knowledge indeed exists, and is useful, but is derivative from story representations. That propositional inferences are drawn from stories we certainly agree. But there are questions of *when* such inferences would be made, and *why* they would be useful.

We see propositional summaries from stories as sometimes serving to *index* those stories at the time of encoding. Thus if someone treats you badly, you may infer that the person has a despicable personality. Finding yourself later in a conversation about mean people, you might be reminded of your tormentor and tell the story of the awful thing the person did.

It is not clear what other functions would be served by having propositions lying about in memory but not participating in propositional logic. If you were an experimental subject or a character witness asked directly for a rating of some attribute of a target person, that would be one use, but it is not very interesting as a mental operation. Thus, the status of the Baumeister-Newman suggestion is not entirely clear. A "secondary" role is anomalous.

On the issue of the importance of role perspectives in scripts and stories, we were quite explicit about role variation in our 1977 treatment of scripts. Neither the diner nor the server could confidently enact their restaurant scripts without mutual reliance. (Imagine the waiter suddenly overcome with hunger, running off to a back room to eat John Smith's order of roast beef!) Whether *all* stories require role players, we doubt. (We are not universally universal.) Is a blind escaped fugitive a role? Do triplets play the "roles" of triplets? How about a man who marries his grandmother?

Finally, while the idea that stories tend to caricature reality is interesting, it too doesn't strike us as always true. Dull stories serve functions, too, and unimaginative people can make stories duller by leveling out interesting details, rather than sharpening them.

Harvey and Martin address a variant of the "secondary proposition" idea by pointing to the concept of *attribution*. Social psychologists have investigated the conditions that lead people to explain a behavioral episode either by attributing it to a disposition of the actor, or to some characteristic of the situation. Mary can run from the dog because (among other things) Mary is fearful, or because the dog is fierce. Such attributions can index the story containing the episode, and can later function to answer the psychologist's questions about the actor or the situation. Whether they enter into any propositional calculus with other propositions in long-term memory, independent of stories, is an open question.

These commentators also highlight the role of images. It seems obvious that a capacity for imagery can be (and is) used by individuals in such tasks as locating places or things, reviewing the attributes of objects, thinking in the shower about correspondence chess games, or putting backyard swings together.

What function might imagery serve in social communication, however? If you want to tell somebody how to find a place or a thing, it is far better to specify a storylike sequence of actions than to try to convey a general map of the terrain. Of course, you could *draw* a map, but even then you would typically put arrows on it, outlining the route. The psychologist who got lost after the Carnegie-Mellon symposium went too far by arguing that mental imagery doesn't exist, but one might argue that imagery is not needed as a substitute for, or even as an embellishment on, storytelling.

However, one of us proposed some time ago (Abelson, 1975) that in listening to stories, people tended to adopt the visual perspective of the protagonist or of an observer. Instructional manipulation of point of view produced variations in memory for details, although this effect was small, and fragile. In a later study (unpublished), subjects were interrupted while listening to stories and asked what was in their minds. Visual imagery was reported extremely often, even when the account didn't seem to call for it (e.g., "John went to lunch"). Does visual imagery complement the storage, retrieval, and/or generation of narratives in some important way?

Rubin thinks so. In his eloquent piece, he raises the imagery issue forcefully, proposing that imagery is a different "natural kind" of knowledge representation than that which forms story structures. It may well be. Rubin also notes the many oral traditions passed between generations, and argues that these ritualistic forms are often nonnarrative. Our implicit setting for storytelling was a friendly conversation among contemporary peers, and although we also considered parent–child interactions, we frankly had not given weight to oral traditions and other forms of cultural transmission.

We emphatically object, however, to his characterization of our view as that of two talking heads in a world stripped of physical things. Rubin is taking the *feel* of the physical world as the *sine qua non* of its presence. That is a position often used to derogate computer simulations of human beings, but it amounts to a preemptive rhetorical strike against *conceptual* representations of the physical world, which are non-trivial.

Mechanical klutzes still know the difference between a hammer and a nail. The illustrative stories we cite contain manifold references to the real world, and starting in chapter 2 of our book (Schank & Abelson, 1977) and continuing throughout, we relied on a set of conceptual primitives which included GRASP, INGEST, EXPEL, MOVE, COME/GO, physical causality, agents, objects, instruments, and so on, such that even a careless reader could not have missed the anchorage in a physical world. Furthermore, we find it appallingly inappropriate to classify us in the same tactical category as Chomsky, from whom we differ on eleven out of every ten criteria that anyone can name. We suppose that Rubin had so warmed up to enumerating all the kinds of knowledge we might have neglected that he was hardly willing to give us credit for including *any* knowledge.

We switch our attention now to the question of how a story told by one person reminds a listener of another story. We wonder whether Hastie and Pennington's laid-back, loose-jointed discussion was designed to satirize our apparent theoretical reliance on clever remindings. If so, we take the point. Conversational partners do not necessarily respond with maximum relevance to each other's stories. That is why we have emphasized telling rather than listening as the primary process in memory transformation. As for the conceptual distinction between overcooked steaks and undertrimmed hair, with only the latter being rectifiable, we had been aware of this lack of parallelism. The striking thing about the haircut experience, though, was that even with repeated attempts to make the hair short, the English barbers couldn't bear to cut off enough to satisfy the customer. The haircut situation was therefore no more rectifiable in practice than was the steak situation.

For the reader who has lost the thread of what is going on here, we close with the comment that Hastie and Pennington have conducted very compelling research on the power of narrative constructions to influence juries, and we love them dearly (we think).

Graesser and Ottati raise doubts about whether conversational partners typically respond with stories to stories, never mind the quality of the response. The conversational situations they analyze for which story-to-story sequences are rare, such as televised interviews and therapist-client interactions, are structured so as to discourage story-based exchanges (as the authors realize). Thus, their evidence is not definitive; nevertheless, their point warrants serious consideration.

We are reminded [sic] of the semantic priming study by Seifert, McKoon, Abelson, & Ratcliff (1986), testing whether a story plot illustrating a common proverb will spontaneously activate a previous story with a different illustration of the same proverb. They obtained evidence for such a reminding effect, but only when subjects were told to pay attention to the themes of the stories as they read them line by line. We take this to signify that stories call up stories in settings that encourage such exchanges (parties, campfires, long airplane rides, and so forth), because in such settings, stories are likely occurrences, and listeners will try to show they have understood the story point by responding in kind. However (we are forced to admit), the initiation of searches for abstract, "cross-contextual" remindings is very probably a controlled, rather than automatic process. (The *intention* to search is controlled, but the *product* of the search could well be automatic.)

There are almost certainly individual and group differences in reliance on remindings. Academics are well-practiced at finding abstract structures embedded in verbal materials, and may, therefore, display special skill in finding cogent stories to keep conversations flowing. This relates to the other major doubt articulated by Graesser and Ottati—the capacity of most people to ask the right questions, recognize anomalies, and so on, in the service of repairing knowledge deficits. Skepticism about John Doe's brainpower is reinforced by evidence that the mass public is depressingly ill-informed about politics (Kinder & Sears, 1985), not to mention economics, science, history, geography, and the fine arts.

We agree, therefore, that folks often miss the point of stories, misunderstand what they hear, and generally degrade the idealized mental life of the hypothetically intelligent understander. Like the teller of dull stories, however, the misunderstander doesn't falsify our theoretical position. He operates at a lower level of story interpretation and responding: Perforce, he has less knowledge.

Harvey and Martin make the unexpected comment that maybe we didn't go far enough in our claims for the preeminence of stories! Having commentators to our left makes us feel not quite the wild radicals we are sometimes made out to be.

Their reference to Fritz Heider was interesting. Heider, known in social psychology for his balance principle, attribution principles, and other seemingly propositional formulations, is nevertheless a quintessential storyteller. Stories about his stories are given by Abelson (1983, 1994).

Harvey and Martin raise a methodological issue that should touch off alarm bells for every researcher who tries to obtain retrospective reports of past behaviors or other autobiographical facts. Due to the fundamentally constructive and recon-structive nature of memory, asking people retrospective questions is hopeless if you want *facts* about the past. A scathing and instructive review of the dangers involved has been given by Dawes (1993).

A prototypic object lesson cited by Dawes involved an evaluation of a particular program to improve students' study skills. There were, in fact, no benefits from this program, but the students enrolled in it reported improvement on class tests. The way they were able to perceive benefits when there were none was to misremember their preprogram test performances as substantially worse than they had been!

Holmes and Murray's discussion of this phenomenon in intimate relationships is quite rich with instructive examples. Peoples' facility at memory revision—with-out conscious awareness—is astonishing. We wonder whether this capacity for convenient self-deceit is so deeply wired that clever therapies designed to improve the accuracy of memory would fail—and be dysfunctional if they succeeded.

Mankowski and Rappaport lay out a fascinating set of forms and settings for the transmission of community sensibilities and cultural knowledge through stories and rituals. The tangibility of their research prospectus is especially valuable, as one sometimes gets the impression from writers about culture that it seeps into individuals without demarcation of place, time, and process.

P. Miller comes at cultural influence from another direction, emphasizing not *what* stories are told, but *how* they are to be rendered. To the extent that "the medium is the message," *how* converts into a *what.*

In the interesting case of cultural norms leading to co-narration, idle curiosity leads us to wonder what happens to the story when the co-narrator is not present. Scott's piece, despite a difference in disciplinary background, and notwithstanding her cryptic "narrative algorithm," makes a plea similar to those that others have made. She would have us include several other kinds of representations besides stories in our conception of knowledge. Under the multidisciplinary barrage of protests and entreaties, our inclination to argue has diminished.

Read and L. Miller have persuasively stated several arguments for the functional preeminence of social relations for humankind. This serves to underscore our emphasis on the imperative of social communication for useful knowledge and memory. We note, however, that whereas we find the argument for the contempo-rary relevance of social factors compelling, the evolutionary argument favoring stories as the primary form of knowledge is unverifiable. There are all sorts of suggestions about the defining period in hominid history when the human mind took its great leap forward from its primate relatives (e.g., the ability to process counterfactuals, or to refer to "embedded worlds," or the linguistic capability of telling others where you left objects such that they could go and find them) and you pretty much pay your money and take your choice.

Nelson was one of the very first psychologists to appreciate the ideas that led to our book (Schank & Abelson, 1977), and to apply them in her research on children's knowledge representations. With her recent research, she has boldly enlarged psychological understanding of the development of the child's capacity for autobiographical memory. We thank her for her complimentary remarks, and take her remonstrations to heart.

Brewer's critique is remarkable. He says that our proposal is certainly wrong, and anyway, it merely reflects the thinking of a long line of wise people. Brewer at various points credits us with an "important line of reasoning," another idea that is "quite likely correct," one that "gives a more complete account" (than the alternative), yet another conception that is "powerful and fundamentally correct," and so on. How could our terrible proposal have so many sterling qualities?

Altogether, we have found this interchange highly productive. The range of topics illuminated by giving storytelling a central role is impressive, and the scope of references to relevant empirical research is gratifying. To a large extent, the disagreements with our critics are matters of presupposition about which forms of knowledge are most interesting and important to work on. Rather than quarreling further, we will leave it at that, with thanks to the editor for providing us this opportunity to state our case.

REFERENCES

Abelson, R. P. (1975). Does a story understander need a point of view? In B. Nash-Webber and R. Schank (Eds.), *Theoretical issues in natural language processing* (pp. 140–143). Cambridge, MA: Bolt, Beranek, & Newman.

Abelson, R. P. (1983). Whatever became of consistency theory? *Personality and Social Psychology Bulletin, 9,* 37–54.

Abelson, R. P. (1994). A personal perspective on social cognition. In P. Devine, D. L. Hamilton, & T. M. Ostrom, (Eds.), *Social cognition: Impact on social psychology* (pp. 15–37). New York: Academic Press.

Dawes, R. M. (1993). Prediction of the future versus an understanding of the past: A basic asymmetry. *American Journal of Psychology, 106,* 1–24.

Kinder, D. R. & Sears, D. O. (1985). Public opinion and political participation. In G. Lindzey & E. Aronson (Eds.), *Handbook of social psychology,* 3rd ed. Reading MA: Addison-Wesley.

Schank, R. C., & Abelson, R. P. (1977). *Scripts, plans, goals, and understanding.* Hillsdale, NJ: Lawrence Erlbaum Associates.

Seifert, C. M., McKoon, G., Abelson, R. P., & Ratcliff, R. (1986). Memory connections between thematically similar episodes. *Journal of Experimental Psychology: Learning, Memory, and Cognition, 12,* 220–231.

Author Index

Subject Index